But

God

But
God

Overcoming Life's Dead Ends:
A Year of Daily Devotions

Cori Kelly

But God

Published by
Inscript Publishing
a division of Dove Christian Publishers
P.O. Box 611
Bladensburg, MD 20710-0611
www.inscriptpublishing.com

Library of Congress Control Number: 2018955234

ISBN: 9781732112513

Printed in the United States of America

JANUARY 1

"Now the Lord is the Spirit, and where the Spirit of the Lord is, there is freedom" (2 Corinthians 3:17).

Take a moment to reflect on the following question before answering: "What do I see in my life that is important but really isn't?" It's a great question to ponder, especially this time of the year with new beginnings and changes being considered. The answer that came to me instantly was just one word, and I was well acquainted with it. It had ruled my life for many years. It was the dreaded *P* word—perfection.

I am a recovering perfectionist. I lived life needing everything to be perfect from my house to my family and, most of all, myself. I had to have a spotless home. My children went to school in matching outfits and well-coordinated accessories. Every meal had to be perfectly balanced and nutritious. Every task, from organizing a closet to overseeing the class Christmas party, was done with great precision and care. I was a slave to perfection.

"But God" stepped in and rescued me from my insanity. He used the example of His Son Jesus who, while perfect in nature, was not a perfectionist. Jesus' attention was always on meeting the needs of others and building relationships. He worried not that His robe and sandals were dirty or that He appeared disheveled. People were what mattered.

Jesus taught us in John 8:32, "Then you will know the truth, and the truth will set you free." Have you answered the question above yet? Is there something in your life that you need to be set free from? Jesus is standing by to help you refocus your life. Why not start the New Year off right and gain your freedom at last!

JANUARY 2

"Do not be like them, for your Father knows what you need before you ask Him" (Matthew 6:8).

I was in a hurry trying to get all the birthday presents wrapped before the party. When I pulled off a piece of tape, it splintered and stuck back on the roll. I can never find those lost ends of tape on the roll. And when I do, they peel off sideways or just shred even more. I tried to make do with the tiny slivers I was pulling off, but it wasn't working very well. Time was ticking, and I was beyond frustrated. A true wrapping nightmare had just begun.

"But God"... the next time I reached for the tape, it was functional again. It had somehow corrected itself, and I was back in business, but not before I felt the Lord kiss me on the top of my head and whisper to me that He always knows what I need even before I ask. God cares about every seemingly insignificant thing that we care about—even malfunctioning tape dispensers! He loves meeting us right where we need to be met. He loves us that much!

Not only did my gifts turn out beautiful that day, but I got a wonderful kiss from God and a reminder of just how much He loves me and cares about my every need.

JANUARY 7

"We must go through many hardships to enter the kingdom of heaven" (Acts 14:22).

Some people mistakenly think that once they become believers, all their troubles will be over. They think there will be no more pain and suffering because they have committed their lives to Christ and He will spare them.

God's Word teaches us entirely different. It tells us that suffering should be considered a gift or a privilege. It tells us that our trials are just as much of a blessing as is our faith. The Apostle James taught that we should consider trials and temptations pure joy because they develop perseverance, maturity, and wisdom in us. Jesus said in John 16:33, *"In this world, you will have trouble."* No one gets a free pass. We will all suffer in this life.

Suffering should never be misinterpreted as God's punishment. God doesn't punish, but He does discipline. If we had to be completely honest, we could probably say that some of our hardships have been from our own poor choices or decisions. Maybe we neglected to consult with God beforehand. Or maybe we heard from God but didn't listen. We do have some control over our suffering.

Never let hardships define you or your faith. Focusing on God and not your problems is what we are called to do. Concentrate on doing your part and let God take care of the rest.

JANUARY 8

"But his delight is in the law of the Lord, and on His law he meditates day and night" (Psalm 1:2).

The word *meditate* is the perfect word to describe what we are to do with God's Word. To *meditate* means to dwell on a thought; to study or contemplate; to turn it over and over in your mind.

God's Word is meant not only to be read but meditated upon. We must absorb it into our hearts and our minds for us to draw encouragement and strength from it. The promises of God are the best defense we have against the trials that we face. Hardships put patience and faith to the test. We need the Word to enable us to persevere and come out the other side. The Word protects and defends us from the attacks of Satan. You can't do battle without ammunition, and God's Word provides that and more.

We can learn how to follow God by reading His Word. Knowing and thinking about God's Word are the first steps toward applying it to your everyday life. That is the ultimate goal of Scripture—to teach us how to live godly lives in an ungodly world.

JANUARY 13

"And this is love: that we walk in obedience to His commands" (2 John 6).

The statement that Christians should love one another is a recurrent New Testament theme. However, the command to love first appeared in Leviticus 19:18 when God was giving Moses the Law. He said to tell the people, "Love your neighbor as yourself. I am the Lord. Keep my decrees."

Knowing God's commands is not enough. We must put them into practice. Love is expressed by showing respect, self-sacrifice, and servanthood. In fact, it can be defined as "selfless living," reaching beyond friends to encompass our enemies and persecutors as well. Love is not a feeling but a choice. We can choose to be concerned with other people's well-being and treat them with respect whether we feel affection towards them or not. If we choose to love others, God will help us express our love to them.

Love is sacrificial. It personally costs us something. Usually, it involves taking a back seat to our own needs and desires and putting others before ourselves. God desires that we love Him first and foremost and then love our fellow man. Love should always be the identifying mark of a Christian. If you are not known for your love, what are you known for? Now might be a good time to examine how you're doing with loving your neighbor. Is it time to act instead of waiting for the right moment or the right feeling to come? Now is the perfect time!

JANUARY 14

"By the seventh day God had finished the work He had been doing so on the seventh day He rested from all His work" (Genesis 2:2).

We all lead hectic and busy lives. It seems we always have an endless To-Do list. We rarely stop and take a breath, let alone have time to sit and reflect. When God rested on the seventh day from His work, He wasn't worn out and needed a break. He simply wanted to kick back and revel in the beauty of His creation. He wanted to stop and smell the roses.

The Greek word for rest is *refreshment*. All of us need times of refreshment on a regular basis. God knew how crazy our lives would be. He knew we would have to take time to refill our empty physical and emotional tanks.

Imagine how delightful it would be if we allowed ourselves the luxury of rest. Why are we always in such a hurry? Why do we feel it is so important to be productive and accomplish our agendas? If we were to be completely honest, we would see that there really is no good reason to push ourselves so hard. And in fact, we are missing out on more important things.

We don't have to sit and do nothing one day a week to observe the Sabbath. We can have a daily Sabbath by simply taking a break and appreciating God's creation. Take a time-out, a deep breath, and a moment to just sit in His presence. Refresh your spirit, and your body will follow. Even if it means sacrificing some other activity, there is nothing more fulfilling than spending a tender moment with the Almighty

JANUARY 15

"To this you were called because Christ suffered for you leaving you an example that you should follow in His steps" (1 Peter 2:21).

It is hard to imagine suffering as Christ suffered for us. He endured unimaginable pain and torture at the hands of the depraved Roman soldiers. Even though we are called to conform to the image of Christ and imitate Him, we really don't want to think about that when it comes to our own suffering. We are too focused on our pain and misery. But the building up of perseverance during hard times is part of God's plan for every Christian. James 1:4 says, "Perseverance must finish its work so that you may be mature and complete, not lacking anything."

Nothing pushes us faster or harder into God's waiting arms than a good healthy dose of pain. If we lived a trouble-free life, what need would we have for God? What better reminder than suffering to make us realize that we can't do this life on our own. If we are to achieve our goal of becoming like Christ, we must be like Him in every way, not just in some ways.

Jesus suffered and died so that we could spend eternity with Him in heaven. And He did so in the humblest way. He did it with patience, calmness, and confidence that God was in control of His future. He didn't take revenge on those who crucified Him. He didn't even curse them. What He did was forgive them, giving us the perfect example of how we can also forgive even the most heinous injustices. If Jesus could love and forgive His enemies, then so can we. Choose to forgive those who have caused you pain and suffering. It will bring you great freedom and reward.

JANUARY 16

"Always be prepared to give an answer to everyone who asks you to give the reason for the hope that you have. But do this with gentleness and respect" (1 Peter 3:15).

Are you prepared to give an answer for the hope that you have? Are you prepared to defend what and whom you believe in? How should you respond when someone comments that there is something different about you? How can you share your faith without turning people off?

Sometimes these answers and conversations can be difficult, as people like to cling to their own beliefs and opinions. Some love a good debate and like to take the theological route and indulge in religious rhetoric. However, it's futile to entertain these frustrating discussions. You can't change someone's mind with facts. The best way to respond when asked about your faith is to tell how having a relationship with Jesus has changed you. Approach it from a personal standpoint. Share genuinely from your heart. No one can dispute your testimony.

On the flip side, what if people aren't asking us to give a reason for the hope that we have? Does that mean that we are not shining our Jesus light in this dark world? Are we not wearing our faith on our sleeve as we should be?

Ask yourself when was the last time someone asked you about your faith. When was the last time someone noticed something different about you and made a comment? Before we can be prepared to give an answer for the hope that we have, we must make sure that our own hope is secure and alive. We must always be ready to share Jesus! Are you ready?

JANUARY 17

"Each one should use whatever gift he has received to serve others faithfully administering God's grace in its various forms" (1 Peter 4:10).

The Greek word for gift is "charismata" which refers to special gifts of grace. God freely gives these to His people to meet the needs of the body (the church). We are given special talents and abilities by God to help others and glorify Him.

Some of the gifts mentioned in Romans 12 are prophesying, serving, teaching, encouraging, contributing to the needs of others, leadership, and mercy. The spiritual gifts that we've been given are not for self-glorification. A gift means nothing if left unopened or ignored. We need to unwrap it and see what God's unique purpose is for us. Pray and ask God how He wants to use the gift that He has given you. How does He want you to use it for His Kingdom?

There are some who question or doubt that they possess any of these spiritual gifts. They feel they have no unique talents or abilities with which to serve Him. However, the Word says that no believer is overlooked in this regard. Some just may not be able to recognize their gift or simply don't know how to use it. Pray and seek God's direction and He will enlighten you and point you down the right path.

JANUARY 18

"I am the good shepherd; I know my sheep, and my sheep know me just as the Father knows me and I know the Father; I lay down my life for the sheep" (John 10:14).

The prophet Isaiah wrote, "God tends his flock like a shepherd. He gathers the lambs in His arms and carries them close to His heart; He gently leads those that have young" (Isaiah 40:11). In Ezekiel 34:11, the Lord says, "I myself will search for my sheep and look after them."

Jesus refers to Himself in Scripture as the true Shepherd. A shepherd had many responsibilities in Jesus' day. He had to meet every need of the sheep as they are incapable of caring for themselves. He had to lead the sheep and keep them well-nourished and out of harm's way. When one went astray, the shepherd went out to find him and bring him back to the fold. Often, the shepherd would have to break the sheep's legs so he couldn't run off again. Then He would carry the lamb until healing took place and the animal could walk again.

The good Shepherd has to break our legs at times for the exact same purpose. He wants to teach us to stay close and show us how to rely solely on Him. He wants us to feel His love stronger than ever as He carries us in the warmth of His embrace. He wants us to depend on our Shepherd just like the sheep depended on theirs. Our healing will take place if we have faith in Him. Rest in His arms and let the mending process begin.

JANUARY 19

"As the body without the spirit is dead, so faith without deeds is dead" (James 2:26).

Faith is not really a noun but a verb. Faith requires more than understanding the truth of God's word. It is more than a simple belief of God's existence, character, and doctrines. Faith must be accompanied by action, or it is not really true faith. It is not enough to just believe in God. James 2:19 says, "Even the demons believe in God and shudder." If a true commitment to Jesus has been made, then action will naturally follow. We will want to serve God because we love Him and want to honor Him.

We can look for opportunities to live out our faith. Volunteering is a great way to demonstrate faith in action. I always told myself I would never be one of those elderly women in blue smocks who volunteer in the hospital gift shop. *"But God"* ... has such a marvelous sense of humor. After moving to a new city and finding myself with too much time on my hands, I knew exactly what I needed to do. I signed up to be one of those ladies in the gift shop!

I discovered I was able to put my faith into action as I interacted with the customers. As they bought their gum and candy, I was able to minister to many people just by listening to their stories and encouraging them. Sometimes I even offered to pray for them. As God had planned, the gift shop turned out to be one of the most rewarding experiences of my life.

Getting out in the world and caring for others is faith in action. We can't be a country club of Christians and stick to our own little groups and comfortable places. How can we make a difference in the world if we never step away from our circle of friends? Jesus didn't minister to the same group of people all the time. He traveled far and wide and went after the skeptics and unbelievers. Shouldn't we be ministering to people just like Jesus did? Maybe it's time to step out in faith and put on a blue smock!

JANUARY 20

"Your beauty should not come from outward adornment. Instead, it should be that of your inner self, the unfading beauty of a gentle and quiet spirit which is of great worth in God's sight" (1 Peter 3:4).

How do you define beauty? In a world that puts so much emphasis on external appearances, many women are tempted to find security and self-worth in physical beauty. But we are not made beautiful by outward adornment, according to God's Word. What makes us lovely and attractive is our character. Peter tells us in this verse that God is not looking for beautiful faces and bodies but a gentle, quiet spirit within us.

We should not be obsessed with our self-image. God doesn't want us to be lazy about our appearance but neither should we be a slave to beauty. Scripture says that our bodies belong to the Holy Spirit and therefore we should respect them and take good care of them. If we abuse our bodies, we are exploiting something that God created and that He treasures.

Along with fostering a beautiful inner spirit, Peter talks about gentleness in this verse. Gentleness is "Christ-like consideration of others." We can learn many things about gentleness just by looking at the life of Christ. Matthew 11:28 says, "He is gentle and humble in heart." These are the things that are of great worth in God's sight. These are the qualities that really matter to God. Outward appearances will fade away, but our inner beauty will shine forever!

JANUARY 21

"Are not all angels ministering spirits sent to serve those who will inherit salvation?" (Hebrews 1:14).

Angels often disguise themselves in the flesh. A man happens to be driving by on a deserted road just when a car breaks down, or a tire goes suddenly flat. A twenty-dollar bill is handed to a poor old woman counting out her pennies in the checkout line. A compassionate traveler buys an airline ticket for a young man who shows up at the airport a day late for his flight.

God can use as us angels as well. I had the privilege of being used by God for this very purpose a few years back. I was driving to the mall on a cold, blustery day when I passed a young mother in a heavy coat struggling to carry a toddler and an oversized bag. After I passed her, I heard God tell me to turn around and go back and pick her up.

As I pulled the car alongside them, I saw that the mother was crying and talking on her cell phone. She was out of breath from the heavy load in her arms. I rolled down the window and asked where she was headed. "The airport," she replied, which was a good five miles down the road. I told her to get in, and I would drive her there. She gladly buckled her toddler in the back seat and climbed in the front. She told me she was trying to get home and her sister had a ticket waiting for her at the airport. She seemed upset and didn't talk very much. I knew I shouldn't pry, so I left her to her thoughts and watched as her tired bundle in the backseat slowly closed his eyes.

As I pulled up to the airport, I asked her if I could pray with her. She said yes, so I prayed and helped them out of the car. As I drove away, I remembered the Scripture verse that says, "He will command His angels concerning you to guard you carefully" (Luke 4:10). I believe I was a ministering spirit that day. I was able to share the love of Christ with a weary traveler who just might have been praying for an angel to come along.

"But God" ...

JANUARY 22

"Let us hold firmly to the faith we profess" (Hebrews 4:14).

Different Bible translations are helpful when studying God's Word. They help to give added insight and perspective. The New Living Translation of this verse says, "Let us cling to Him and never stop trusting Him." This adds a new dimension by using the word *cling* in place of the words *to hold firmly*. The word *cling* implies a closeness that cannot be separated.

Holding onto our faith seems easy when life is going along smoothly. But when raging storms blow into our lives, our faith can take a beating. We have to hold on and fight to stay afloat. Hebrews 6:19 says, "We have this hope as an anchor for the soul, firm and secure." We have to trust Him even in gale force winds.

I had a friend who lived with the constant threat of losing her home because her husband was out of work. Every week there would be notes from the bank threatening foreclosure. But she clung firmly to her faith and trusted that God was in control. She trusted that God was her ultimate provider, and she had nothing to fear. She clung to God's promise that no matter what, He would take care of her and her family. She had her eyes fixed on Jesus and persevered in her faith.

My friend was a walking testimony with her strength and unwavering trust. It's not always easy, but God tells us we can get through anything if we keep our focus on Him. We will surely stumble and fall if we keep our focus on our trials and our circumstances. Always hold firmly to your faith and cling to the One who walks beside you!

JANUARY 23

"God is not unjust; He will not forget your work and the love you have shown Him as you have helped His people and continue to help them" *(Hebrews 6:10).*

Many places in Scripture remind us of the command to serve one another with the love of Christ. One way to embrace this is by praying and asking God to provide you with a divine appointment. Ask Him to put someone in your path that you can minister to. I have a friend who does this on a regular basis and the ways that God uses her are unbelievable. Is it inconvenient at times? Can it rearrange your day? Will some people and situations be challenging? Of course! God never promised us that His work—our work—was going to be easy.

I was leaving the hospital after my volunteer shift one day and was totally focused on getting home before it started to storm. As I was walking to my car in the drizzle, I saw an older woman who appeared lost. I thought about passing her by since I was in a hurry with the threatening weather moving in. However, I felt God prod me to stop and ask if she needed some assistance. She spoke broken English, but I gathered that she couldn't find her car. I asked if maybe she had come in from a different entrance. She shook her head yes, and I immediately knew where I needed to take her. The thunder was rolling by now and the sky on the verge of exploding. I tried to point her in the right direction, but it was obvious that wasn't going to work. It was then that I realized here was my divine appointment for the day. I walked her all the way back through the hospital to the medical office parking lot as she thanked me over and over.

That woman was not the one who was blessed that day; I was. The Lord held off the rain until I was safely tucked away in my car and on my way home. There is no more satisfying feeling than knowing that you made a difference in someone else's life, if just for a moment. Serving others doesn't have to be some big ordeal. If we wait for the big opportunities, we will miss all the little ones God sends along the way.

JANUARY 24

"The Lord God made garments of skin for Adam and his wife and clothed them" (Genesis 3:21).

God's grace and mercy are truly overwhelming. You may not have noticed His amazing grace in this Scripture verse at first glance, but it is there, big as life. It is the very essence of the entire passage.

Adam and Eve had just committed the biggest sin of all time, a sin that forever introduced evil and suffering into our world. They blatantly disregarded God's instructions and ate from the tree that God told them specifically not to eat from. He gave them just one rule to follow, and they chose not to obey it. Can you even imagine God's disappointment when He went to find them afterward? Here He had given them a utopia to live in, and they blew it!

After disobeying God, Adam and Eve no longer deserved to live in the garden of Paradise, so God exiled them forever. *"But God"* ... in His grace and mercy sent them on their way with one small gift. At the time they only had fig leaves to cover themselves. But God still loved and cared for them, and so He made them new garments from animal skins so that their modesty would be preserved. He could have sent them away in total shame and nakedness. "But God" in His goodness showed them favor and kindness.

It is so reassuring to know that no matter what we do or how many times we've failed, God still loves us and extends His grace towards us. God's treatment of us is not contingent on our behavior. He can never love us any more or any less than He does right now. Nehemiah 9:17 says, "But you are a forgiving God, gracious and compassionate, slow to anger and abounding in love." We don't deserve anything and yet He still gives us everything.

JANUARY 25

"Let us throw off everything that hinders and the sin that so easily entangles and let us run with perseverance the race marked out for us" (Hebrews 12:1).

The Apostle Paul compares living out our faith to running a race. He actually refers to it as a marathon. The Christian life involves hard work. It requires us to give up whatever endangers our relationship with God. Paul tells us to throw off everything that hinders us from being close to Him and stay in the race.

Marathoners and Christians have a lot in common. They both have to run at a steady pace to preserve their stamina. They both persevere through pain and discomfort even when they feel like they've hit a brick wall. They both must take care of themselves and replenish their bodies along the way. They both are dedicated to their mission even if it takes everything in them to cross that finish line.

I ran my first race—a daunting 5K—in my late forties. I didn't think about winning. I just wanted to see if I could do it. I wanted to see if I could just make it to the finish line. I started out slow, proud that I had stepped up to the challenge. Runners flew by me on either side as I diligently made my way along the beaten path. I didn't get caught up in comparing myself to them or their speed. My mission was simply to cross that finish line.

Jesus is eagerly waiting for us at the finish line in heaven. He can't wait until we cross over and can hold us in His arms and tell us what a great job we did. If we are to run a successful race, we must keep our eyes on Jesus standing at the finish line waiting for us. Acts 20:24 encourages us with these words: "However, I consider my life worth nothing to me if only I may finish the race and complete the task the Lord Jesus has given me—the task of testifying to the gospel of God's grace." I am looking forward to my next finish line and the reward of seeing Jesus face to face. Oh, what a prize I will behold!

JANUARY 26

"Do not be afraid of them; the Lord your God himself will fight for you" (Deuteronomy 3:22).

There have been many times in my life where, in the heat of the battle, I forgot that I wasn't alone in the fight. God promises in His Word that He will not only fight for us, but He will go before us. It says in 2 Chronicles 20:15, "For the battle is not yours, but God's." And in Exodus 14:13, "Do not be afraid. Stand firm and you will see the deliverance the Lord will bring you today. The Lord will fight for you; you need only to be still." To remain still means to be patient and trust that God has everything under control. Of course, that's a hard thing to do when you're engaged in combat. But relying on God's promises is our best ammunition.

A little boy in our church had been battling a rare blood disorder that required a bone marrow transplant. It had been an intense fight for his life. However, his parents never stopped believing in God's ability to heal their son. They trusted that God was going ahead of them into the battle. They didn't place their confidence in physicians, procedures, or medications. They knew God would be faithful and lead them where they needed to go. They trusted and followed Him through the miraculous healing of their son.

Don't forget when you're caught in the crossfire that you have a God who is already fighting for you. He has gone before you in combat. He will deploy His mighty weapons and cut off the enemy. Our job is to just remain still and trust. God will bring the victory and provide restoration. Our God is a mighty warrior willing and able to be our conqueror. Allow Him to assume that role and rest in the peace that comes from turning your battle over to Him!

JANUARY 27

"In my distress I called to the Lord; I cried to my God for help. From His temple He heard my voice; my cry came before Him and into His ears" (Psalm 18:6).

David loved to play his instruments and worship God. He wrote this song after the Lord delivered him from his enemies in answer to his cry for help. Many people can't put their pride aside to ask for help. They think they can pull themselves up by their bootstraps and soldier on in their own strength, or they turn to family and friends for the comfort and guidance that only God can provide. Psalm 108:12 says, "For the help of man is worthless." God is the only One who can meet all our needs.

David is one of my biblical heroes. I connect with him because he suffered from depression at times in his life just like I do. I have prayed that same "help me" prayer, just like David, in my pain and suffering. God hears our every cry and plea. He is pleased when we admit we can't survive on our own because then we can rely on Him. This helps draw us closer to Him so we can learn to lean into Him. He lovingly reassures us that we've come to the right place for help!

Humility should be one of the hallmarks of the Christian faith. It is only the sin of pride that prevents us from humbling ourselves to admit that we need God. We are not weak because we ask for help. On the contrary, it takes a lot of strength and courage to ask for assistance. David wasn't weak. He was the greatest King in the Bible. He knew he wouldn't be where he was or what he was without God's help!

JANUARY 28

"For without Him who can eat or find enjoyment? To the man who pleases Him, God gives wisdom, knowledge, and happiness" (Ecclesiastes 2:25-26).

People interpret the word happy in many ways and according to the circumstances of their life at the time. They allow life to dictate their joy and contentment instead of acknowledging the only true source of all good things. The world's view of happiness comes and goes with the changing tides. But God's happiness permeates our hearts for all eternity.

True fulfillment and happiness can only come from being in a relationship with God. Without Him, satisfaction is a futile search. Only in God does life have true meaning and pleasure. Without Him, nothing satisfies. The happiness that the world offers has no staying power. It can be here today and gone tomorrow. The happiness that Jesus offers is fixed and solid. Nothing or no one can take it away from us.

There is one caveat, however, to experience this promise of happiness. Scripture says, "To the man who pleases God" this happiness will be awarded. This means we must live our lives not for ourselves but for God. Being happy has nothing to do with us and everything to do with God. Give up trying to find it and let it come to you by way of a personal relationship with Jesus. Only then will you fill that hole in your heart and stop that vacuum from sucking the air out of your soul. When you choose Christ, you are choosing a happy fulfilled life. It is the most significant life-altering decision you will ever make!

JANUARY 29

"But remember the Lord your God for it is He who gives you the ability to produce wealth" *(Deuteronomy 8:18).*

The term "self-made millionaire" is frequently used in our society today. We are only too eager to take credit for our accomplishments and flaunt our achievements. We take great pride in ourselves. But, nothing is self-made in this life. If it weren't for God giving us the abilities and His hand of blessing upon us, we would never be able to achieve anything.

God is in total control of our lives and can bless or take away. 1 Samuel 2:7 says, "The Lord sends poverty and wealth; He humbles, and He exalts." Our talents and successes don't come by our own merit. John 15:5 says, "Apart from me you can do nothing." God wants to see us succeed. He wants us to have nice things in life and enjoy them. He wants us to live life abundantly. But He also wants and expects us to acknowledge that it is only by His hand that we have anything at all.

God wants us to overflow with thanksgiving for every good thing He has given to us. Do we remember to thank Him for His generous provisions? Do we thank Him for the many gifts and abilities He has given us to live such successful lives? We must get in the habit of practicing an attitude of gratitude if we want God's continued hand of generosity upon us. There is nothing that exists that is self-made. God is the maker and provider of everything. His stamp is on every success and achievement in our lives.

JANUARY 30

"Train yourself to be godly" (1 Timothy 4:7).

How do we train ourselves to be godly? When you think of the word *training,* you might think of people working out at the gym. It could be the athlete who trains for a triathlon, the bodybuilder who trains for a contest, or maybe the gymnast who is training for a competition. These athletes can't just show up and expect to perform well, let alone win. They can't assume they are ready for the challenges ahead without practice. They have to put in the time and effort to get ready. They must work hard, be dedicated, and exercise huge amounts of self-discipline. Their success depends on their training.

Godliness is the same as physical training. It requires the same commitment of time, energy, and diligence. It is not some by-product of our faith. We just can't pray to be godly and achieve it. We have to work at it. Further, in the book of Timothy, Paul tells us to, "Pursue godliness." The word *pursue* is a verb, and verbs suggest action. You can't pursue something and be passive at the same time.

Why do we spend so much time working on our physical bodies and so little time on our spiritual bodies? A spiritual workout is much more important for our total well-being.

Do you have a spiritual workout routine? Are you in training to be the godly person Christ intends for you to be? You can practice godliness by making time to read and study the Scriptures, to pray, to worship, to fellowship with other believers, and to share your faith with others. These disciplines, if practiced regularly, will keep you in great spiritual shape!

JANUARY 31

"But your iniquities have separated you from God; your sins have hidden His face from you so that he will not hear" (Isaiah 59:2).

Reuben was one of Jacob's twelve sons. Scripture doesn't say much about him except that he was the first-born of his large clan. In the Jewish culture, the first-born was given a great blessing by his father as well as inheritance rights. This was all in store for Reuben until the day he sinned by defiling his father's marriage bed. This one bad choice cost him everything. Reuben was disinherited and excluded from his place of honor in the family. In a weak moment, Reuben sacrificed all that was good in his life.

This is a powerful example of the consequence of sin. The first place we battle with sin is in the mind. Temptation enters, and we have to decide immediately what to do with it. Are we going to act on it as Satan would love for us to do or be strong and run far away from it, which would have been a much better choice for Reuben?

God gave us tools to use to avoid moral failure. He gave us a Spirit-filled mind to empower us to withstand temptation. He gave us armor to put on every day to do battle with the flesh. He also gave us Scripture which is the most powerful weapon of all. Even Jesus used Scripture to battle temptation when Satan tried to trip him up.

It's hard to think about the consequence of sin in the heat of the moment. That's why it is so important to be ready all the time. If Reuben had been better prepared, things might have turned out much differently for him. Always be ready to stand against temptation. Never give Satan a foothold by showing your weakness.

FEBRUARY 1

"Be joyful always; pray continually; give thanks in all circumstances for this is God's will for you in Christ Jesus" (1 Thessalonians 5:16-18).

I have asked God this question many times in my life: "Lord, what is your will for me?" We are told in His Word that God has a plan and a purpose for each of us. Yet I have felt uncertain at times of what that means for me.

Thankfully, Scripture has an answer for whatever questions we struggle with. We don't have to wonder or guess about anything in our lives. The answers to all of life's questions are gathered together in one book for us. The answer to this question is found right here in this verse. 1 Thessalonians tells us very clearly what God's will is for us. His will for us is to "be joyful always, pray continually and be thankful in everything, for this is God's will for you in Christ Jesus."

God's design for us is a spiritual steadfastness. It is a determined resolve to live by the commands He has set before us in His Word. His will and purpose for all of us is to choose joy, pray consistently, and always give thanks no matter what we feel. This is God's will for you and for me and for every believer who truly seeks to live a godly life.

FEBRUARY 2

"Ask God to fill you with the knowledge of His will through all spiritual wisdom and understanding" (Colossians 1:9).

Wise King Solomon knew the value of insight and understanding. When God posed the question, "Ask for whatever you want me to give you," the King replied, "Give me wisdom and knowledge" (2 Chron. 1:7). Would any of us give God the same answer if asked to share the true desires of our hearts?

We are exercising great wisdom when we pray for wisdom. James 1:5 says, "If any of you lacks wisdom he should ask God." Wisdom is not just acquired information or know-how. It is not theology or facts. It is the everyday application of living for God. What should I do in this situation? How should I handle that conversation? Do I need to confront this person?

The acquisition of spiritual knowledge is of little use unless we can apply it to our lives. Wisdom produces a transformed attitude which then rolls over into righteous living. It enables us to make choices and decisions that line up with God's best for us.

Colossians 1:10 says that we pray for wisdom "In order that we may live a life worthy of the Lord and may please Him in every way, bearing fruit in every good work and growing in the knowledge of God." Wisdom teaches us how to please God and live a life worthy of Him. God made it so simple for us to accomplish this task. All we have to do is ask.

FEBRUARY 3

"May the words of my mouth and the meditation of my heart be pleasing in your sight, O Lord my Rock and my Redeemer" (Psalm 19:14).

What better way to begin each day than by asking God to help us live our lives in honor of Him? David is praying that everything he says and everything that he does be pleasing to God. What a beautiful prayer!

All our thoughts and actions are born in the mind. We can't say or do what we haven't thought of first. It is difficult to keep our minds pure in the world today. Satan seeks to corrupt it on an ongoing basis. The evil one makes it his full-time job to jeopardize our relationship with our Father. So, we must make a conscious effort to keep our minds focused solely on God.

Colossians 3:2 says, "Think about the things of heaven, not the things of earth" (NLT). It is so easy to get caught up in the circumstances of everyday life. We must be intentional about keeping our focus on God. This doesn't come easy as we are so incredibly busy and pulled in so many different directions.

David also loved to meditate on God's Word. Maybe that's why he was known as "a man after God's own heart." Reading and meditating on God's Word pleases God and encourages us to live out our faith. We can't live out what we don't know. A Bible sitting on a shelf does us no good. Pray and ask God to fill you with a passion for His Word and the desire to become an eager student. You will be blessed, and God will be glorified!

FEBRUARY 4

"Everyone should be quick to listen, slow to speak and slow to become angry for man's anger does not bring about the righteous life that God desires" *(James 1:20).*

The Bible doesn't tell us that we should never be angry, but it does point out that it should be handled properly. If vented carelessly, anger can hurt others and destroy relationships. If bottled up inside, it can cause us to become bitter and resentful. If not dealt with, it can be like a cancer that will eat us up on the inside and metastasize to every area of your life.

Anger can cause hostile feelings toward someone and cause us to want to retaliate. When we've been hurt we naturally want to take revenge. However, Scripture tells us, "Vengeance is mine says the Lord" (Romans 12:19 KJV).

I had an experience once where someone had hurt me so deeply I didn't think I could ever get over it. The pain was so intense that it literally consumed me. I didn't think I would ever be able to get past it, let alone forgive the person. And yet I knew that I was causing my own suffering by rehearsing the incident over and over in my head, feeding my anger.

Then one day it hit me. I didn't have to try to get over this on my own. In fact, I couldn't get over it on my own. I needed God's help if I was ever going to heal and move forward. I began praying that God would not only soften my heart towards this person but also that He would soften theirs as well. I began to pray for the person I was angry with. In the process, I discovered that it's hard to have spiteful feelings towards someone you are praying for. Slowly but surely all that incapacitating anger started to seep away as I prayed for this person. The process of forgiveness had begun as I relied on God to do what I couldn't in my own power.

FEBRUARY 5

"Trust in the Lord with all your heart and lean not on your own understanding. In all your ways acknowledge Him and He will make your paths straight" (Proverbs 3:5-6).

When we have important decisions to make, sometimes we feel that we can't trust anyone—even God. *"But God"*... always knows what is best for us. We must trust Him completely and allow Him to lead and guide us in the right direction. We must be willing to listen to Him and be corrected by Him. Every area of our lives must be submitted to His authority.

There are many times that we don't particularly like the path that God has us on. We don't like our current circumstances or the testing God's allowing us to go through. That is when it is wise to remember this verse and trust that God knows what He's doing. Trusting Him is all He ever asks of us.

We can't possibly understand all the things that God does in our lives or in the world. God never intended for us to understand Him and His ways completely. There are mysteries of God that no one will ever know. Deuteronomy 29:29 says, "The secret things belong to the Lord our God." God doesn't want us to doubt and question. He wants us to trust that He has everything under control. We need God's presence in our lives, not His explanations.

FEBRUARY 6

"Whatever you do work at it with all your heart as working for the Lord and not for men" (Colossians 3:23).

I often think about this verse when I am doing housework. Instead of thinking how monotonous the work is, I try to shift my thoughts from the mundane work over to the positive side. Everything we do can be done for His glory. Every time we thank Him for something we are glorifying Him. So, as I am cleaning, I thank Him that I am healthy enough to bend over the tub and the toilets and scrub them. I thank Him that I have such a beautiful home to take care of. I thank Him for my husband who provides for me and is always so appreciative of my efforts.

Working to serve others is an act of worship to God. Our service—whether to our family or the community— is pleasing to Him and brings Him great glory. God has given all of us work to do. And He expects it to be done with the right perspective and attitude.

We serve an audience of one. It matters not if others are impressed with us. Our focus should be on pleasing God and not the world. I don't particularly care for work day at our church. To be honest, I'm also not crazy about taking my turn in the nursery on Sundays. But when I stop to remind myself that I am serving God and not man, I can enjoy what I'm doing. God wants us to be cheerful givers and cheerful servants in everything we do.

FEBRUARY 7

"The Lord was grieved that He had made man on the earth and His heart was filled with pain" *(Genesis 6:6).*

Adam and Eve are responsible for introducing sin into the world forever. Their disobedience brought evil into existence. When man began to increase on the earth, wickedness started abounding. The Bible gives vivid descriptions of how depraved humanity had become. David foretold this in Psalm 14:3. He wrote, "All have turned aside, they have together become corrupt; there is no one who does good not even one."

How did something that God created and said was good turn so corrupt? All of creation was pure perfection as God intended it to be until Adam and Eve decided to listen to the devil and disobey God's command. Now all mankind would suffer the consequences. Sin will always be prevalent in the world until Jesus comes back and restores it as it once was in the Garden. But until that day, all of creation will suffer great tragedies and injustices.

Human sin is God's sorrow. God's precious creation rebelled against Him, and His heart was filled with pain and sadness. God doesn't regret creating humanity. He didn't make a mistake. God does not lie nor does He ever change His mind; however, He does mourn when we turn our backs on Him and go our own way. Adam and Eve fell for the lie that they could be greater than God if they just ate that apple. Don't allow yourself to be tempted by such false promises. Stand firm in your faith and listen only to the voice of God.

FEBRUARY 8

"Above all, love each other deeply because love covers over a multitude of sins" (1 Peter 4:8).

Love is a "no matter what" proposition. It is not predicated on good behavior. Just like Jesus can't love us any less for our bad actions, we can't love people any less for theirs. Unconditional love is what we are called to practice. Loving people *no matter what* should be our vision statement.

Feelings can't be controlled. Emotions can just take over. But what we do with those feelings and emotions is what is important. We can't control how we feel, but we can control our actions and reactions. We have a choice as to how we're going to respond to everything that happens to us. We can choose grace and mercy or anger and vengeance.

Sometimes it takes dying to our own desires to make the right choices. It takes courage to be the bigger person. *"But God"* ... promises to be that strength and courage when we need it. 1 Corinthians 16:13 says, "Be men of courage; be strong. Do everything in love." Love should cover over every hurt ever inflicted upon us. If Jesus' love covered over all the injustices done to Him, we can too.

It's challenging to follow in Jesus' footsteps. But the Bible never promised us that it would be easy. In fact, it promises the complete opposite. It tells us we will experience trials and tribulations. However, 1 John 5:4 reassures us, "For everyone born of God overcomes the world."

Love no matter what. Forgive no matter what. Choose God's ways no matter what. It's the only right action we can choose. Don't base truth on feelings—base truth on truth! God is our source of truth, and He will provide all we will ever need.

FEBRUARY 9

"And if Christ has not been raised our preaching is useless and so is your faith" (1 Corinthians 15:14).

The Resurrection of Christ is one of the most debated events in the Bible. There will always be people who say that it didn't happen. They simply refuse to believe that Jesus rose from the grave three days after His crucifixion.

What is not debatable is that there were hundreds of eyewitnesses to this fact. Jesus appeared to Peter and the Apostles on Easter Sunday. And after that, He appeared to over 500 believers (1 Corinthians 15:6). This same testimony is given by all the Gospel writers.

Jesus' half-brother James did not believe that Jesus was the Messiah before the Resurrection (John 7:5). He was like the Apostle Thomas who doubted and needed proof. Thomas told the other Apostles that unless he saw the nail marks and the wound in Jesus' side, he would not believe. Not long after that, Jesus appeared and told Thomas to reach out and touch the evidence and stop doubting. Then He said, "Because you have seen me you have believed; blessed are those who have not seen and yet have believed."

The Resurrection of Christ is at the center of the Christian faith. Because Christ rose from the dead as He said He would, we know that He spoke only truth. He is the One True God! There is no other person nor another god who can make this claim. Putting your faith in anyone or anything else is a useless faith. Only Jesus Christ can provide life after death. Take a stand and reject useless faith and grab hold of the truth!

FEBRUARY 10

"This is the confidence we have in approaching God: that if we ask anything according to His will He hears us" (1 John 5:14).

I had been scheduled to go on a vacation with a friend for months. I was excited until I developed a serious back problem and was somewhat incapacitated. My activity level was way down, and I began to doubt whether I should go. But my friend had purchased the ticket, and I didn't want to disappoint her. So, I began to pray that something beyond my control would happen that would prevent me from going. I guess what I was really hoping for was God to intervene and provide me with a gracious way to avoid going.

Then one morning in my quiet time the Lord showed me this verse and suggested that perhaps I was praying for the wrong thing. He suggested that maybe I should try praying for His will to be done instead of mine. Truth be told, I've always thought that praying for God's will to be done was somewhat of a risky prayer because of the possibility of not getting my own way. But I obeyed and earnestly changed my prayer to, "Thy will be done."

It became obvious all too soon that God's plan for me was to go on the trip. I wasn't there long when God gave me another Scripture verse in Mark 6:31. It said, "Come with me by yourself to a quiet place and get some rest." I ended up having one of the most restful vacations I've ever had as well as some amazing personal time with the Lord. He poured into me every day through His word and spoke to me when I was out walking albeit at a snail's pace. He revealed His next project for me, which I credit to being obedient to His command to go on the trip.

If we pray for God's will to be done, it is always what

is best for us. I thought what was best for me at the time was staying home. But in the end, I saw that God's will was much better than mine. I now have more confidence that He always has my best interests at heart. I think our prayer requests must entertain God sometimes as we think we know what we need instead of Him.

FEBRUARY 11

"Be joyful always, pray continually, give thanks in all circumstances, for this is God's will for you in Christ Jesus" (1 Thessalonians 5:16-18).

There is a misconception by many that prayer is something of a duty we have to perform as Christians. Some people may even look at it as an obligation to be fulfilled every day. However, Scripture tells us the way to pray is more about our hearts and our attitudes than an act to be performed.

Prayer needs to be on a very personal level. It should involve our hearts intimately connecting with God. Our prayers should be encased in gratitude as it says in this verse. Thankfulness should not fluctuate with our feelings or circumstances. It might be a challenge sometimes to live this out in our lives. Being joyful and thankful can often go against our natural inclinations. So, we have to be deliberate about our gratefulness and expressing it to God.

Fostering a mindset of gratitude transforms us into worshipful beings that truly please God. Nothing can transform our hearts quicker than praising God. We were created specifically for this very reason. He loves the personal exchange that takes place during these special moments. Develop the habit of praying and worshipping unceasingly. You will experience more joy than you ever dreamed possible.

FEBRUARY 12

"And we pray this in order that you may live a life worthy of the Lord and may please Him in every way, bearing fruit in every good work, growing in the knowledge of God" (Colossians 1:10).

Just as physical fitness requires commitment, perseverance, and hard work, so it is with spiritual fitness. It just doesn't happen spontaneously. It takes great effort and consistency with both these endeavors. This is where most people fail in their quest for fitness. They start out with a bang, but, in time, their commitment slacks off. They begin to skip workouts, and soon they haven't seen the inside of a gym in months. It takes a great deal of discipline and determination to keep the goal in focus and stick to it.

Spiritual fitness works the same way. It takes the same time and effort as physical conditioning. To begin this process, we have to first make the commitment to become spiritually fit and then stick to a program that will help us get there.

The first exercise we must do is to read God's Word. This is essential to our success. God gave us His Word for our health and well-being. We can't live a healthy lifestyle without it! Prayer is the second exercise we must perform. This takes a non-negotiable decision to be faithful in spending quiet time with God. Making excuses will sabotage the entire process.

Just as physical conditioning can be difficult and inconvenient at times, we can expect the same as we get in spiritual shape. We have to make a choice up front that we will not let excuses get in the way. We must put God first in our day and stay true to our commitment. This is the only way we will achieve spiritual growth and fitness.

FEBRUARY 13

"Whoever does not love does not know God, because God is love" (1 John 4:8).

The word *love* gets tossed around so easily. The Bible says that God is love yet we love so many things. We say we *love* a dress or we *love* a restaurant, or we *love* a movie. It is not a word we use with reverence. We throw it around casually. But it really is a holy word.

There are hundreds of references to the word *love* in the Bible. They all pertain to how much God loves us and how His love for us is unconditional, unfailing, and abounding. The most important Scripture verse in the Word related to love is what is known as "The Greatest Commandment." When one of the teachers of the law came to Jesus and asked Him what was the most important law, Jesus replied, "Love the Lord your God with all your soul and with all your mind and with all your strength" (Mark 12:30). He continued and told them the Second Greatest Commandment, which is to "Love your neighbor as yourself."

Love is not a feeling. It is a choice we make. We can choose to love God, and we can choose to love our neighbor. We are called to obey God's commandments, and we are promised great joy in return. The prophet Malachi described it this way: "'Test me in this,' says the Lord Almighty, 'and see if I will not throw open the floodgates of heaven and pour out so much blessing that you will not have room enough for it.'" Choose love. It will never return to you empty but steeped in the blessings of the Almighty.

FEBRUARY 14

"Don't be afraid. Just believe" (Mark 5:36).

Jesus spoke these very words to a synagogue ruler who had come and asked Jesus to heal his dying daughter. The ruler came to Jesus and fell at His feet and said, "Please come and put your hands on her so that she will be healed and live" (Mark 5:23). Jesus was focused on something else at the time which kept Him from leaving right away. In the meantime, an official of the ruler came and told Jesus to forget it. He said that His daughter was already dead. But Jesus told the ruler not to be afraid and to believe.

Jesus went on to the ruler's house anyway and told those grieving that the child was not dead but simply sleeping. He went to the girl, took her by the hand, and told her to get up. She immediately arose, astonishing everyone as they witnessed this miracle.

Faith is the foundation that miracles are made of. My biggest miracle occurred many years ago and involved the saving of one of my children's lives. My teenage son was missing for three agonizing days. He was finally found on the morning of the third day. He was alive but had suffered many injuries.

Many missing children stories don't end up like ours. Usually, hope fades quickly after the first 24 hours. *"But God"*... performed a miracle in our family and gave our son back to us. That miracle went on to lead a normal healthy life. Miracles still happen today. Don't fear. Just believe!

FEBRUARY 15

"He tends His flock like a shepherd; He gathers the lambs in His arms and carries them close to His heart; He gently leads those that have young" *(Isaiah 40:11).*

There exists a popular picture of Jesus with a sweet little lamb wrapped around His neck. It is a beautiful and peaceful picture. Jesus is tenderly carrying the animal in such a way that you can't help but feel the love and tenderness. The lamb resting so comfortably on Jesus adds to the wonder of the scene.

Shepherds used to break the leg of a wayward lamb to keep it close to the flock. Then the shepherd would carry the animal until it could walk again. This is how God cares for us. When we are broken and can't go it on our own, God carries us until we heal and can stand on our own again.

The Good Shepherd always takes care of the broken. He is right there waiting to pick us up and carry us. He is faithful to care for us and guide us back to the flock after we are strengthened and healed. If you need to rest in the arms of Jesus just like the hurting lamb, simply ask Him, and you will soon find yourself basking in His warm embrace. He will carry you until you are completely healed and ready to do life again.

FEBRUARY 16

"Because of the Lord's great love, we are not consumed for His compassions never fail. They are new every morning; great is your faithfulness" (Lamentations 3:22-23).

I've often wondered how the Apostle Peter felt after the rooster crowed. He had denied knowing Christ three times just as the Lord had predicted. Was he totally eaten up with remorse? How would he ever be able to face Jesus again?

It's rather easy to understand the fundamentals of forgiveness. But do we fully experience it in our hearts? Do we experience the freedom and peace that comes from true forgiveness? Jeremiah 31:39 tells us that God will remember our sins no more. He will never bring them up to us again. They are wiped away forever.

But do we forgive ourselves? If God can wipe our slate clean and remember our failures no more, how come we can't? Why do we continue to beat ourselves up over and over? We are the only ones who can do the reminding, so we know who the culprit is when those memories come popping back up.

There is a lesson in every one of our failures. Peter got a lesson on forgiveness and unconditional love when he was reunited with Jesus after His Resurrection. Maybe he learned to be stronger when tempted to sin again. Maybe he learned that failing is part of succeeding. One thing is certain; Peter embraced the task that Jesus had given him to feed His sheep. He is responsible for starting the first church and went on to be martyred later in life. Peter indeed discovered just how great God's love, compassion, and faithfulness were. They never fail even after a rooster crows three times!

FEBRUARY 17

"Submit to God and be at peace with Him; in this way, prosperity will come to you" (Job 22:21).

The word *submit* in the Bible tends to make some people cringe. They tend to conjure up all sorts of visions of being slaves or servants. They mistake the word submission for control. This is so far from the truth. Submitting to someone is a voluntary act. It is a choice we make to yield to and respect authority. The definition of submitting is to "yield without murmuring," to do what we're asked without complaining.

Scripture goes on to say that if we submit to God, we can be at peace with Him. Some think of peace as absence from war or strife. This is the world's view. Jesus' peace can live in us even when everything around us is in turmoil. Spiritual peace does not depend on circumstances or things going our way. Peace is a by-product of living in a right relationship with Jesus. He is the only true source of peace. But we must submit to receive that gift of peace in our lives.

Submission and peace go hand in hand. Submission really is just turning the wheel of your car over to Jesus and moving over to the passenger side. Giving God control over your life is the first step in this process. Paul writes in Philippians 4:6, "And the peace of God which transcends all understanding will guard your hearts and your minds in Christ Jesus." Submit your life to God, and He will fill you with the most unfathomable peace you have ever known.

FEBRUARY 18

"Many are the plans in a man's heart, but it is the Lord's purpose that prevails" (Proverbs 19:21).

Someone once told me that if you really want to make God laugh, tell Him your own plans. I have run full steam ahead of God so many times in my life. I've done things that I thought shouldn't be done and not done things I should have done.

I had a game plan laid out for my life. I had goals set and things I wanted to accomplish. But I never stopped to pray about these desires or involve God in the decision making. I selfishly neglected to get His input on what might be His will for my life. Wise King Solomon addressed this perfectly in Proverb 16:9: "In his heart, a man plans his course, but the Lord determines his steps." I had determined my steps and left God totally out of the equation.

Mistakes are wonderful teachers. I have learned from many a failure not to make plans for my life. I do not concern myself with the future anymore. I don't focus on my goals but on what God has in store for me each day. I have relinquished control of what I think is best for me and trust in God's plans alone.

It's hard to let go and let God! It's an aha moment when we finally discover that it's not about us. We are not the center of our universe. It's so freeing when we finally come to realize that our steps are totally directed by God. We can trust Him in every aspect of our lives because we know it was meant to be. Jesus teaches in Matthew 6:34 that "We don't have to worry about tomorrow for tomorrow will worry about itself."

FEBRUARY 19

"I am the Way, the Truth, and the Life. No one comes to the Father except through me" (John 14:6).

Some people think that if they lead a good life and have a good heart that they will share eternal life with God. Some even think that God is so good He could not possibly let anyone perish. God is indeed a good God, and He intends that no one is left behind. But He left the choice up to us. It's called free will. If we want to see the Father, we have to embrace the Son.

Scripture is very clear on the subject. Galatians 6:7 (TLB) says, "Don't be misled. Remember that you can't ignore God and get away with it." God knows the difference between lip service and true devotion. Our hearts must be fully committed to Him.

Jesus offers us the way to heaven. He is not one way among many but THE WAY. Scripture is replete with verse after verse of this truth. The main theme in the book of John is the identity of Jesus as the son of God and the path to eternal life. One can hardly read this gospel and not be convinced that Jesus was who He said He was. He did what He came to do, which was providing us the way to live eternally with our Father. He opened the door and beckons us in. Will you choose Jesus and the assurance of heaven one day?

FEBRUARY 20

"I planted the seed, Apollos watered it, 'But God' made it grow. So, neither he who plants nor he who waters is anything, but only God, who makes things grow" (1 Corinthians 3:6-7).

Sometimes we feel like it is our responsibility to lead others to Christ. We sow the seeds of faith and then expect them to immediately pop up and bear fruit. When nothing happens, we think that our efforts have been wasted.

There are no superstars in God's Kingdom. We all share in the task of planting and watering the seeds of the gospel. However, we have no control over the condition of people's hearts. We have no way of knowing whether what we've sown has taken root. Some hearts are simply impenetrable. Some hearts are shallow, and the seed can easily be snatched away. And some are so scarred that they receive the seeds only for them to be swallowed up in the darkness of their wounds.

The salvation of others is not up to us. It is only through the work of the Holy Spirit that new life is produced. Only God can take those seeds we've planted and make them blossom and bear fruit. We are simply the planters that God uses to begin the process of germination.

Don't be discouraged by someone's rejection or lack of interest when you are trying to sow seeds of faith. You never really know what has penetrated their hearts and minds. We may never know who we influenced by our sowing until we get to heaven and see the fruit of our labor.

FEBRUARY 21

"The voice of the Lord is powerful; the voice of the Lord is majestic" (Psalm 29:4).

The voice of God spoke all of creation into existence. God said, "Let there be light." God said, "Let there be an expanse between the waters." God said, "Let there be lights in the expanse of the sky." Merely by speaking, God brought all things into being. The powerful and majestic voice of God brought forth all of life. He created the entire universe in six days, and then He rested on the seventh to kick back and enjoy His handiwork.

Job gives us another dimension of God's voice. He tells us, "How faint the whisper we hear of Him." God's voice is commanding, but it can also be quiet. It can whisper things in our hearts and in our minds. God normally doesn't use a booming voice to grab our attention. He has a much gentler approach which usually involves the advice found in Psalm 46:10: "Be still and know that I am God."

We have to silence our minds to be able to hear from God. Just like we sometimes can't hear our own kids amid the noise and distractions, we can't hear from God when our minds are clogged up with the day-to-day stress of life. Getting alone in a quiet place with God will enable you to hear those faint whispers. He is waiting to whisper to you as soon as you are still enough to hear Him.

FEBRUARY 22

"Apart from me, you can do nothing" (John 15:5).

Jesus is teaching about the vine and the branches in this passage. Jesus calls Himself the vine, and He calls us the branches. He tells us that the branches cannot grow or produce fruit without being connected to the vine. He adds, "Anyone who parts from me is thrown away like a useless branch and withers" (15:6). A branch that is disconnected from the vine is dead and lifeless.

Scripture says we can do nothing apart from God. He wants to be at the center of our lives enabling us to do what we need to do. Every accomplishment is the result of God's intervention. It is God who gives us the ability and the talent to achieve our goals and dreams. If we are successful, it is because of God! He is responsible for every good thing in our lives.

We need to be diligent about giving credit to God for our blessings. If it weren't for Him, we would be in a much different place. Everything comes from God, and our response should always be a great big thank you. Don't ever let pride seep in and try to rob you of the praise that is rightfully God's. Proverbs 16:18 says, "Pride goes before destruction and a haughty spirit before a fall." God should get the credit for every good thing in our lives.

FEBRUARY 23

"Rejoice in the Lord always. I will say it again—Rejoice!" (Philippians 4:4).

The Apostle Paul wrote this verse while shackled in a Roman prison. The tough situations he repeatedly found himself in did nothing to thwart his passion for rejoicing in the Lord. He constantly taught the early churches to be content with life despite the circumstances that surrounded them. Paul lived what he preached. He rejoiced if he was being blessed or if he was in chains. His love for Jesus and His desire to continue his mission of spreading the gospel was all that mattered to Paul.

Our attitudes do not have to reflect the state of our circumstances. Paul was always full of joy because he knew that no matter what happened Jesus was with him. He lived his life with the full assurance that God was in control and would take care of him.

It's easy to get discouraged when we are in unpleasant situations. But we need to look no further than Paul for encouragement. In all his sufferings he never lost sight of God. His faith and trust remained steadfast through thick and thin.

If you have lacked joy lately maybe it's not your circumstances but your perspective. The prophet Habakkuk tells us in verse 3:18, "Yet *[But God]* I will rejoice in the Lord; I will be joyful in God my Savior" (italics mine). This is one of the strongest affirmations of faith in all of Scripture. Habakkuk is saying that he chooses to be joyful no matter what life brings. He knows his faith will carry him through anything. When you wake up tomorrow morning say to yourself, "Today I choose joy—no matter what!"

FEBRUARY 24

"The mind controlled by the Spirit is life and peace"
(Romans 8:6).

The battle over good and evil takes place in our minds. As humans, we are all sinners by nature. Isaiah 53:6 says, "We all like sheep have gone astray; each of us has turned to his own way." When we think about ungodly things, we are being controlled by our sinful nature. But when we allow our minds to focus on the things of God, we are then being controlled by His Spirit. Our minds naturally gravitate towards our sinful nature, so it truly is a battle keeping it on the right track.

Just as we can train our bodies physically, we can also train our minds. Christian author Joyce Meyer wrote a book on this very subject and gives some great advice. She tells us that, "We don't have to think on what we're thinking on."[1] In other words, you don't have to continue to think a bad thought. You have the power and ability to choose what you will allow into your mind.

The training of anything takes practice. Our expectations can't be met all at once. If you want to transform your mind spiritually, a good place to begin is with prayer. Pray and ask God to help you have a mind controlled by the spirit. Ask Him to help you remove the bad thoughts and nurture the good. Use Scripture to encourage you. A mind filled with God's Word is less likely to struggle with sinful thoughts.

---

1   Meyer, Joyce. *Battlefield of the Mind* (Warner Faith, 1995)

FEBRUARY 25

"The god of this age has blinded the minds of unbelievers so that they cannot see the light of the gospel of the glory of Christ" (2 Corinthians 4:4).

Satan is the god of all evilness in the world. He is the archenemy of God and the unseen power behind all unbelief and ungodliness. His mission is to deceive and blind us all to the truth.

The devil rules in this present age. He is responsible for all wickedness. His Mission is to entice everyone into his camp and away from God. He works hard looking for pawns that he can use in his schemes to bring more and more terror and darkness into the world. And he seems to be doing a good job of it!

We must be careful to recognize how Satan is trying to blind us and pull us away from God. He is always at work trying to tempt us with sin and corrupt our minds. He knows if he can get a foot in the door it won't be long before he can take over the room. We have to be vigilant about keeping our hearts and minds solely focused on Christ and refuse to listen to the father of all lies.

The good news is that Satan will be destroyed in the end along with all pain and evil. Jesus is coming back to take His rightful place as King and Ruler, and there will be victory for all believers. Jesus will take His own to live with Him in eternity.

Don't succumb to the devil's lies. Take a stand against him and tell him to get lost. Open your eyes to the truth and refuse to be fooled any longer. The rewards of this choice are life-changing and eternal. God wants to prepare a place for you in heaven with Him. Open your eyes to the light of the gospel of Jesus and get your room reserved today.

FEBRUARY 26

"But the Lord's unfailing love surrounds the man who trusts in Him" (Psalm 32:10).

A father tells his son that it's time for him to become a man. So, he takes him far into the woods at night, sits him on a tree stump and then blindfolds him. The father tells him he must sit there until he senses the first ray of light.

It was a long and scary night for the young man. The woods were full of all kinds of eerie noises. The leaves rustled all around him, and animals cried out in the wilderness. He couldn't wait for the arrival of dawn. When it finally came, he took off his blindfold and, lo-and-behold, the first thing he saw was his father sitting on a tree stump not far from him. He had been there all night guarding and protecting him from any potential harm.

Isn't that just like the relationship with have with our Father in heaven? Even though we might not see or hear Him, He is always with us! His presence is present all the time. His unfailing love surrounds us every minute of every day.

Sometimes it takes blind faith to believe that God is sitting on that stump right next to us. It takes faith not to worry and trust God's got everything under control. It takes believing completely and wholeheartedly. God is sitting right beside you on that tree stump in your own wilderness.

FEBRUARY 27

"And we know that in all things God works for the good of those who love Him and who have been called according to His purpose" (Romans 8:28).

I have struggled with depression all my life. I used to shake my fist at God for this thorn in my flesh and plead with Him to take it away. I would whine about the unfairness of it all and feel sorry for myself for having to live with such a real but misunderstood disease. "Why Me?" became my theme song.

"But God" ... kept bringing me back to this verse in Romans, and I began to see my affliction in a different light. I wondered how I could use my thorn as a platform to help others. I soon realized that living with depression had groomed me to be a passionate mental health advocate. I became very outspoken about my illness because I knew there were people out there like me who needed to hear they were not alone in their struggle. I have since used my thorn to give talks to groups of women about not being ashamed of their depression and how faith can play a big part in living with the disease. I told them my secret for being able to persevere and live with hope. Jesus is and will always be my source of strength as I soldier on in this fight.

If we don't have our faith to help us, what do we have? Jesus is the greatest therapist we could ever ask for. He is always available to listen to us without our making an appointment. He gives us hope when we have absolutely none. He shows us that there is a light at the end of the tunnel if we hang in there. He is our life preserver in the storm.

God has a purpose for everything and everyone. Everyone has a thorn that God gave them to use for His glory. Thorns are not a curse but a blessing because they can be used to help others while glorifying God. The thorn in your flesh is a divine opportunity given to you by God as part of His plan. How will you use it for His glory?

FEBRUARY 28

"Lord, you know everyone's heart" (Acts 1:24).

Some days when I sit down with the Lord to have my quiet time my head starts swimming with all the people and needs I want to pray for. I am compelled to make sure I bring all my concerns before the Lord and not leave anyone or anything out. Then a friend said to me one time, "Don't you realize that God already sees what's in your heart and what's on your mind. He's already got this before you utter one word." That comment brought me enormous freedom. If God has counted every hair on my head, then He must know me well.

The Lord knows everything about us better than we do. There is nothing that can be hidden from Him. He knows our thoughts and feels our emotions. There is not one corner of our heart that we can hide from Him. God sees it all.

It is pointless to try and cover anything up from God. Denying your feelings is also a waste of time because God sees right through them as well. He sees our struggles. He is longing for us to unburden our hearts so we can rest in peace. Remember He knows your heart inside and out, but He wants you to willingly share it with Him. Will you stop hiding and open your heart to Him?

MARCH 1

"But we are not of those who shrink back and are destroyed, but of those who believe and are saved" (Hebrews 10:39).

The book of Hebrews is a book focused mostly about faith. The tenth and eleventh chapters give great examples of the undying faith of the Old Testament Patriarchs. The author, the Apostle Paul, also addresses some fundamental truths of Christianity.

Paul, like Jesus, was a straight shooter. They told the truth and nothing but the truth. Sometimes people turned away from their teaching because it could be convicting at times, and looking inward can be painful. We might not like what we see.

This verse is an example of how Paul doesn't mince words. In the New Living Translation, it says, "But we are not like those who turn their backs on God and seal their fate. We have faith that assures our salvation." He who rejects God will face punishment. God tells us, "I will take vengeance. I will repay those who deserve it."

The consequences of turning our backs on God are serious and affect where we will spend eternity. But if we believe and have faith, our salvation is assured. We will be spared from God's wrath, and we will have the security of knowing that we will live with Him in heaven one day.

Two choices with two very different outcomes. Which choice have you made? Do you know for sure where you will spend eternity? We never know what tomorrow holds.

MARCH 2

"Find rest, O my Soul, in God alone; my hope comes from Him" (Psalm 62:5).

The book of Job is packed full of wisdom and inspiration. After Job was assaulted physically by Satan, he lay suffering on an ash heap being ridiculed by his wife and friends. But he said to them, "Though He (God) slay me yet I will hope in Him." No matter what happened to poor old Job, he was not going to give up and curse God. He maintained his faith throughout his entire ordeal. Job had the confident assurance that God would save him from his suffering and restore him back to health.

We claim to have hope in Jesus, but then we doubt that He will do what He promises in His Word. We believe He can do all things yet our hope wavers like a flag on a windy day. Romans 8:24 says, "But hope that is seen is no hope at all. Who hopes for what he already has."

Job's challenge is our challenge today. Will we wait patiently and confidently while God works out His plan? I had a Bible Study teacher tell me one time that she prayed for her husband's salvation for 40 years. She never gave up on him or lost hope. She was confident that he would see Jesus face-to-face one day. He did give his life to Jesus in the end.

It took decades for my teacher's prayer to be answered, but the lesson we can take from this is God is faithful and does answer our prayers. Why did it take so long for God to answer? There are things in this life we will never understand. There are mysteries of God that we will never grasp while on this earth. We can't begin to understand the mind of Christ or His purposes. We are simply called to have faith and trust in God.

MARCH 3

"By day the Lord went ahead of them in a pillar of cloud to guide them on their way and by night in a pillar of fire to give them light so that they could travel by day or night" (Exodus 13:21).

When the Israelites were wandering through the desert, they were guided along both day and night by either a pillar of cloud or a pillar of fire. When the pillar of cloud appeared in the daytime, that was their signal to pack up camp and move on. It also protected them from the broiling sun of the desert. At night they traveled by a pillar of fire to light their way and to remind them of God's continual presence with them. They never had to worry about getting lost or road construction up ahead. The cloud and the fire were their compass—their GPS system.

God gave us our own GPS system to use on our journey through this desert called life. It's called the Bible. There are guidance and direction to be found there for everything. We don't ever have to wait for pillars of fire or pillars of clouds. God's Word is always available to us.

It must have felt strange for the Israelites to follow a puffy cloud and the glow of fire. But I am certain they traveled confidently knowing they were protected and cared for. It's much easier to walk in confidence when you know who is leading—when you trust the person up front.

Is your pillar out in front of you? Are you following it or trying to make the journey on your own? Don't run the risk of getting lost in the desert. Keep your GPS plugged into the Lord and He will lead the way.

MARCH 4

"The Lord delights in those who fear Him; who put their hope in His unfailing love" (Psalm 147:11).

The word *fear* in Scripture does not mean to be afraid of God. When the Bible talks about fear in relation to God, it means to have a reverential awe and respect for Him. It means to honor and glorify Him. It has nothing to do with dread, fright, or foreboding.

Fear is the opposite of faith. You can't be afraid of God and trust Him at the same time. If we truly trust Him with our lives, then we must live like we believe it. Fear is a tool Satan uses to trip us up. One of the most quoted Psalms is 23:4, which says, "I will fear no evil, for you are with me." Another translation reads, "I will not be afraid, for you are close beside me." Fear has no place in a believer's heart.

Wise King Solomon talks a lot about fear in the book of Proverbs. In 1:7 he writes, "The fear of the Lord is the beginning of knowledge." Faith in God produces knowledge and knowledge gives birth to wisdom. Wisdom is the insight we need for living godly lives, making godly decisions, and avoiding pitfalls. The fear of the Lord is the first step to peace and fulfillment in life. Allow the Lord to delight in you as you place your faith and trust in Him.

MARCH 5

"If any of you lacks wisdom, he should ask God" *(James 1:5).*

Scripture tells us that there was none wiser than King Solomon until Jesus came. One of the things that made him so wise was that he loved God with all his heart and walked in all His ways. He served Him dutifully and was obedient to His commands.

How did Solomon become so wise? Scripture tells us that God appeared to him in a dream one night and said, "Ask for whatever you want me to give you" (1 Kings 3:5). Solomon replied, "But I am only a little child (he was 20 when he took over as king) and do not know how to carry out my duties. So, give your servant a discerning heart to govern your people and to distinguish between right and wrong." Solomon didn't ask for wealth or prolonged life. He simply asked for the gift of wisdom. So, God agreed and granted Solomon a "wise and discerning heart."

When choices and decisions need to be made, we need to go to God first and ask Him, "Is this a wise thing for me to do? Considering my past, present, and future, is this a good decision I'm making?" God will answer when you call on Him. Just don't forget to let God be the first person you call to seek advice.

MARCH 6

"Come to me all you who are weary and burdened and I will give you rest" (Matthew 11:28).

Carrying a heavy load is not an easy task. One of my granddaughters was still asking to be carried around at the age of 3. Not having the ability to say no, as most grandparents would agree, I struggled with those 30 pounds of love and could only carry her for so long until my arms and back gave out. My strength and power were exhausted.

However, Jesus isn't referring to physical burdens in this verse. He is talking about the weariness that results from emotional trauma. He is referring to that suitcase of problems we tend to carry around with us everywhere we go. He is talking about the problems we have struggled with for years and can't seem to let go of.

Jesus is ready and waiting to take those suitcases from us. But we must be willing to give them up. Sometimes we think we can handle everything on our own. We think *I got this*. But then life begins to fall apart, and we wonder why we didn't turn to God before. Why didn't we turn to the only One capable of helping us?

"But God"... only He can handle our burdens. We can't do this life on our own. Furthermore, we weren't meant to. Decide today to bring your burdens to Him and then leave them there! God will take care of them and offer you the freedom you have been searching for all your life.

MARCH 7

"Trust in the Lord with all your heart and lean not on your own understanding, but in all your ways acknowledge Him, and He will make your paths straight" (Proverbs 3:5).

Our understanding of life and how it all fits together is so limited. We do not see the big picture like God does. He sees our whole lives like a giant parade being visible all at once from the beginning to the end. We can only see it from the curb watching it slowly pass by float by float.

God always knows what is best for us, so we must trust Him completely in everything. Our understanding will never be equivalent to God's, so we would be foolish to expect it. His perspective is far greater and smarter than ours.

God tests us, so we can learn to rely on and trust in Him. It is not a sign of weakness to need God. It takes a humble person to acknowledge their need for Him. It takes real humility to be honest and admit we need guidance and direction to stay on the right path.

There is nothing weak or shameful about needing to rely on God. He is actually very pleased when we finally wave the white flag and ask Him to get involved. He rewards those who seek Him and acknowledge His goodness. Make Him a part of everything you do, and He will make your paths straight.

MARCH 8

"I am the Way, the Truth, and the Life" (John 14:6).

Why does Jesus refer to Himself as the Truth in Scripture? The answer can be found beginning in the Old Testament. Prophets predicted that a Savior would come down to earth and through His death and Resurrection bring salvation to all men. Those predictions by the Prophets, plus hundreds more, solidified the truth about Jesus. The truth was fulfilled through Him; thus, He embodied the word *truth.*

The gospel is sometimes referred to as the Truth in Scripture. The Apostle John used the word truth 25 times in his book and always links it together with Jesus. The gospel is focused on the truth of Jesus and His saving grace. It is the very essence of the Good News.

As the Truth, Jesus is the reality of all of God's promises. John says in 1:14, "The Word became flesh and made His dwelling among us. We have seen His glory, the glory of the One and Only who came from the Father, full of grace and truth."

The world offers many opinions and variations on the truth. They are caught up in darkness and unbelief. No one can offer eternity except the real Truth—Jesus. What is the barrier that is holding you back from accepting the real Truth? Maybe it's time to remove that wall once and for all and make room for "The Way, the Truth, and the Life" to come in.

MARCH 9

"He cuts off every branch in me that bears no fruit while every branch that does bear fruit He prunes so that it will become even more fruitful" (John 15:2).

What is the purpose of pruning flowers and plants? What results from lopping off withered petals and stripping old stems away? Any gardener knows that this is the only way to get the plants to grow bigger and fuller. To increase their splendor, they have to undergo this harsh process.

God has to prune us in the same way so that we can grow in our faith and be more productive for His Kingdom. Sometimes the pruning is a snip here or a snip there, nothing too painful or traumatic. But sometimes He has to prune us all the way down to our roots to enable a new birth to take place. It can be a difficult process but a necessary one for our spiritual lives to thrive and be fruitful.

The results of pruning should be evident. There should be new growth or some reaping that has taken place. Jesus said that He cuts off every branch that bears no fruit. It might be time for some of us to do a little gardening. This might be a good opportunity to examine ourselves and see if we are bearing any fruit. Are you growing in your spiritual life? Are you sowing into the lives of others? John 15:8 says, "This is to my Father's glory that you bear much fruit showing yourselves to be my disciples." One of the best ways to glorify God is by producing fruit and blessing Him with the harvest.

MARCH 10

"I have set the Lord always before me. Because He is at my right hand, I will not be shaken" (Psalm 16:8).

Fixing our eyes on Jesus is the only way to remain unshaken in this tumultuous world. Placing Him at the center of our lives will keep us strong and steady. Nothing can lead us astray if we keep the Lord firmly enthroned over our lives.

A dancer can't do a successful spin unless she picks a focal point and keeps her eyes glued to it as she twirls. If she loses her focus for one minute, she will lose her balance and fall. That spot in front of her is the key to her success.

We are all like dancers in this respect. As we turn and spin through life, we must stay focused on that one thing—on that one person. Jesus will keep us steady on our feet if we keep Him in front of us. Those who choose not to train their eyes on God will not achieve the abundant life He has promised all believers. God is and should be our only focal point if we truly want to live happy and successful lives.

MARCH 11

"This happened that the Scripture might be fulfilled"
(John 19:24).

When Jesus was born, the Father had His whole life carefully planned out for Him. God had a mission and a destiny for Jesus, and He would see to it that everything would happen according to His plan.

In the recordings of the Crucifixion, one verse was repeated several times. It was, "This happened that the Scripture would be fulfilled." There were 28 prophecies fulfilled in Jesus' Crucifixion. It was all predicted and recorded in the Old Testament. These prophets were in constant communion with God and recorded the words He spoke to them. They were the vessels He used to give the world a glimpse of what lies ahead.

Our lives are fashioned in the same way. God has everything pre-planned for us for a specific purpose. Just like Jesus, we were born with an important task to carry out, custom fit to the way God created us.

As our lives unfold, we can say that God's prophecy is being fulfilled. God's sovereign intentions are taking place in our lives every day. He is always at work orchestrating the next event. He had it all mapped out from the beginning of time.

How will you respond to God's plan for your life? Will you choose to be obedient to God's calling like Jesus? Will you commit to finishing the work He's given you to do? Why not embrace your assignment and commit to using it for God's glory?

MARCH 12

"Love covers over all wrongs" (Proverbs 10:12).

Hurts happen in life. Someone hurts our feelings and doesn't give us the apology we think we deserve. Or, we take offense to a comment someone said about us. Then we want to rehearse the painful scenario repeatedly in our minds until we're further convinced that we are victims of injustice. We can, however, choose to react differently. We can choose the way of love instead.

We must make a choice when wrongs happen. Will we hold onto the hurt and let it affect our relationships? Or, do we forgive and let it go? The person who offends is most likely oblivious to the feelings of the offended. They're not losing any sleep over it because they're not aware of any problem. We are the ones tossing and turning in our beds at night holding on tight to our pain and suffering. But what exactly are we accomplishing by holding onto this hurt except to make ourselves completely miserable?

We have no power to change people or make them see things our way. We only have power over ourselves and the choices we make. It's our humanness that makes us feel totally powerless to forgive and do the right thing. That's why we need God's help. Only He can give us the desire and the fortitude to forgive. Isaiah 40:29 says, "He gives strength to the weary and increases the power of the weak."

Hurts are a part of life. They will always exist and try to sabotage our relationships. Just remember, Scripture tells us God is love and love conquers all. If you choose God, you *must* choose love.

MARCH 13

"Be very careful then how you live—not as unwise but as wise, making the most of every opportunity because the days are evil" (Ephesians 5:15-16).

If we're not vigilant, we will miss an opportunity to make a positive difference in someone's life due to being so focused on our own lives and our own agendas. Divine opportunities often come disguised as interruptions.

A good example of this is the story of the Good Samaritan. Two men passed by an injured man because they were in a hurry and too consumed in themselves to stop. They clearly had no interest in helping the man as they passed by. But the Good Samaritan lived his life with his eyes open to the people and needs around him. He didn't think twice about interrupting his day by helping a man in need. He seized the chance to allow God to work through him to minister to a hurting soul.

I was unexpectedly called to be a full-time babysitter when my new granddaughter was born. I was not expecting to revisit my child-rearing years in retirement. *"But God"*... obviously had other plans. At first, I couldn't stop thinking about all the things I would have to give up: shopping, lunch with friends, projects I wanted to work on. But then I realized what a divine opportunity God had given me. God gave me the privilege of sowing into this little one's life. My attitude came full circle, and I poured myself into her and made every minute count. The bond we now share because of this divine opportunity is incredible.

Divine opportunities come our way every day. We just have to be open to them and willing to make some sacrifices. God will always reward us when we put other's needs before our own. Who will you bless today?

MARCH 14

"The Lord is my Shepherd; I shall not be in want. He makes me lie down in green pastures. He leads me beside quiet waters. He restores my soul!" (Psalm 23:1-2).

God is the master of restoring souls. As the Living Water, He knows our constant need to be refreshed, and He knows what will revive us. When we are feeling dry, the best thing we can do is lie down with our Shepherd and allow Him to recharge us.

Besides relying on the Shepherd to renew us, we can be proactive in keeping our souls healthy. One of the best ways is to read God's Word. His Word is living water to all who drink from it. Another way is to develop an attitude of gratitude. Being grateful lifts our spirits and fills us with unspeakable joy. Finding things to thank God for and being appreciative of His blessings works wonders in our hearts and minds.

Seeing God work in the lives of others can encourage us as we witness firsthand the goodness and the faithfulness of God. Hearing someone share an answered prayer or tell how God just ministered to them is wonderful nourishment for our souls.

If you feel like you need some restoring, seek the Shepherd and take a moment to smell the rich green pasture surrounding you. Stop and listen for the Living Water running beside you. Jesus is right there waiting to lead you where you need to go!

MARCH 15

"The greatest among you will be your servant"
(Matthew 23:11).

Greatness was no prerequisite for God calling our fore-fathers into service. God used sinners from every walk of life to accomplish His purpose. King David was an adulterer, Moses was a murderer, and Jacob was a master deceiver. Yet they all were chosen by God to accomplish great things for His Kingdom. Some, however, were not very excited about God's plans to use them.

When God gave Moses the command to go and deliver the Israelites from Egypt, Moses wasn't all that thrilled about the prospect. In fact, he said to God, "Who am I that I should go?" (Exodus 3:11). Even when God promised that He would go with him, Moses still argued with Him and said, "O Lord, I have never been eloquent neither in the past nor since you have spoken to your servant." Did you notice how Moses called himself God's servant yet was not willing to be obedient to His call?

Moses' story is a prime example of how God will never ask us to do something that He hasn't already equipped us to do. Our job is to put one foot in front of the other and walk in obedience. If we are to be good and faithful servants, we must believe that God's plans are trustworthy and that He knows exactly what He's doing.

God sees our greatness even when we don't. He sees our potential and has a plan for our lives. He has given us everything we need to serve Him. We just need to take that leap of faith like Moses and trust in God's promises.

MARCH 16

"I want you to know brothers that the gospel I preached is not something that man made up; I did not receive it from any man nor was I taught it; rather I received it by revelation from Jesus Christ" *(Galatians 1:11-12).*

Some people believe that Paul was the greatest evangelist in the New Testament. He was the most prolific writer, having written thirteen of the 27 New Testament books. Paul may have written the words on paper, but He did not truly *author* the books. Paul writes in 2 Timothy 3:16, "All Scripture is God-breathed." Paul, in his humbleness, affirmed God's sovereignty as the only author of Scripture.

Although Paul used his own mind, talents, language, and style, he only wrote what God wanted him to write. He only recorded what He heard God tell him to record. That is why we can be certain that Scripture is totally trustworthy because God was in control of its writing. Paul's recordings are known today as the Pauline Epistles.

We should study God's Word so that we will know how to lead godly lives. However, our knowledge of Scripture is not useful if we don't allow it to strengthen our faith and lead us to do the work that ultimately brings glory to God. The words God spoke to the writers of the Bible are just as relevant to us today. Read and heed the precious gift of the Word of God.

MARCH 17

Many are the plans in a man's heart, but it is the Lord's purpose that prevails" (Proverbs 19:21).

We all have dreams and aspirations. We all have goals and plot our lives accordingly. But how many times do we pause before we make our plans and ask God's opinion on the matter? How many times do we ask Him what He wants us to do?

Sometimes God agrees with our plans but just not our timing. God answers all our prayers in one of three ways: yes, no, and not yet. Things that we want to happen ASAP sometimes turn into months of waiting before there are any answers. However, when those answers come, we can look back on all that waiting and see that God's timing was indeed perfect.

A good verse to remember if you're in a holding pattern of some kind, waiting to hear from God, is Jeremiah 29:11. "For I know the plans I have for you,' declares the Lord, 'plans to prosper you and not to harm you, plans to give you hope and a future.'" God hears you and will answer you. Even if it's not the answer you want to hear, trust that God only wants the best for you. His ways are always better than ours!

MARCH 18

"You intended to harm me, 'but God' intended it for good to accomplish what is now being done, the saving of many lives" (Genesis 50:20).

The story of Joseph in Genesis is a great example of a *"But God"* moment. Joseph had to endure much injustice in his young life. He faced abandonment by his brothers, false accusations made against him, and imprisonment for many years for a deed he never committed. He could have chosen to be very angry with God. Instead, He trusted that God had a higher purpose for Him. And indeed, He did. Through a series of God-ordained events, Joseph ended up being vizier over all of Egypt and was credited for saving the people of Egypt from a severe famine in the land.

Joseph himself summed up his life like this. While speaking to his brothers who had sold him into slavery, he told them, "You intended to harm me... *'But God'* intended it for good to accomplish what is now being done, the saving of many lives."

We have to believe that everything that happens to us is happening for a reason and that God will bring good from it. All our challenges in life are for a single purpose—to give glory to God by our testimony.

MARCH 19

"The man who formerly persecuted us is now preaching the faith he once tried to destroy" (Galatians 1:23).

If anyone has ever doubted that God can transform a life they need look no further than Paul. The Apostle Paul went from being a persecutor and murderer of Christians to one of Jesus's most instrumental Ambassadors of the Gospel. *"But God"* ...

Paul's transformation took place on a simple country road as he was traveling to the town of Damascus. One question, one moment in time and the old Saul was gone, and Paul was born. All it took was a flash of light and the voice of God asking Saul why he was persecuting Him.

It was an honest question, yet Saul had no answer. It makes one contemplate if people today know why they persecute God. How can you reject someone you don't even know? Paul didn't know Jesus until he had an up close and personal experience with Him. You have to get close to someone before you can get to know them.

Saul didn't have an answer for Jesus, but he did have a response. He shot back with a question of his own, "Who are you, Lord?" He was curious enough at that point to consider: who was this Lord who had called to Him?

Have you been rejecting God for no reason? Have you turned your back on Him because of some past hurt or a prayer that went unanswered? Maybe this is your Damascus moment. God is calling to you and asking you to leave your old self behind on that dusty road and allow God to make you a new person.

MARCH 20

"Therefore, I tell you do not worry about your life"
(Luke 12:22).

The medical community has done various studies on worry, and they have proven that worry can, in fact, shorten our lifespan. Findings reveal that worry and stress not only affect longevity but can also cause a myriad of health issues and diseases. It seems Jesus was one-up on science when He preached this sermon. He knew worry would damage us physically, mentally, and spiritually.

Worry is the opposite of trust. We can't worry and trust at the same time. Either we're going to give our problems and concerns over to God, or we're going to hang onto them ourselves and live in a shroud of anxiety. Being nervous and apprehensive solves nothing and only adds to our frustration. Worry can't change a thing except to add stress to our bodies, which goes along with what the scientists are telling us.

Jesus asks further on in this passage, "Who of you by worrying can add a single day to his life?" When worry rears its ugly head, read Psalm 55:22 and trust David's great wisdom. He wrote, "Cast your cares on the Lord, and He will sustain you." We need to give our burdens over to Him, and He will take care of the rest. Don't waste another minute doing something that has no benefit and will most likely shorten your life expectancy. Don't worry; just trust, and God will take care of the rest.

MARCH 21

"You are right in saying I am a King. In fact, for this reason I was born, and for this I came into the world, to testify to the truth. Everyone on the side of truth listens to me" (John 18:37).

Jesus' life was coming to an end. It was night, and the soldiers came to arrest Him after He was betrayed by Judas. Jesus willingly went with the soldiers and was taken to stand before Pilate, the Roman governor. After Pilate questioned Jesus, he told the people that he found no basis for any charges to be brought against Him.

After an unfair and illegal trial according to Jewish law, Pilate finally condemned Jesus to death. He was charged with a crime that He didn't commit. He was an innocent man accused of an offense that was fabricated against Him. Jesus didn't argue or fight back. He willingly submitted Himself to the Romans and their decision.

Have you ever been falsely accused of something or treated unjustly? I was accused of something in high school that I didn't do and suffered unfair consequences that I didn't deserve. However, unlike Jesus, I didn't forgive so easily. I carried that betrayal around like some badge of honor for years. Then one day someone asked me, "How is it that Jesus forgives you and you can't forgive others?"

Are you holding forgiveness hostage towards someone? Have you been the victim of an injustice and can't seem to get over it? Even after being falsely accused, Jesus willingly laid down His life for us. We are not called to ransom our lives, but we can certainly treat others with the same grace and mercy that Jesus modeled. Jesus tells us through His sacrifice on the cross that no injustice is unforgivable. Everyone is worthy and deserving of forgiveness, regardless of their crime.

MARCH 22

"My grace is sufficient for you, for my power is made perfect in weakness" (2 Corinthians 12:9).

I cannot do this life on my own. I am not ashamed to admit that I'm not self-sufficient. I need a Savior who can walk with me through this crazy life. Some people consider needing help as a sign of weakness. This is not true and a lie that Satan wants us all to believe.

Our human weakness provides the perfect opportunity for God to display His divine power. The weaker I am, the more I need God. I can't muster up any strength on my own. I need God's help to empower me. He loves for us to cry out to Him and admit our frailty. That's when He can step in and say, "It's okay, beloved. I have you, and I will take care of everything. Just rest in me and watch what I can do."

The Apostle Paul suffered a physical ailment that he referred to as a thorn in his flesh. He prayed and asked God to remove it three times, but that wasn't in God's plan. God's answer was, "My grace is sufficient." In other words, I will help you deal with it and be glorified in the process.

If you are suffering, don't ask God why He has afflicted you. Instead, ask Him to teach you about His grace and pray for Him to fill you with His strength. Paul ended this passage with these words, "Therefore I will boast all the more gladly about my weaknesses so that Christ's power may rest on me. That is why, for Christ's sake, I delight in weaknesses, in insults, in hardships, in persecutions, in difficulties. For when I am weak, then I am strong." Will you allow others to see your need for God so that they will also have hope for their weaknesses?

MARCH 23

"But those who hope in the Lord will renew their strength. They will soar on wings like eagles, they will run and not grow weary, they will walk and not be faint" (Isaiah 40:31).

I had a revelation one day while down in the pit of depression. It helped me forever as I struggled through life with mental illness. I realized that when I'm flat on my back down in that hole, the only place I really had to look was up. Being in the shadow of darkness forced me to focus on the speck of light above me. I reminded myself that Light brings death to darkness. I knew then that God was with me and had the power and ability to pull me up from that pit of despair. I just needed to trust Him and believe in His promise of healing restoration.

God wrote in Isaiah 49:23, "Those who hope in me will not be disappointed." When I discovered hope through the Light of Jesus, I never felt abandoned or alone again. The next time I found myself back in the pit of darkness, I had hope because I knew that God would rescue me. He had done it before, which gave me the ability to persevere.

We can trust that God will do what He says He will do. We can put our faith in His promises. If you're in a pit right now, look up! God will give you all that you need to make it through. You will soon soar on wings like eagles in the light and with the hope that God is waiting to pour into you.

MARCH 24

"Love the Lord your God, listen to His voice and hold fast to Him" (Deuteronomy 30:20).

Nothing brings me greater joy than to hear God's still small voice whispering in my inner being. It honestly feels like a piece of heaven opening, and I get a taste of what I'll be hearing when I get there.

I always try to be in tune to God's voice, but the stresses of life can take over sometimes, and I can't hear anything but noise and confusion. Distractions have a way of keeping us from things that are far more important. Often, we can't hear God's voice because we're too busy talking, and He can't get a word in edgewise.

My morning devotional allows me the time and attention to be still before God. I've also learned how to commune intimately with Him as I go throughout my day. I share my thoughts with Him and listen for His voice of encouragement. I pause often and thank Him for every little blessing, even the simple things like a good parking place or quickly finding the perfect gift I need. I ask for His direction during the day or how I should handle a situation. I involve Him in every aspect of my life.

The more I make Him a part of my life, the better the chance I have of hearing from Him. Just as sheep respond to the shepherd's voice, we need to learn how to respond to our Shepherd. Ask Him to help you recognize His voice and to be responsive. Listening is as much a part of our faith as praying.

MARCH 25

"I am the Lord your God who teaches you what is best for you, who directs you in the way you should go" (Isaiah 48:17).

Having a teachable spirit is crucial for our spiritual growth. Jesus was always in teaching mode throughout His ministry, and He wants to fulfill that role in our lives today. He wants to teach us everything we need to know about how to live godly lives.

It's a challenge to let someone else take over and direct your steps. Surrendering your desire to be the leader is difficult because it transfers all control over to them. It's just basic instinct for us to want to run the show—to run our own lives. But the question is: how do we know in our finite human minds what is really best for us? We don't see the big picture like God does. We only see momentary glimpses and snapshots. Therefore, God is much more knowledgeable about the direction that is best for us. We don't know what is up ahead. We can only live in the moment.

A hiking trip could put the hikers at great risk if they lost sight of their guide. A mountain climbing expedition could be put in grave danger if the climbers couldn't see their Sherpa up ahead. A ship might be lost at sea if the sailors ignored their compass. We have a great guide and compass, and His name is Jesus. All we have to do is keep Him in full view. He is always out in front leading the way. If you follow Jesus, you can be certain that you're on the right path!

MARCH 26

"O Lord my God, I will give you thanks forever" *(Psalm 30:12).*

Thankfulness opens the door to feel more of God's presence in our lives. Thanking God is acknowledging His goodness and faithfulness. It is telling Him that we appreciate all that He does for us. To thank God is to honor and glorify Him.

Practicing thankfulness also creates a positive mindset. It is virtually impossible to be grateful and negative at the same time. Gratefulness leads to joy and peace deep down in our souls. Nothing can sweep away a bad mood faster than gratitude.

Being thankful is a habit that can be learned just like any other habit. The more you put it into practice, the better you will become at it. We have to be deliberate and train our minds to focus on God's goodness. We have to redirect our thinking from the things that pull us down to the things that lift us up. We should memorize and rehearse Scripture verses that center on thankfulness to encourage this way of thinking. Negativity won't stand a chance against such a pre-determined mindset.

It's never too late when it comes to change. Begin to discover things that you are grateful for and tell God! Make it a daily habit of thanking Him for at least five things every day. If you have sight enough to read this, you already have the first one!

MARCH 27

"Be still before the Lord and wait patiently for Him"
(Psalm 37:7).

The definition of patience is to endure pain and trouble without complaining. Unfortunately, we all fall victim to being complainers at times. Waiting doesn't come easy for most of us, and we feel ourselves getting irritable and frustrated in the process. Yet God tells us to wait patiently for Him. We are to wait patiently while we anticipate our prayers being answered or we need direction in a certain area. God's timing is usually much different from ours, but be assured His is always perfect.

Some of us live impatiently for some future event instead of living in the present. When we live for tomorrow, we miss today and sadly we never get it back. Each day is a precious gift that we need to appreciate. Our focus needs to be on today and what God is doing in our lives at this very moment. Jesus said in Matthew 6:34, "Tomorrow will worry about itself."

Abraham waited for his son Isaac to be born for 25 years. He and Sarah were 100 years old when they became parents. Hebrews 6:15 says, "And so after waiting patiently, Abraham received what was promised." If we endure without complaining, as Father Abraham did, God's promises will come to fruition in our lives. Just be still and keep trusting God for everything in your life.

MARCH 28

"The mind of sinful man is death, but the life controlled by the Spirit is life and peace" (Romans 8:6).

The battle between trying to live a godly life vs. living according to the world's standards takes place in the mind. Before we ever sin, we have to first entertain that tempting thought. This is where we go astray and fall into sin's snare. Satan loves to plant sinful ideas in our minds. Then it is up to us to choose either to entertain those thoughts or reject them.

The world and all its moral corruption try to infiltrate our minds daily. We must be intentional about what we think about. Sometimes, it seems like a constant battle trying to keep our minds pure and focused on God. However, this is what we are called to do. And yes, it's a tough job! Thankfully, we have the help of the Holy Spirit to enable us to transform our thinking and keep it on the right track.

We have a clear choice to make. What are we going to allow in our minds? Which of these two mindsets will we follow? The one that leads to spiritual death or the one that offers everlasting life and peace? God leaves the decision up to us.

MARCH 29

"For God has been gracious to me and I have all I need" (Genesis 33:11).

If you have ever doubted that God blesses the undeserving, the story of Jacob will change your mind. Jacob—one of the twin sons of Isaac, who is one of our great Forefathers—had a very bad habit of deceiving people. His name, in fact, means "deceiver." He had a long list of deceptions to his credit. The most famous one was conning his brother Esau out of his birthright as the eldest son. Jacob pretended to be Esau when Isaac was giving out the family blessing before his death. He then lied to his brother again later when he told him he would follow him to an agreed upon city and then went his own way.

"But God" ... even when we are unworthy and undeserving of God's kindness and faithfulness, He shows us grace and mercy. Even though Jacob lied and deceived many, God still blessed him and used him for His mighty purpose. The twelve tribes of Israel were all the sons of Jacob!

There is nothing God can't turn around and use for His good. God doesn't look at the sin in our lives; he looks at our hearts. His plan will prevail no matter what we've done in our past. God is a God of grace and new beginnings. Lamentations 3:22 says, "Because of the Lord's great love we are not consumed, for His compassion never fails." Great is thy faithfulness O Lord!

MARCH 30

"A man is not justified by observing the law but by faith in Jesus Christ [...] For if righteousness could be gained through the law, Christ died for nothing!" *(Galatians 2:16, 21).*

The second chapter of Galatians has been referred to as the core of the gospel message. The Apostle Paul tells us that the only way we can become righteous and justified is by grace through faith in Jesus Christ. There is no other way or person through whom we can be saved.

Following a set of rules and observing rituals does not make us right with God. If we believe that, we are essentially making a mockery out of the cross. If we could have been reconciled with God simply by obeying rules, then Christ died for nothing. None of us can be good enough to earn a spot in heaven. God's standard is perfection that we can never achieve. So, He gave us the gift of faith through His grace, so we can be made right with God. No human effort can contribute to our salvation. Titus 3:5 says, "He saved us not because of righteous things we had done, but because of His mercy."

If you feel like something is lacking in your life, it may be that you just need to be made right with God. God created us with a Jesus-shaped hole in our hearts that can only be filled by Him. He gives us a choice to either live with empty hearts or allow the love of Jesus to come in and fill it. Pride is the only thing standing in your way of living the fulfilled life God has ready for you.

MARCH 31

"I urge you to live a life worthy of the calling you have received" (Ephesians 4:1).

What is our calling? Ephesians 2:10 tells us, "For we are God's workmanship created in Christ Jesus to do good works which God prepared in advance for us to do." What are the good works Paul is referring to? What calling have we received?

We were all born with a purpose. God has a task for each one of us both personally and for the church in general. We were all called to full-time ministry the day we were saved and gave our lives to Christ. Serving God is not optional. We have all been ordained as ministers and disciples to go out and bring hope to a hurting world.

We are all in the program and have a part to play in God's kingdom. Each of us is designed for a special purpose. To get a feel for what your purpose might be, ask yourself some questions. For instance, what am I good at? What comes naturally to me? What do I have a passion for? The answers to these questions might help you to identify how you were meant to serve God and His Kingdom.

As Christ's Ambassadors, we should live worthy of the calling God has placed on us. We are Christ's representatives on earth. We should consider it a privilege to serve Him and to be able to bring Him glory. That is our calling, and it is worthy of our devotion.

APRIL 1

"I have made the Sovereign Lord my refuge; I will tell of all your deeds" (Psalm 73:28).

A refuge can easily be pictured as a port in a raging storm. Think of how the port acts like a shelter providing safety for the ships as the fierce winds blow, and the rains pummel down. A port in a storm provides what the ships need for survival.

We can easily identify with those ships. We need to have protection as well against those nasty storms in our own lives. We can do this by having a solid relationship with Jesus and depending on Him to be our refuge. David wrote a beautiful song of praise in 2 Samuel chapter 22:31. It says, "He is a shield for all who take refuge in Him. For who is God besides the Lord? And who is the Rock except our God?"

We all need a safe place to run when the storms of life start blowing around us. Where will we turn? To whom will we run? Jesus is the only one who can vigilantly keep watch over us. He promises to be our refuge and our shield. The prophet Nahum wrote in 1:7, "The Lord is good, a refuge in times of trouble. He cares for those who trust in Him." God will always be there for us rain or shine. He promises never to leave us nor forsake us. Jesus will see us through every stormy sea. His life preserver is poised and ready to be tossed out to you. Grab hold of Him and hang on!

APRIL 2

"Enter His gates with thanksgiving and His courts with praise; give thanks to Him and praise His name" (Psalm 100:4).

Thankfulness should be a daily habit—a way of life. We should give God thanks every day regardless of our circumstance or how we feel. God's Word tells us to be thankful "in all things." The good and the bad. This doesn't mean that we should thank Him for a painful situation or problem. However, we should be able to find something to thank Him for in the midst of it. If nothing else, you can be thankful that He has given you yet one more day to live and breathe.

When coming out of a trial or a difficult circumstance, it may take some time to see God's purpose behind the suffering. But when all is said and done, the good will be evident. We will be able to look back and see how our faith and trust in Him have grown. Spiritual growth is the fruit that God wants to harvest from every one of our hardships.

I developed a significant back problem while finishing this book. I was really struggling with giving God thanks in this circumstance! How could I praise Him for being bed-ridden at such a crucial junction? I couldn't even sit at my desk and type. *"But God"* ... showed me how to improvise and set things up so I could work from my bed lying down. He gave me something to be very thankful for amidst my infirmity.

God has taught me through the years that sometimes He has to make us be still so that His purposes can be accomplished in our lives. I may never have finished this book if not for God calling a timeout. Being grounded from life's normal activities allowed me to complete the task God had given me to do. His will was fulfilled through my painful circumstances.

APRIL 3

"Clothe yourselves with humility toward one another because God opposed the proud but gives grace to the humble" (1 Peter 5:5).

Being humble can be a challenge. We tend to want to puff ourselves up to look good in front of other people. We like taking all the credit for our successes. We have a strong desire to show off our nice things and boast about our achievements. But doing these things is the opposite of the behavior that God expects from us. He defined humility when He sent His Son to be the perfect example of humbleness.

The night before Jesus died, He had dinner with His disciples. It was customary in that day when entering a home to leave your sandals at the door and wash your feet. The dusty roads made for some very dirty feet back then! Jesus told His disciples that He would be the one to wash their feet. The King—the Savior of the world—stooping down and doing a job that was usually left to the lowliest of servants in the home! John 13:5 describes the scene: "After that, he poured water into a basin and began to wash His Disciples feet, drying them with the towel that was wrapped around Him." He then told them, "I have set you an example that you should do as I have done for you."

We are called to clothe ourselves in humility and serve one another just as Christ served others. We may not have a chance to wash any feet, but we should always be aware of the needs of those around us.

APRIL 4

"Those who know your name will trust in you, for you, Lord, have never forsaken those who seek You" (Psalm 9:10).

David truly had a heart for God. His Psalms reflect the deep love and admiration he had for Him. He wrote more about God's goodness and faithfulness than anyone else in Scripture. His words are encouraging and can lift up even the heaviest of hearts. You can always find a spiritual boost visiting David in one of his Psalms!

When David referenced knowing God's name, what he was really saying was that we should be able to relate to God intimately. To have a close and personal relationship with God is to acknowledge Him as Lord of your life and to live out that acknowledgment. We can know something from an intellectual standpoint but not necessarily relate to it personally. Knowing God is a spiritual experience, not just how much information we know about Him.

If you really want to discover the Lord, open your Bible, and start reading. Take the time to get to know Him just like you would any new friend. Spending time together is vital to any relationship. Make room for God, and He will make room for you!

APRIL 5

"And my God will meet all your needs according to His glorious riches in Christ Jesus" (Philippians 4:19).

There is a huge difference between a need and a want. God never promised to indulge all of our desires, but He has promised to meet all of our needs. We will never be able to supply all our needs on our own. God didn't create us to be self-sufficient. He made us to depend solely on Him.

Some people believe they can get by in life on their own. That's exactly what they are doing—getting by. They are not experiencing the true joy and peace that comes from allowing God to be in control of their lives. They are missing out on the true fulfillment and satisfaction that can only come through the glorious riches in Jesus Christ.

God not only provides everything we need but if we follow Him closely, He blesses us with our desires as well. Just like we love to spoil our kids and grandkids, God loves to do the same for us. It brings Him great joy to shower us with gifts.

We will never receive everything we want in this life. However, by trusting in God, our wants will soon fade and be replaced with appreciation for what He has already given us. We will realize that our wants were never that important anyway. Paul sums it up best for us in Philippians 4:12, "I have learned the secret of being content in any and every situation, whether well fed or hungry, whether living in plenty or in want." Live in contentment and bask in God's peace!

APRIL 6

"You will be made rich in every way so that you can be generous on every occasion and through us, your generosity will result in thanksgiving to God" *(2 Corinthians 9:11).*

The abundant life Jesus refers to in Scripture is achieved through sacrificial giving. This is a beautiful piece of godly wisdom. The act of giving should be a part of every Christian's life. Generosity can transform hearts and lives and reflect Jesus working in us for the good of His Kingdom. Giving is a wonderful way to honor and glorify God.

Imagine if we all performed one act of generosity or kindness every day. It wouldn't have to be a material thing. It could be just a smile, holding a door, or helping someone take a package to the car. We don't necessarily have to do acts of kindness; we can be acts of kindness. What a completely different world we would live in if we practiced such a divine concept.

Generosity produces great joy in our lives. Don't we always get more pleasure out of giving a gift than receiving one? God designed it this way so we would be encouraged to bless others.

Next time you're in a Starbucks drive-thru line, think about buying the person's coffee behind you. Or, anonymously treat someone to a meal in a restaurant. There are countless ways to express generosity. Pray and ask God to put opportunities in your path to be a light and a gift to someone else.

APRIL 7

"It is finished" (John 19:30).

These three words, spoken by Jesus on the cross just before He died, culminate the mission Jesus was sent to earth to accomplish. The word *finish* in the Greek means "complete" or "paid in full." Jesus paid the price in full for our sins so we could be reunited with the Father in heaven one day.

Imagine receiving a huge bill in the mail. The amount owed is so steep you know there is no way you will ever be able to pay it. Now imagine that same bill coming in with a bright red stamp across it saying, "Paid in Full." That bill represents our lives and how Jesus paid in full what we owed. We are now free from the debt of sin, and we can start over with a clean slate.

How could mankind ever be reconciled to God after sin entered the world? *"But God"* ... sent His One and Only Son to earth to be born in a manger and die on a cross to fix the problem. Jesus made a way for us to be with God in heaven by His death and Resurrection. We are now debt-free and can look forward to a glorious reception in heaven. Has your bill been *paid in full* yet?

APRIL 8

"I am the Lord's servant" (Luke 1:38).

These are the words Mary spoke after the angel had visited her and told her she will be with child and give birth to a son. Mary only asked one question: "How will this be since I am a virgin?" The angel explained that the power of the Most High would come upon her and she would bear the Son of God. Without any further questions or comments, Mary simply replied, "I am the Lord's servant. May it be to me as you have said."

I don't think I would have taken this news as graciously as Mary. I think I would have said something like, "Say what? Who? Me?" But Mary didn't try to make excuses or complain about how unworthy she felt. She simply believed the angel and trusted God. Her first response wasn't to think about herself or what others would think. Her only response was that if God was asking her to do something, she was going to do it.

What is your response when God asks you to do something? Is it the same as Mary's? Or do you weigh and balance, procrastinate, and argue? Mary knew this wasn't going to be an easy assignment. She knew the ridicule and ostracizing that would take place. Yet, she was willing to be obedient to God's calling. We all need faith like Mary's, faith that says we will do whatever the Lord asks of us without any questions or doubt. Faith that simply says as Mary said, "May it be to me as you have said."

APRIL 9

"And the peace of God which transcends all understanding will guard your hearts and your minds in Christ Jesus" (Philippians 4:7).

Peace can be described in many ways. It can be a feeling of well-being that resides in our souls. It can be a calmness that exists no matter what is going on around us. It can be that inner tranquility that tosses all worry aside. Experiencing peace in our lives truly does transcend our human understanding.

We can't experience true lasting peace without Jesus. In Scripture, peace is referred to as one of the "Fruits of the Spirit" (Galatians 5:22). It is a by-product of being in a relationship with Christ. It is the harvest gathered from being committed to and living for Him.

God's peace will always be different from the world's peace. We will never live in a world free of war and chaos until Jesus comes back. However, we can experience personal peace irrespective of what is going on around us. The gift of peace is available to everyone. We just need to immerse ourselves in Christ, and we will receive this precious gift.

APRIL 10

"Devote yourselves to prayer being watchful and thankful." (Colossians 4:2).

The power of prayer is nothing short of amazing. Prayer is as simple as talking to God. It can be done anywhere at any time. It has no boundaries or restrictions. We can pray about anything and everything.

The Apostle Paul taught that we should always incorporate thanksgiving into our prayers. He taught that rather than reciting a list of requests we need to take the time to thank God for all His many blessings. Our prayer life should be more about praising and thanking God than rolling out our laundry list of needs. Matthew 6:8 says, "Your Father knows what you need before you ask Him."

God will always answer our prayers, maybe not in the way we expect Him to or want Him to, but He will always give us a response. Even though we don't like it, sometimes the answer is simply no or not right now.

Persistent prayer is an expression of our faith and trust in God. It is honoring Him because we realize we can't do this life on our own and need His help and direction. If you are discouraged because some answers to your prayers seem to be coming too slowly, remember that His delays always work to our benefit. Never give up hope. Just keep praying and trusting that God always knows what's best for you.

APRIL 11

"Come to me all you who are weary and burdened and I will give you rest" (Matthew 11:28).

Life can get very wearisome sometimes. It seems we are excessively in demand on a daily basis and our load feels heavier and heavier. When it becomes too much, it can affect us physically, mentally, and spiritually. *"But God"* ... quite clearly gives us the antidote for this problem.

God promises us a respite if we hand over our burdens to Him. He promises to free us from worry and replace it with rest. The word *rest* conjures up a myriad of feelings. Words like relaxation, a break, a breather, a time-out, all come to mind. When you put a toddler in timeout, you are essentially removing him from his stressful environment and putting him in a place where he can be quiet. I think adults could benefit from some time-outs. When we become over-burdened and overwhelmed, it might be a good idea to remove ourselves from the situation and go to a quiet place to think and pray.

Jesus reassures us of the wisdom of bringing our burdens to Him in Matthew 11:29. He says, "For I am gentle and humble in heart and you will find rest for your souls." If you are looking for rest, look no further than Jesus. He is the answer to all of our burdens!

APRIL 12

"Surely God is my salvation; I will trust and not be afraid" (Isaiah 12:2).

Trusting is a challenge when it seems like everything is spinning out of control. Our minds know the meaning of trust, but sometimes our hearts are slow to catch on. Intellectually, it makes perfect sense, but applying it to our lives can sometimes become a stumbling block. Fear gets in the way and wants to rob us of our ability to trust in God.

Trust is defined as the firm belief in the honesty and reliability of another person. The two words that are synonyms with trust are faith and hope. It's interesting how these words—faith, hope, and trust—are all linked together by definition, almost as if it's impossible to have one without the other.

When you find yourself staring in the face of trouble, it's time to put your faith and trust into action. Fear should have no place in our hearts if we are truly trusting God. When we experience fear, we have placed our hope in something or someone other than God. We must keep our focus on God and rely on His Word to encourage us and keep things in the right perspective.

APRIL 13

"Praise the Lord O my soul and forget not all His benefits" (Psalm 103:2).

Offering praise to God is not something we do only when we receive good things from Him. Praise should be embedded in every heart. Being thankful and exercising gratitude should be a daily occurrence. The New Living Translation says, "Praise the Lord, I tell myself, and never forget the good things He does for me." Notice the words: *I tell myself.* What this means is that praise may not come naturally, so we must make it a point to practice praising God every day.

It is easy to complain and find fault with life, but, we have plenty to be thankful for. God can always be praised for forgiving our sins, loving us unconditionally, and the biggest gift of all, salvation! We receive all these things without deserving any of them.

If life is tough right now, and you can't find anything to be truly grateful for, read the entire 103rd Psalm. There is a list of God's promises there as well as wonderful descriptions of the essence of His character.

Remind yourself daily to incorporate praise into your life. Nothing is more pleasing to God's ears than our utterances of thanksgiving. We should never take for granted the God we serve and who is so faithful and good to us.

APRIL 14

"They are more precious than gold, than much pure gold; they are sweeter than honey, than honey from the comb" (Psalm 19:10).

I received a wonderful spiritual insight one day simply cutting up an apple—an ordinary task that served as a beautiful illustration of how God views us. It also reinforced a hallmark truth of our faith that God can save us even when we're tainted.

I had grabbed an apple out of the refrigerator and noticed it had a rotten spot on the top. So, I cut the spoiled section off but thought the rest of it still looked good enough to eat, so I tasted it. I was surprised to find that it was still very juicy and sweet as honey. God intervened at this point and whispered, "Salvation is like that apple. After the rotten part (sin) is cut away, the remainder is just like it was before the decay occurred. Better than good. Exceedingly and abundantly good. Fresh and sweet like honey."

I found it interesting that the Lord referred to the saved part of the apple as honey. I later learned that honey was a precious commodity in biblical times. It was a key ingredient in every Jewish household as it never spoiled or lost its flavor. It was also considered a treasured gift of honor. God was comparing us to honey and all its priceless qualities!

God is always one teaching moment away from what we think are the mundane things in our day. Learn to look for Him in the ordinary and discover the spiritual lesson behind it!

APRIL 15

"Share with God's people who are in need" (Romans 12:13).

One day, I came across a woman working in a retail shop who seemed to be having a particularly bad day. It was obvious from her comments to fellow employees and her sad countenance that she was deeply troubled. After she checked me out and I walked away, I was prompted in my Spirit to go back and give her one of the cards of encouragement that I carry in my purse for such occasions. I asked one of the other employees her name, wrote it on the envelope, and placed it on the counter for when she returned.

After I left, I prayed that the note would brighten her day and give her a new perspective. I prayed that she would feel God's presence and find the hope that she seemed to need at the time. I wanted her to know that she was loved by a Heavenly Father who cared about her and wanted to fill her with His peace.

God sends divine opportunities our way so we can lift each other up and share with those in need. We can be a light just by a soft touch or a kind word to someone. If we truly love people the way Christ loves us, we should be able to minister to God's people in need. The grace of God should always be something we share and pass on to others.

APRIL 16

"Write in a book all the words I have spoken to you"
(Jeremiah 30:2).

I started journaling back in 2001, and it has been one of the most rewarding experiences of my life. I have filled 30 journals (and counting). I have loved every minute, every word, and every page that I've filled. Journaling has taught me so much about myself and about God. I have always told my friends that writing is the best free therapy and God is the best therapist we could ever ask for!

I was having my quiet time and journaling one morning when I really felt the Lord nudge me to share what I wrote in my journal that day with my Bible study group. I wasn't sure why, but I know when God asks us to do something, He always has a plan.

So, I took my journal with me and read the passage to the group. When I finished, the woman next to me leaned over and whispered, "Thank you. I really needed to hear that today."

God uses our passions to bless others. That day He used my passion for journaling to give a much-needed word of encouragement to someone. We both received a blessing that day—the one who was obedient to God's nudge and the one who needed to hear a word from the Lord.

APRIL 17

"He will have no fear of bad news; His heart is steadfast trusting in the Lord. His heart is secure; he will have no fear" (Psalm 112:7-8).

It's maddening when Satan or people, in general, try to plant negative or destructive thoughts in our minds. The worst thing we can allow into our minds is fear. Notice the word *allow* in that sentence. The only way fear can take hold of us is if we allow it. That's why we're told in this verse to make sure our hearts are steadfast and focused on God.

Allowing fear into our hearts and minds is, in essence, saying to the Lord, "I don't trust that you have things under control." We have to believe that God is who He says He is and will do what He says He will do. Otherwise, our faith is of no use.

We are called to cast off fear as well as our anxiety. Psalm 46:1-2 says, "God is our refuge and strength, an ever-present help in trouble. Therefore, we will not fear." Remaining steadfast is a choice we make. Are we going to give in to the temptation to question whether God knows what He's doing? When we trust God completely to take care of us, we will find that fear has no place in our lives.

APRIL 18

"Let us draw near to God with a sincere heart in full assurance of faith" (Hebrews 10:22).

We must consider a few things before attempting to draw closer to God. We have to be sure our hearts are completely sincere before we approach a holy God. We must check ourselves and make sure that we have undivided allegiance to Him. We should ask ourselves if we have faith and trust in Him alone for everything. Are our lives built on the foundation of His Son? Approaching God with anything less would make us out to be a hypocrite.

The Israelites in the Old Testament had some problems drawing near to God from time to time. They would turn to idol worship, and God would destroy them. The prophet Ezekiel in 13:23 tells us why God did this. It says, "And then you will know that I am the Lord." He let them know without a shadow of a doubt who the One True God was.

Israel was God's chosen people, and as many times as they turned away from Him, He always forgave them and restored them back in His good graces. We can expect God to do the same for us. If we are repentant and seeking to draw near to Him, we can be assured that He is pulling us to Him. Always approach the Lord with a full assurance of faith and He will surround you with His presence.

APRIL 19

"The Son of Man must be delivered into the hands of sinful men, be crucified and on the third day be raised again" (Luke 24:7).

As I celebrated Easter recently, I thought about how we really need to acknowledge this holiday more than one day a year. One Sunday in the spring falls short of the daily gratefulness that should be a part of our lives. We have been saved by His miraculous victory over death!

Jesus could have climbed off that cross at any time. But His love for us kept Him there writhing in agony and gasping for His next breath. He knew He had to complete the mission God the Father had given Him. When Jesus rose on the third day, He changed our destinies forever. Without the Resurrection, salvation would not have been possible, and our fates would have been sealed. The Christian faith would have died out without the miraculous work of Jesus on the cross.

We can be born again through the Resurrection. We have been given the gift of faith and eternal life by Jesus' sacrifice. Do you believe this? Are you willing to risk your eternal destiny on your answer? This question is the most important question you will ever have to answer in your lifetime. Do you believe this? God wants your answer to be yes. He wants you to be with Him in heaven one day. Will you choose to be with Him as well?

APRIL 20

"A gentle answer turns away wrath" (Proverbs 15:1).

Proverbs is a book about wisdom. This verse would be a good one to copy and carry around in your pocket. The tongue can be a dangerous thing if we don't keep a careful watch over it. Proverbs 13:3 says, "He who guards his lips guards his life."

I once heard a great shaving cream analogy about how words can affect others. Our words can be compared to the foam that comes out of the can. Once the foam is out, you can't put it back in. Words are that way too. Once they leave our mouths, they can't be taken back. I can't count the number of times I wished I could have put that foam back in the can!

Gentleness really makes a difference in our speech. Have you ever tried to argue in a whispering voice? A soft, gentle reply will diffuse many an argument. Have you ever noticed how a child loves to have a secret whispered to them? They immediately get quiet and listen very intently. This advice works great when disciplining a child as well. Responding to a child's tantrum with a gentle whisper will go a long way towards calming them down and quickly resolving the issue.

All our words impact people. Whether they are spoken gently and encouragingly is up to us. Gentle answers are more effective and can build a person up while harsh answers can hurt and even scar. Think about that shaving cream the next time you are tempted to unleash potentially fatal words. They will never fit back in that can!

APRIL 21

"But you brought my life up from the pit, O Lord my God. When my life was ebbing away, I remembered you, Lord, and my prayer rose to you" (Jonah 2:6-7).

In Bible times, pits were used to trap animals. The animal was tricked into stepping on a covering over the pit, thus falling into it and being captured. Satan works in the same way today. He is the ultimate trickster! He lures us to the coverings over his slimy pits of sin. He loves to trip us up, and he accomplishes this by his lies and deceit. When we're at our lowest point, it doesn't take much convincing to accept the hopelessness he feeds us. We can get well acquainted with that nasty old pit really quick.

There is an old story about a farmer who threw his stubborn old mule down into a pit and was going to bury him alive. But with each shovel full of dirt that was thrown down on him the stubborn old mule just shook it off and tamped it down under his feet. He stomped and pressed with each new heap of dirt until finally, he was standing eye to eye with the overwrought farmer.

We have to learn to be like that donkey. When the evil one heaps his shovels of lies and deception on us, we have to shake them off and stomp them into the ground. We can climb out of that nasty old pit just like that diligent mule and look a defeated devil right in the eye. I imagine he will be just as surprised as the old farmer.

APRIL 22

"Let us not love with words or tongue but with actions and in truth" (1 John 3:18).

I had a crazy busy day ahead. I had doctor's appointments and a list of errands to run. As I was flying around going through my to-do list, I received a text message from a friend who was in town. She wanted to know if we could meet for coffee. My first reaction was, "O Lord, not today. You know this particular friend is a talker and I have things to do." But I felt God's nudge, and so I agreed to meet with her.

Over coffee, I quickly realized that my friend was in deep trouble. She had gone off all her bipolar meds and was extremely depressed. During our time together, I was able to convince her of the urgency to get back on them. She had a history of attempted suicides, and I was overwhelmed with concern for her. She was due to stay in town a few more days, but the next morning I got a text from her saying she had returned home specifically to call the doctor and get back on her meds. I was on my knees thanking God for this intervention!

When interruptions interfere with your agenda, think of them as God wanting you to take a time out and focus on someone else who may really need your help. God doesn't interrupt our day for no reason. He knows how valuable our time is.

Speaking of which, God multiplied my time that afternoon when I left my friend. I was able to accomplish all I had to do and then some. He will always bless those who put others before themselves. God honors obedience and sacrificial living.

APRIL 23

"My grace is sufficient for you for my power is made perfect in weakness" (2 Corinthians 12:9).

Our human weakness provides the ideal opportunity for God to display His divine power. We can be completely distraught over a situation and yet be filled with His peace. That is God's grace being sufficient! We feel weak in that we are helpless to change anything in our lives. *"But God"*... is giving us the chance to demonstrate our trust in Him and in His power. We have to believe that God will take care of us and has everything under control.

Weakness is really a good thing. We wouldn't need God if we were self-sufficient. Don't ever feel bad or guilty when you are feeling weak. You are humbling yourself before the Lord and asking Him to step in. You are exchanging your pride for humility.

Paul concludes this passage by saying, "Therefore I will boast all the more gladly about my weaknesses so that Christ's power may rest on me. That is why for Christ's sake I delight in weaknesses, in insults, in hardships, in persecutions, in difficulties. For when I am weak, then I am strong." The next time you feel weak cling to this Scripture verse and rest assured that God's power is at work in your life.

APRIL 24

"Do everything without complaining and arguing so that you may become blameless and pure, children of God without fault in a crooked and depraved generation" (Philippians 2:14).

When we complain and argue it accomplishes nothing except making people angry and resentful. We indulge in this sinful behavior because our pride tells us that we have to be right and our opinions are the only ones that matter. We have to make our point, and we work hard to get others to agree with us regardless of the hurt feelings that might be left behind in the aftermath.

Sometimes we even complain and argue with God. We are unhappy with our circumstances, and we think He isn't working fast enough for us. God interprets this as, "I am not content, Lord, and you need you to fix it."

God welcomes our questions and concerns but not our complaints. Being unhappy with our lives is really telling God that we are unhappy with Him. It is a sign of our lack of faith and trust in Him. If we truly trust Him like we say we do, then we must trust Him in every area of our lives and do it without arguing.

When you are tempted to complain, open your Bible to 1 Thessalonians 5:16. The Apostle Paul writes, "Be joyful always, pray continually; give thanks in all circumstances for this is God's will for you in Christ Jesus." God's will for all of us is that we would always be filled with joy and that we should never let circumstances dictate our level of contentment. He wants us to pray about everything and be grateful even for the things we may not understand.

Joy and thankfulness can't live in the same house as complaining and arguing. If we focus on God and foster gratitude, we will be less tempted to complain.

APRIL 25

"Fix these words of mine in your hearts and minds. Teach them to your children, talking about them when you sit at home and when you walk along the road, when you lie down and when you get up" *(Deuteronomy 11:18-19).*

If we want to teach something, we first must have the knowledge to pass on. We need to be educated before we can educate. If we want to teach our children about God, we need to know about God. We need to be familiar with His Word and understand Scripture. We can only teach our children after we first teach ourselves.

When the oxygen mask drops down in an airplane, the adult has to put theirs on first before they can tend to the child. If the parent doesn't ingest the air first, they won't be able to give it to their child. God's Word is like that mask. It can only bring life to your child if you inhale it first.

It is also important to teach our children by our actions as well. Being a godly example is as vital to their spiritual growth as teaching them God's Word. The apostle James wrote, "Do not merely listen to the Word and so deceive yourselves. Do what it says." Teaching your children about God is a responsibility every parent should take seriously. Live your faith out loud in full view of your children. They will learn more about God from your actions and how you treat other people.

APRIL 26

"Am I now trying to win the approval of men or of God? Or am I trying to please men? If I were still trying to please men, I would not be a servant of Christ" (Galatians 1:10).

Do you seek to please God or your neighbor? This is what this Scripture verse is really asking. Do you care a little too much about what others think of you? Are you constantly trying to win their approval or words of affirmation? All you really need concern yourself with is what God thinks of you.

It is so easy to get caught up in egotistical thinking. The world tells us it is all about us and we should strive to indulge our every whim. Our culture and media preach that we should be the center of our own universe. Nothing could be further from the truth! God should be the only One at the center of our world, and He should be the only One we need be concerned about pleasing. The truth is: *it's not about us!*

If you think you may be caught up in this kind of self-absorbed thinking, you might want to ask yourself some questions. "Do I constantly look for the approval of others? Am I a people pleaser? Do I always want everyone to like me?" These questions will determine whom your real focus is on.

The only approval we should be seeking is God's. Our self-worth does not come from other people. It comes from a God who loves us unconditionally and wants our focus to be solely on Him. Don't live to please others; live to please God!

APRIL 27

"A heart at peace gives life to the body, but envy rots the bones" (Proverbs 14:30).

Have you ever met someone who just seems like a shell of a person? They seem to be present only in their physical bodies. Their eyes are lifeless, there is no joy in their voice, and their countenance seems heavy. It seems like they are enduring life rather than living it.

As I stand at the door and greet people when they come into church, I see some lifeless faces—smiles that lack joy and eyes that cry out for help. It saddens me to see this, but I am glad that they are walking through the door and coming to church. I pause and pray that they would find Jesus that day and open their hearts to Him.

Some people seem content to just plod along to get through life. If only they could get a glimpse of just how different the quality of their lives would be if they came to know Jesus. One intimate moment with the Savior and they would be transformed forever. They would have a brand-new life filled with love and light and joy.

Jesus will set us free from whatever hurts we are carrying if only we ask Him. He is the only One who can give life to the body and give us a heart at peace. If life doesn't seem to be working for you, maybe it's time to open your heart to the only One who can bring change and new beginnings. What do you have to lose but the pain and suffering that you've been living with?

APRIL 28

"At daybreak, Jesus went out to a solitary place"
(Luke 4:42).

Even Jesus needed a time-out occasionally. The Bible recorded many occasions when Jesus needed to get away to pray and be alone with His Father. He needed to be encouraged and reenergized. We sometimes forget that Jesus was also a man and had human needs, thoughts, and emotions just like we do. Jesus needed time with His Father so that He could continue to carry out the mission that He was given to do.

Do you have a special place where you can be alone with God? It doesn't have to be on a mountaintop or on a secluded beach. It's not really the place that matters but the time. My place is simply an ordinary brown chair in the corner of my bedroom. It is our special place. We meet there together every morning. I read my Bible, journal, pray and rest in the majesty of God's presence.

No matter how busy or crazy life is we should always be willing to carve time out of our day to spend with Jesus. If He could take time out from His work to be with His Father, then so can we. It's just a matter of making it a priority and then being committed to it. Are you ready to make time with Jesus a priority in your daily routine? It will soon become the most treasured part of your day!

APRIL 29

"Make every effort to enter through the narrow door because many, I tell you, will try to enter and not be able to" (Luke 13:24).

What is the narrow door Jesus is referring to? Quite simply, it is the passage that leads to the Kingdom of Heaven. Jesus is warning us that many people are disillusioned. They think that if they are good and follow all the rules, they will be able to come through the door. However, Jesus says, "Many, I tell you, will try to enter and will not be able to. Once the owner of the house gets up and closes the door, you will stand outside knocking and pleading, 'Sir, open the door for us.'"

There will come a day when the owner—Jesus—will say time is up and close the door. This life on earth is not forever. We are given plenty of time and opportunities to decide if we are going to follow Jesus through heaven's door.

In Ephesians 2:8, Paul explains what is required to enter through the door. He writes, "For it is by grace you have been saved, through faith—and this not from yourselves, it is the gift of God—not by works so that no one can boast." Paul is saying that it takes more than just faith to enter into the Kingdom. It's not enough to just believe in Jesus. We have to have an ongoing personal relationship with the doorkeeper and follow in His ways.

The only way through that narrow door is by giving your heart to Jesus and living your life for Him. None of us can predict when the day will come that the door shuts for the last time. Make sure you are on the right side when it does!

APRIL 30

"Rejoice in the Lord always. I will say it again: Rejoice! Let your gentleness be evident to all" *(Philippians 4:4-5).*

Paul is writing this letter to the Philippians from a Roman prison. He is being held prisoner in the worst of circumstances, and yet he is writing about rejoicing in the Lord. He is suffering, yet he wants the people to know the importance of being joyful. Paul's outlook teaches an important lesson. Our attitudes do not have to reflect what we're going through at the time. Paul was full of joy because he knew that no matter what happened to him, Jesus was with him, and that was all he needed to know.

It's easy to get discouraged in difficult situations. However, Paul wants us to remember that our joy has nothing to do with anything on the outside. It comes from the inside and having Jesus living in us. Fixing our eyes on Jesus is what enables us to rejoice, no matter what.

Our attitudes do not have to reflect our outward circumstances. We can choose to get discouraged, or we can give thanks for having Jesus always by our side. We can be a great testimony to others by how we handle difficulties in our lives. Choose joy, and you will be a powerful witness for the Lord.

MAY 1

"Why are you so afraid? Do you still have no faith?"
(Mark 4:40).

One afternoon as Jesus finished teaching the crowd that had gathered, He decided that He and His Apostles needed to take a boat ride. They all piled in the boat, and Jesus promptly found a comfortable cushion and soon was able to catch up on some much-needed sleep. A furious storm arose, and the boat nearly capsized. The disciples couldn't believe that Jesus was sleeping through all these frightening forces of nature. They woke Him up and asked Him, "Teacher, don't you care if we drown?" (Mark 4:38). Jesus got up and rebuked the wind and the waves. Then He turned to His disciples and asked them what happened to their faith. Why were they so afraid when He was in the boat with them?

There is a wonderful truth in this illustration that I just recently discovered. Jesus was already in the boat when the storm blew in! He was right there ready and able to rescue the others. Jesus is already in our boat as well when our storms kick up. He will always come against whatever it is that is trying to harm us. But we have to do two very important things while we wait for Jesus to calm the storm. We have to have faith and trust that He is capable of taking care of the problem. There is no room for fear in faith. They can't be in harmony with one another. You either have one or the other.

What will you do when your boat starts to flood? Will you call on Jesus to save you or just keep bailing water on your own? You will not be able to keep up with the rising water, but Jesus can. Pray and ask Him to calm your storm and see how fast the wind and the waves settle around you.

MAY 2

"Speak the truth to each other" (Zechariah 8:16).

There are many ways in which we can speak the truth. If your best friend asks you how you like her new dress and you respond, "Nice material but it makes your hips seem a bit wide" your answer may have been honest but not necessarily positive. The truth could have been expressed in a far gentler way. It would have been much better to say something like, "It really shows off your figure nicely, but it's not my favorite color on you."

Sometimes not speaking the truth can be harmful to a person and detrimental to a relationship. If a fellow believer is engaged in sinful behavior, Scripture tells us that we are to confront them. We are called to always speak the truth of God's Word regardless of how it may be received.

God's Word tells us that there is only one way to carry out this command, and that is to be sure to speak the truth with love and gentleness. Colossians 4:6 says, "Let your conversation be always full of grace." Our conversations must always be flavored with grace and affirmation. Always tell the truth but tell it like you would like to hear it.

MAY 3

"You are my Lord; apart from you, I have no good thing" (Psalm 16:2).

What are the good things the Psalmist is referring to? Are they wealth, success, or perhaps material possessions? These are all good things and certainly to be considered as blessings from God. But these are not the things that this Scripture verse implies.

The Word says that the good things in life are love, joy, peace, patience, kindness, goodness, faithfulness, gentleness, and self-control (Galatians 5:22). These are called "Fruits of the Spirit," and they are the by-products of being committed to Christ and living a life devoted to Him. Apart from Him, this harvest of fruit is not attainable.

Material things may bring temporary fulfillment but not the consistent inner peace that we crave in our spirits. It is unrealistic to think that other people or things can provide the fulfillment that only God can. He is the only One who can fill our deepest desires.

Everything the world wants to give us is empty compared to what God offers us. He is the ultimate source of the only things that truly matter in this life. God is responsible for every good thing we have in our lives!

MAY 4

"He who has ears to hear let him hear" (Luke 8:8).

Have you ever heard someone tell a child to put their listening ears on? You might hear the phrase used in preschools or Sunday school classes as the teacher tries to corral the little ones to get them to pay attention.

Jesus is preaching a parable when He closes with this verse. He admonishes His listeners to not just hear the words He is speaking but to take them to heart and apply them to their lives. The definition of the word *hear* is, "To learn by the ear and listen with favor and compliance." Hearing involves acknowledging what we've heard. Then it requires a reaction on our part. Otherwise, as the saying goes, "It goes in one ear and out the other."

Some people make up their minds about Jesus before ever truly hearing what He has to say. They read Scripture with a cynical eye and an ear that does not really want to hear the truth. God wants us to be open to His message. He wants us to take His words and allow them to infiltrate our hearts.

God knows that having ears to hear is a choice we all have to make, and we can either be active or passive about it. We can listen and believe God's Word, or we can choose to live denying it. Choosing to hear God's Word will give you new life both here on earth and for all eternity.

MAY 5

"May the words of my mouth and the meditation of my heart be pleasing in your sight O Lord, my Rock, and my Redeemer" (Psalm 19:14).

Our words, thoughts, and actions originate in our minds. Think about it. We can't say or do what we haven't already thought of first. It is challenging to maintain a pure mind and have our every word be pleasing to God. The world and Satan seek to constantly corrupt us. The evil one will do everything he can to jeopardize our relationship with the Lord. Colossians 3:2 says, "Set your minds on things above, not on earthly things." The New Living Translation reads, "Let heaven fill your thoughts. Do not think only about things down here on earth."

It's easy to get caught up in the circumstances of everyday life. We get busy and distracted and focused on daily demands. But we can be purposeful in directing our thoughts to the right places. One such way is by practicing thankfulness and reflecting on God's goodness and faithfulness. This will help keep our minds focused in the right place and on the right person.

Would you change the way you talk if you knew that every word was heard by God first? How many words a day do you think you would speak if they were only words that were pleasing to Him? It might be a quiet day for some of us! Think about your words and how they will affect others before you speak them. Our mouths should always be vessels that bring God glory!

MAY 6

"It is fine to be zealous, provided the purpose is good, and to be so always and not just when I am with you" (Galatians 4:18).

People can be zealous over a myriad of things. They can be passionate about their careers, their hobbies, fame, or success. It's easy to be zealous for worldly things. It's common today to see people standing on their soapboxes shouting about some perceived injustice in the world. But are these the causes that Scripture is encouraging us to be zealous for?

Being zealous for Jesus is what Paul is referring to in this passage. It's fine to be eager and enthusiastic about something we care about. But if we feel led to climb up on a platform, our subject should be the Good News of the gospel message.

The Apostle Paul was a huge zealot for Jesus. He was unstoppable. He went through shipwrecks, sicknesses, beatings, imprisonment, even surviving being stoned. But he preached the gospel through it all. He looked at his misfortunes as divine invitations to speak more boldly about Christ. Paul always used his hardships to further God's Kingdom.

What are you zealous for? What dominates your thinking and your time? Is it a political cause or devotion to a job? Do you use your trials and suffering to draw attention to yourself or to God? We were all created with the capacity for zealousness. God just asks that we focus it on Him!

MAY 7

"Whoever can be trusted with very little can also be trusted with much" (Luke 16:10).

How easy it is to take things for granted, especially all the blessings that come from the hand of God. When those gifts come, we are full of thanksgiving and praise for His grace and generosity. Then after a time, we forget what we've been given and simply begin looking forward to the next thing or something bigger.

It was my granddaughter's birthday, and as usual, I overindulged my sweet little girl. I fulfilled her wish list and then some. She loved everything and was as happy as any six-year-old could be. However, a few days later when she came over for dinner, she asked me if I had any more presents for her. I explained to her that I had already given her all her gifts at her party. She walked away disappointed as I tried not to bite the end of my tongue off!

I wonder if God could have related to my frustration. As His children don't we act the same way sometimes? We are excited to receive His blessings at the time, but the joy soon wears off, and we find ourselves looking forward to the next one. If we are so quick to forget His past generosity, how eager do we think He is going to be to reach out His hand of blessing in the future?

I think this is what Jesus is referring to in this passage. How can He trust us with much if we can't be satisfied with little? We should never cease to feel thankful as we look back on all that God has given us. Gratitude should never fade with time. The more we sincerely thank God and praise Him for His goodness, the more He will want to shower good things upon us.

MAY 8

"Bear with each other and forgive whatever grievances you may have against one another. Forgive as the Lord forgave you" (Colossians 3:13).

How many times do you need to forgive someone, especially if that person commits the same offense over and over? The Apostle Peter came to Jesus one day and asked Him that very question. He said, "'Lord, how many times shall I forgive my brother when he sins against me? Up to seven times?' Jesus answered, 'I tell you not seven times but seventy-seven times'" (Matthew 18:21-22). Jesus was telling Peter that forgiveness is unlimited and not conditional. It is times without number.

We all have challenges in this area. Someone does what we think is unforgivable and we adopt an air of self-righteousness. We feel like we have been wronged and did nothing whatsoever to deserve such treatment. What we need to remember is if God can forgive us of all our sins and failures time and time again, how can we not extend this same grace to others?

Jesus calls us not only to love others but to forgive them as well. There are no exceptions or extenuating circumstances. We must choose the path of forgiveness and walk it. Peace and freedom are waiting for us at the end of the road.

MAY 9

"You are my hiding place; you will protect me from trouble and surround me with songs of deliverance" (Psalm 32:7).

Hiding places provide a sense of safety and protection. Children will run and hide when they're afraid or when they get into trouble. They will usually pick the same place over and over to hide in because it becomes familiar to them and they feel comfortable in that place.

Adults have hiding places too. Some hide behind insecurities or weaknesses. Some choose dangerous places like drugs or alcohol. Some hide behind their jobs or careers. People turn to these places and things because they do not know any other way. They don't realize that there is a God who wants to be their hiding place. He wants to be the One to take away all their fears and replace them with comfort and strength. He wants them to seek Him when they feel weak and afraid.

If you are searching for a safe haven, God is right there with you waiting to provide one. He is everything you need now and forever. Let God be your hiding place. He will soon become your favorite place to find comfort and rest.

MAY 10

"The Lord will guide you always; He will satisfy your needs" (Isaiah 58:11).

A need is a necessity, something we can't live without. Food, shelter, and clothing all fall in this category. Things that are essential for survival are true needs. However, people often confuse the word *need* with *want*. But they are two very different words with two very different meanings. A need is vital for life, and a want is a craving or desire for something that is typically indulgent or unnecessary.

We all have wants. We would be kidding ourselves if we claimed to never desire some personal gift. The problem becomes when the wants take over the needs. We develop bad habits where we spend too much money or invest it in the wrong places. We are lax in our self-gratification skills. We want what we want, and we want it now or yesterday

A preacher once asked his congregation this question: "If God never blessed you with another thing would you still love and serve Him for the rest of your life?" This question should make us take a serious look at how we view God. How would we feel about Him if His hand of generosity was removed?

Scripture tells us that our deepest needs in life are spiritual ones. According to Matthew 6:25-33, even our physical needs are met when we put God first. If we have God, then we have all we will ever need. It is okay to desire other things, but God should always be all we need!

MAY 11

"I raised you up for this very purpose, that I might display my power in you and that my name might be proclaimed in all the earth" (Romans 9:17).

Do we live our lives by chance or with intent and purpose? Are we letting life just happen or are we actively pursuing a goal? We can't wait around and expect life to give us meaning. We must make an effort to give meaning to life. Some people try to find their purpose in their own personal lives. However, to find our real purpose, we have to take the focus off of ourselves. We will never live a meaningful life if we keep looking inward. Living for self will only lead to emptiness and a lack of fulfillment.

We all have to stand before God one day and answer this question: "Did you live your life to please me or to please yourself? What were you most focused on?" We will all have to give an account of how we spent our time. Did we use it for God's glory or for our own?

When we stand in front of Jesus one day, we should desire nothing more than to hear these words: "Well done thy good and faithful servant." Our purpose in this life will then have been accomplished. Are you waiting for life to give you meaning or are you actively pursuing giving meaning to life?

MAY 12

"Surely as I have planned, so it will be, and as I have purposed, so it will stand" (Isaiah 14:24).

Did you know God had a plan for your life even before you were a seed within your mother's womb? Did you know He already knew your name and called you by it before you took your first breath? God knew you from the beginning of creation and had a course already mapped out for you. It is so amazing to think that the God of the Universe knows each of us so intimately.

Some of what God has planned for your life may not be easy. It probably is not what you would have chosen by a long shot. Maybe you keep God at a distance because you feel you have been treated unfairly and don't deserve such trials. Maybe you are struggling with the way that God has directed your life.

God promises in His Word that He works all things for good for every believer (Romans 8:28). You must believe that things will look much better after the dust settles. You will be able to see that He always had your best interests at heart, even when you didn't understand what He was doing. Most of the time the greatest blessing we discover from our trial is how our faith and trust in God grew to a whole new level. Every challenge and hardship we face is meant to do one thing, and that is to grow us closer to our Heavenly Father. He tests us so we can prove our love and loyalty to Him.

Will you pass your next test with flying colors or continue to be hard-hearted and stiff-necked like the Israelites in the desert?

MAY 13

"No one is like you, O Lord; you are great, and your name is mighty in power" (Jeremiah 10:6).

Although everything else had a beginning, God has always been. He always was, always is, and always will be. There is no one like our God. He is the Creator and Sustainer of life. He is the Beginning and the End. No one and nothing can compare to Him.

God only had to speak the words for the world to be created. His divine power set the universe into motion. His majesty and workmanship can be seen and heard all throughout His vast creation. A beautiful sunset or a newborn baby are but two examples of God's divine masterpieces.

Many false gods are worshipped in our world today. But they are not the One True God. Think about it. Did any of these other gods become man, die on a cross, and rise again? Did any of them perform the signs and miracles that Jesus did? Do any of them promise eternal life in heaven?

There is none like our God. He holds the world in the palm of His hand and rules it sovereignly. He is the only One worthy of our praise, honor, and glory. 1 Chronicles 16:25 says, "For great is the Lord and most worthy of praise; He is to be feared above all gods. For all the gods of the nations are idols but the Lord made the Heavens; Great and mighty is He!" Amen and Alleluia!

MAY 14

"They are darkened in their understanding and separated from the life of God because of the ignorance that is in them due to the hardening of their hearts" (Ephesians 4:18).

Stubbornness and a lack of knowledge will cause some people to shut their minds off to God and harden their hearts towards Him. Maybe something painful happened in their lives, and they blame God for it. Maybe they bought into the lies that the evil one has fed them. Maybe they just won't believe because they want proof.

The Bible tells us that such people are living in darkness and are far from God. They are living in a state of confusion and doubt because they refuse to accept the truth that is written in God's Word. That is why Paul says it is only our ignorance that prevents us from understanding and becoming a believer.

If you have questions and doubts about God, I would encourage you to pick up a Bible and do your own research. You can't refuse or argue something you aren't familiar with. Start with the book of John. You will soon find that eyewitnesses alone prove its validity. There are hundreds of witnesses to all the miracles Jesus performed during His time on earth. There are the hundreds of fulfilled prophecies in the Old Testament, and of course, there are the archaeological findings. The challenge really isn't proving the Bible is true; it's proving it isn't! An atheistic journalist by the name of Lee Strobel set out to do that very thing, and after interviewing dozens of religious scholars, physicians, and scientists ended up becoming a believer! [2]

God wants you to come into His light and believe in His Son. You have the real Truth. You have the proof. Don't remain in the darkness any longer. Jesus is waiting for you to come into the light and be united with Him.

---

2 Strobel, Lee. 1998. *The Case for Christ: A Journalist's Personal Investigation of the Evidence for Jesus*. Grand Rapids, MI: Zondervan.

MAY 15

"But I am like an olive tree, flourishing in the house of God" (Psalm 52:8).

Olive trees were abundant in Jesus' day. They thrived easily and were described as having great splendor. Olive trees can live for hundreds of years and are known for their productivity and longevity. They have deep roots and are not easily uprooted. The prophet Jeremiah called them, "Beautiful to see and full of good fruit."

King David described himself as an olive tree. He considered himself a flourishing servant of God. The trees are purposeful and healthy just like he was. The roots of David's faith ran deep, and he was intimately connected to the Creator. He had the strength to withstand just like that olive tree.

If we are to be productive for the Kingdom of God, we must be like the olive tree. We must become productive in our communities and in our service to God. We must invest our time and our resources wisely. Like the olive tree and like David we must be deeply rooted in our faith and able to bear fruit. Nature again provides us with a great spiritual lesson from which we can gain truth and application. All of creation can be our classroom if we open our minds to it like David.

MAY 16

"'Neither this man nor his parents sinned,' said Jesus. 'But this happened <u>so that</u> the work of God might be displayed in His life'" (John 9:3).

The words *so that* are much like the title of this book. They could probably be interchanged. There is a statement that usually follows the "so that"s in Scripture. It is, "that God may be glorified." Jesus is saying that all the "so that"s in life are for the sole purpose of glorifying God.

My most recent experience with a "so that" happened not long ago. I was suffering from a major health issue, and I was not a happy camper. So, I prayed and asked God to help me have a positive attitude and be a good example of perseverance. I wanted to be able to bring God glory in my circumstances. I wanted the work of God to be displayed in my life just as Jesus explained to His disciples.

The one thing that helped me through was knowing I would have a powerful testimony at the end. I have learned through years of walking with Christ that God never wastes experiences in our lives. He looks at them as opportunities for us to exercise our faith and our trust in His sovereign plan. I knew that the "so that" would come eventually.

Remember to look ahead to the "so that"s when trials come knocking at your door. Jesus gave the answer to the why question we always seem to ask in tough times. It happened "so that" the work of God might be displayed in your life. This answer should bring us great comfort in our time of need.

MAY 17

"This is what the Lord says to you: do not be afraid or discouraged because of this vast army. For the battle is not yours, but God's" (2 Chronicles 20:15).

We are all familiar with the story of David and Goliath. Goliath stood over nine feet tall thus earning him the nickname "giant." David was only a boy at the time he went out to fight this towering menace. Goliath entered the battle with this pint-sized foe covered in bronze from head to toe and armed with a spear and a shield. David was dressed only in his shepherd clothes carrying a slingshot and a stone.

Where did David's confidence come from? How did he muster up the courage to face such a formidable enemy? There is only one answer. It was because of his faith that David could stand before Goliath. He did not place his trust in his human abilities but simply in the power of God. He believed that the God who saved him from the lions and the bears while he tended sheep would save him in this battle as well.

We need only to be still in our battles and let God fight for us. Just like He went before the Israelites in a pillar of cloud in the desert He goes before us leading and guiding us. Don't take on your enemies by yourself. Enlist the One who can go before you, and you will have the victory.

MAY 18

"Because we have sought the Lord our God has given us rest" (2 Chronicles 14:7).

King Asa of the Old Testament was the great-grandson of King Solomon. He reigned over Judah for 41 years. Scripture says, "Asa's heart was fully committed to the Lord all of his life." These were tumultuous years for the king as wars were constantly breaking out between the different tribes. But as he relied on the Lord, He rescued him from all his enemies and brought peace to the land.

Like his great-grandfather, Asa also had great wisdom. He called to the Lord one day and proclaimed, "Lord there is no one like you to help the powerless against the mighty. Help us, O Lord our God, for we rely on you and in your name." King Asa knew that the only way to rule his kingdom with success was to look to God and His direction.

God showed many kings in the Bible that if they were faithful and humbled themselves before Him, He would give them and their people peace and rest. It is the same with us today. It takes a heart of humility to ask for help. If we can lose our pride and admit that we can't do life on our own, He will step in and give us the strength we need. Seek the Lord as Asa did and find the peace and rest that you've been searching for.

MAY 19

"And God will wipe every tear from their eyes"
(Revelation 7:17).

What a great comfort to know that God has wiped away every tear we have ever shed. Scripture tells us that He catches each one in the palm of His hand. I can envision the Lord bending down close and kissing our wet cheeks just like a mother does to her crying child. Jesus feels our every emotion, and I'm sure His deep compassion for us stirs Him to cry right along with us.

Our God never looks at us as weak or lacking in faith when we cry. He knew we would need to be able to weep so we could relieve some of the pressure when we're hurting and struggling. He knew our tears would be cathartic and enable us to feel renewed and refreshed. God anticipated our every need when He created us, and He knew our tears would serve a good purpose.

When you feel the tears coming on, don't hold back. Remember that God is right there with you ready to catch each one and share in your suffering. His Kleenex is poised and ready for you.

MAY 20

"Honor one another above yourselves" (Romans 12:10).

When I struggle with the ability to love and honor someone, I go to God and ask Him to change that person. I ask Him to convict them of their ungodly behavior and set them straight. I'm sure that if God could just stop them from irritating me and make them more aware of my needs, I could love and honor them as I should. God just has to bring them to their senses.

This almost comical scenario is called *self-righteousness*. It means I come first and I have the right to judge others. In reality, the first person we need to ask God to change is ourselves! Heart transformation can only happen through humility and sacrificial living. To live sacrificially is to put others before ourselves. It's putting their needs and desires above ours. This is what it means to honor one another.

Change begins with obedience and action. We can't let entitlement sneak in and tell us we deserve to be treated better. Really? What about Jesus? Didn't He deserve to be treated better? How did He respond to those who dishonored Him?

Jesus showed love and compassion towards everyone. He just didn't think about it, He proved it. Stop and ask the Holy Spirit to transform your heart so that you can love and honor others like Jesus. Ask the Holy Spirit to empower you to live sacrificially and to honor those around you.

MAY 21

"And the God of all grace, who called you to His eternal glory in Christ, after a little while, will Himself restore you and make you strong, firm, and steadfast" (1 Peter 5:10).

Peter sometimes uses the words *a little while* when writing about suffering. Wouldn't we love to know what God's definition of *a little while* is? We know that His timing is totally different from ours. Peter addresses this as well in the third chapter. He says, "With the Lord, a day is like a thousand years and a thousand years are like a day." *A little while* to God could be days, weeks, months or even years. There is no way for us to understand what the purpose is behind His divine timing.

Our job in the waiting period is to remain strong, firm, and steadfast. This sometimes tends to wax and wane as we go through the different stages of our trials. Our resolve may vacillate back and forth as the trial seems endless. We trust for a little while, and then we get discouraged and go back to worrying.

Our *little whiles* may wear us down, but we must press on in our faith and trust that God has everything under control. He sees the big picture. He sees the tapestry on the finished side. God will bring restoration. His grace is enough to see us through.

MAY 22

"Yet I am always with you; you hold me by my right hand. You guide me with your counsel" (Psalm 73:23-24).

Every time God's hand is mentioned in Scripture, it always refers to His right hand. It's interesting that the right hand is symbolic of a blessing. When we greet people, we always shake with our right hands. I don't think the correlation is coincidental. Greeting someone with a handshake is a sign of our desire to bless them with a welcome, a congratulation, or an offer of kindness.

God's counsel is also mentioned in this verse. 1 Kings 22:5 says, "First seek the counsel of the Lord." Sometimes we forget to go to God first when we need direction, and we seek guidance and advice from others. We pick up the phone and call a family member or a close friend and talk to them about the situation before we seek God's opinion. While our friends may give us advice, it may not be what God would have chosen for us. His counsel is the only true source of direction we can trust.

We don't want to do what others think we should do. We should want to do what God wants us to do. His direction should be the only direction we seek. No one knows what's in our best interests… *"But God."* When you need counsel go to the right place and to the right person.

MAY 23

"I will give them an undivided heart and put a new spirit in them. I will remove from them their heart of stone and give them a heart of flesh" (Ezekiel 11:19).

An undivided heart is fully and completely committed to God. It is a heart united with God's as one. Our hearts are not whole until we are joined with His. Luke 16:13 says, "No one can serve two masters. For you will hate one and love the other or be devoted to one and despise the other." Ezekiel is saying that you can't have half of your heart devoted to God and half of it devoted to something else. True devotion requires 100% commitment.

When our hearts are united with God's, it is through the work and the power of the Holy Spirit. He moves in and begins the reconstruction process of joining our hearts together with God's. He turns our hearts of stone into hearts of love which brings new life. The Holy Spirit's job is to transform us to be more like Jesus. And the more we become like Jesus, the more of the Spirit's power is poured into us. The Holy Spirit is the one who shapes and molds our hearts to be faithful followers.

An undivided heart requires us to choose God over everything and everyone else including ourselves. We must let Him be in control of our hearts and our minds. Letting go and letting God is key to our transformation.

MAY 24

"If your brother sins against you go and show him his fault just between the two of you" (Matthew 18:15).

Confrontation is hard. Some people go to great lengths to avoid it. They would rather talk to another friend about it rather than the person who is involved. Conflict is unavoidable in relationships. Hurts happen, and feelings get trampled on. But they must be dealt with right away, or barriers will be created that will be hard to penetrate.

It is never a good idea to sweep an offense under the rug. It will just cause a bump that you will eventually trip over in time. In the natural realm, a wound must be taken care of immediately, or infection could set in and threaten the life of the person. Word wounds are no different. They will eventually threaten to destroy the relationship if not taken care of properly.

Jesus lays the groundwork in this verse for resolving conflict. When someone hurts you go to that person and talk to them. Work it out immediately before the wound starts to fester in your heart. Keep your accounts with people short. This will avoid disagreements being blown out of proportion.

If you're struggling with a hurt, pray and ask God to help you resolve the issue. Ask Him to help you let go of anger and bitterness and allow forgiveness to enter your heart. Ask Him to work with you right now to help you remove the stubbornness and the excuses you've been using to avoid the situation. God wants you to remove that barrier and free you from your burden forever.

MAY 25

"Here I am! I stand at the door and knock. If anyone hears my voice and opens the door, I will come in and eat with Him and He with me" (Revelation 3:20).

When there is a knock at your front door, you have a few choices. You can ignore it and hope that the person goes away. Or you can peek around the curtain to see who it is and then decide whether to open it. Or you can throw the door wide open and greet your visitor with a warm hello.

When the Bible talks about Jesus knocking on the door, it is really referring to Jesus knocking on the door of our hearts. When we hear His knock, we have those same options. We can either ignore Him or throw the door wide open and welcome Him in. Jesus is always knocking and waiting for an invitation to be invited in.

Jesus will never force open the door to our hearts. He is a gentleman and will always respect our choices and decisions. This is called free will, which God has given to everyone.

Jesus knocks on every door. He doesn't pick selective ones or make random choices. He knocks on all of our doors. He wants all of us to throw our doors wide open and ask Him in. What will you do when you hear Jesus' knock? Will you open the door or pretend you're not home? It's a free will choice that only you can make.

MAY 26

"If you hold to my teaching, you are really my disciple. Then you will know the truth, and the truth will set you free" (John 8:31).

Jesus had twelve Apostles that He hand-picked to come alongside Him as He began His ministry. Jesus also called them His disciples because anyone who followed Jesus was known as a disciple. The word *disciple* in the Latin means pupil or student. As Christians, we are all disciples and should be actively learning just like the Apostles. We do this by studying Scripture and asking the Holy Spirit to teach us.

If you are Jesus' disciple, then you have been given the assignment of carrying out what He called The Great Commission. He states in Matthew 28:19, "Therefore go and make disciples of all nations." This simply means to go and spread the news about Jesus to the world. We are to be Christ's ambassadors and share with others what He has done for us. There is a whole world out there that needs to hear the Good News so that they are also able to share eternity with Christ.

We need to speak up and give our personal testimonies so that we can sow the seeds of faith and salvation. Then we must pray that those seeds take root and bear fruit for His kingdom. If we are Christ followers, we have been given a life-changing message to carry out to the world. Let us all be true disciples and proactive in spreading the Truth of the Gospel!

MAY 27

"Everyone who quotes proverbs will quote this proverb about you: like mother, like daughter" *(Ezekiel 16:44).*

Even though this verse may sound like just an old adage, there is a powerful insight behind it. This passage is talking about the Israelites' repetitive rejection of God. The prophet Ezekiel is speaking about the unfaithfulness of the people through generations and making the point that sin can be passed down.

Just like there are hereditary likenesses in families, there are spiritual ones as well. The Israelites passed the struggle of maintaining their faith from one generation to the next. We are no different. The same thing can happen today in our families. There is an old adage that says, "Children learn what they live with." What a true statement! Our children will reflect the attitudes and behaviors we model for them. If we are angry all the time, chances are they will be too. If we are harsh and unforgiving, they will most likely follow in the same footsteps.

We don't just pass our DNA along to our kids. We pass our beliefs, our morals, and our values. If we don't model Jesus to them and bring them up in a loving Christian home, what will they have to pass down to their children? Give them a firm foundation found only in Christ, and they will have nothing but good things to pass on to their children.

MAY 28

"What good is it if a man claims to have faith but has no deeds? Can such faith save him?" (James 2:14).

Many people believe that if they simply live a good life, they will see heaven one day. They think that if they treat others well and do kind things, they will indeed arrive at the pearly gates after taking their last breath.

The Bible, however, teaches the truth about how to have eternal life and the privilege of living in heaven with God. James explains that intellectual acceptance and belief in God is not enough. We have to take that faith and live it out, or it's not really faith at all. James calls faith without action *dead faith.*

There has to be outward evidence of our faith. Do we share it with others? Do we talk about God to family and friends? It has to be obvious to the outside world that we are living our lives for Christ or we must question whether we have made an honest commitment to Him.

Are you a fan or a follower of Christ? Fans watch and observe from afar. They don't get involved in the game nor do they have any control over the outcome. Followers get intimately involved. And unlike fans, they have the full assurance that their outcome will be a room in heaven in God's heavenly kingdom.

MAY 29

"Let those who love the Lord hate evil for He guards the lives of His faithful ones" (Psalm 97:10).

Jesus was not afraid to use the word *hate* in the proper context. The Bible clearly says that Jesus hates all sin and evil. In Proverbs chapter six there is a list of things He hates, like pride and a lying tongue, to name a few. We are to hate all sin and evil as well. The Apostle Paul tells us to "Avoid every kind of evil" (1 Thessalonians 5:22).

When Jesus returns, He will conquer all the evil in the world. He will have the victory over all sin! But in the meantime, we can fight back by praying for all those who do evil. We can pray that they will find God and that the hatred that fills their hearts would be replaced by love.

The rest of this verse reads, "For He guards the lives of His faithful ones." We should never live our lives in fear of evil. We have to trust that God is always guarding us and has His hand of protection on us. There is no room for fear in faith. And there is no room for sin and evil in our lives.

MAY 30

"The Lord had opened a door for me; I still had no peace of mind" (2 Corinthians 2:13).

I always believed that when God opened a door, we were supposed to walk through it. I never really considered that maybe this was not always the case. When I read this verse, Paul opened my eyes to some great insights that address this issue.

Paul had many open invitations and opportunities to preach in many places, but he couldn't accept them all. Even though the requests were all there and the doors were open for him to go, Paul had to use the wisdom and discernment God gave him to make the right choices.

I once prayed that God would open the door for me to pursue a relationship that I knew deep down was not healthy. I never stopped to think that maybe God had a better plan for me. I wanted my way, and that was that. Well, God let me have my way, but it wasn't long before I realized there was going to be a huge learning curve involved in this answered prayer. I began very quickly to suffer the consequences that came when I insisted on being in control instead of seeking God's will. That open door ended up in a dead end because I wasn't meant to walk through it. I just did it on my own.

God gave us the gift of discernment for a reason. When we choose to go our own way, we are rejecting His wisdom and trusting our own. We should never commit to something that doesn't feel right even if the door has been opened to us. If peace eludes us, there is a reason behind it, and it's usually a heads-up from God. We would be wise to follow God's promptings and guidance and not to depend on our own.

MAY 31

"The Son is the radiance of God's glory and the exact representation of His being, sustaining all things by His powerful word" (Hebrews 1:3).

One of the most important reasons to read Scripture is to get to know God better. We will never know Him completely as there will always be a shroud of mystery that surrounds Him. But we should never stop trying to discover more about Him.

I was looking to learn recently why God gave such precise measurements for how He wanted His temple built. What was His purpose for such specific instructions on every length, width, and cubit in the building process? I know all Scripture is useful for teaching, so what was I to learn from this about God?

Meditating on Scripture is so important. I ponder things I don't understand until the Holy Spirit intervenes and makes it clear. I was doing this when the answer was revealed to me. God is a God of detail. A God of precision. Everything He does is exactly how He wants it and how it is supposed to be. He is always spot on.

God cares about our bodily temples in the same way. He cares about every little detail of our lives. Things we might think are trivial or insignificant matter to God. He is a God of exactness. When our prayers are answered, they are answered exactly the way they should be. God never makes mistakes or misjudges a situation. What He orchestrates in our lives is precisely how it is supposed to be. This should be comforting for us because we don't have to worry or guess about anything. Everything in our lives right now is exactly how it should be.

JUNE 1

"Now I have put my words in your mouth" (Jeremiah 1:9).

God is speaking to the prophet Jeremiah in this verse. He appointed him as a prophet to the nation of Israel, but Jeremiah wasn't so sure he wanted the job. He said, "Ah, Sovereign Lord. I do not know how to speak; I am only a child." He was trying to give God the same excuse Moses tried to use when he said, "O Lord, I have never been eloquent in speech."

Some people don't believe the Bible is the truth because they say it was written by men. Yes, men did record Scripture. However, these men only served as the conduits or the vessels that God used to relay His message. 2 Peter 1:20 says, "Above all, you must understand that no prophecy of Scripture came about by the prophet's own interpretation. For prophecy never had its origin in the will of man, but men spoke from God as they were carried along by the Holy Spirit". God is the Creator and the Sustainer of life as well as the sole author of the greatest book ever written.

The book of Jeremiah repeatedly says, "The Word of the Lord came to me." Jesus spoke, and Jeremiah wrote it down and repeated it to the people. He was a voice for the invisible God. We can be the voice of God as well when we share the gospel and encourage others in their faith. God will put the words in your mouth just like He did the prophets when you speak up for Him.

JUNE 2

"Be very careful then how you live—not as unwise but as wise—making the most of every opportunity because the days are evil" (Ephesians 5:15).

Wisdom is not just possessing knowledge and information. It means seeing things from God's point of view. It is understanding His divine perspective. Wisdom has to do with insight and spiritual applications.

James chapter 3 defines wisdom. James writes, "The wisdom that comes from heaven is first of all pure, then peace-loving, considerate, submissive, full of mercy and good fruit, impartial and sincere." Wisdom has nothing to do with us and everything to do with God.

James tells us how to get wisdom in two little words in chapter 1:5: "Ask God." That's it. That's all we have to do to acquire wisdom is to simply ask God for it. If you want to know what God wants you to do, read your Bible, and He will let you know. He will speak to you in the depths of your heart through His Word. We don't have to stumble around in the dark looking for answers. We just need to turn to the light of His Word and have His guidance and direction illuminated to help us make the right choices.

God is willing and able to impart wisdom to all those who seek to live godly lives. Need a healthy dose of wisdom? Call on God. He has the perfect prescription!

JUNE 3

"This is the day the Lord has made; let us rejoice and be glad in it" (Psalm 118:24).

Life is all about making choices. Every day we are faced with a myriad of decisions we have to make. One of them involves our attitudes. Are we going to choose an attitude of joy or are we going to be Debbie Downers rehearsing all the negative aspects of our lives? Looking at the glass half empty is standard for some people. It is challenging for some to wake up in the morning and rejoice and be glad they're alive to see another day!

At the conclusion of the Last Supper, Jesus ended the evening by singing a hymn with His Disciples. It is thought that this Psalm was what they sang together. They rejoiced and gave thanks to the Lord. They proclaimed that God was their strength and their song. They worshipped Him for His goodness. The evening was filled with wonderful music and worship.

Think about this for a minute. Here is Jesus getting ready to be betrayed into the hands of His enemies and face crucifixion. Yet His apostles are all gathered around Him rejoicing and singing praises. They are not concerned about tomorrow. They are living in the moment, pouring out love and gratitude for the man standing right in front of them.

Jesus is giving us yet another great example of how we can find something to be thankful for even in the bleakest of times. We can choose to rejoice and be glad for every new day. Or we can throw back the covers, put two feet on the floor and be a Debbie Downer! Which one will you choose today?

JUNE 4

"Walk in all the ways I command you that it may go well with you" (Jeremiah 7:23).

This verse is quoted in several books of the Bible. God is commanding us to skip the lip service and walk out our faith. If we do, then He tells us, "It may go well with you." That is not to say that our lives are going to be problem free. Suffering is a part of life just as death is a part of life.

If we choose not to obey God's Word, then we can probably expect life to be even more of a challenge. Life is hard enough as it is. So, why would we want to make it even harder by ignoring God? Deuteronomy 5:33 adds clarification as it tells us to, "Walk in all the way that the Lord your God has commanded you so that you may live and prosper and prolong your days."

I can truly say that all is well with my soul. Not because I've mastered this whole obedience thing. None of us can keep all of God's commands. We need the power of the Holy Spirit to help us stay on the right path. Life goes well for me only because I have Jesus. All is well with my soul because I enjoy peace and joy no matter what the circumstances. I love that God doesn't expect perfection from us—only faithfulness and a willing heart. I can freely give that to Him as I seek to follow Him in all His ways.

JUNE 5

"Let him who boasts - boast in the Lord" (1 Corinthians 1:31).

The word *boast* means to talk about oneself with too much pride or to brag about something. It's so easy to get caught up in bragging especially when it comes to our personal accomplishments or our kids. We have an innate desire to want to share our successes with others. It's part of our human nature to want to show off and impress people.

However, God's Word tells us we need to take the focus off ourselves and put it on God. He is the one responsible for all our successes and blessings. He gave us the ability, the talents, and the gifts to accomplish all that we have done and will ever do. If you are successful, you only have God to thank for it. The Word tells us, "Apart from God we can do nothing" (John 15:5).

Our boasting should always be in the work of Jesus and what He has done for us. Paul is warning us to be careful about who we give credit to for what we have. Our motives should always be examined carefully. To whom are you honoring and giving glory—yourself or God?

JUNE 6

"A man's life is not his own. It is not for man to direct his steps" (Jeremiah 10:23).

It is such a relief to know that I don't have to be in control of my life. For some, that may not be good news or what they want to hear. But God is ultimately in control of this world, whether we believe it or not. Nothing happens apart from His knowledge or providence. Our lives truly are not our own. He gave us life, and He can take it away at any time.

I love not having to worry about sitting in the driver's seat. I can kick back and simply trust in His plan for my life. He plots my course and determines my every step. I can make all the plans I want, *"But God"*'s agenda will prevail. Someone once told me that if you really want to make God laugh—tell Him your plans.

I rest in the fact that God always knows what's best for me. When I look back on some prayers that went unanswered, I am thankful that God had a better plan for me. I couldn't see it at the time. Sometimes it takes a look in the rear-view mirror to see that God always knows what we need. Allow God to direct your steps and see what great places He takes you!

JUNE 7

"Teach me knowledge and good judgement, for I believe in your commands" (Psalm 119:66).

You must have a passion for learning, or you won't grow in your faith. Faith that isn't growing is stagnant and will never go anywhere. If you don't feel the desire to read your Bible and study His Word, pray and ask God to encourage you in the desire to get to know Him. He wants nothing more than for His children to draw closer to Him and what better way than to attend His classes every day.

Nicodemus, who was part of the Jewish ruling council, came to talk to Jesus one night and addressed Him as "Rabbi." In the Hebrew, this is another name for Teacher. Nicodemus is telling Jesus that he knows He is a Teacher who has come from God. Isaiah 48:17 says, "I am the Lord your God who teaches you what is best for you, who directs you in the way you should go."

You can make a choice to become a committed student of God's Word. Romans 11:33 says, "Oh the depth of the riches of the wisdom and knowledge of God!" Will you be a willing student and allow God to teach you His wonderful truths?

JUNE 8

"Your Word is a lamp to my feet and light for my path" (Psalm 119:105).

Natural darkness and spiritual darkness are similar. The Apostle Paul said, "First the natural then the spiritual" (1 Corinthians 15:44). Natural darkness can be an unpleasant place, just like its spiritual counterpart. Have you ever walked across a dark parking lot alone at night? You probably felt anxious and fearful. Have you ever gotten up at night and staggered across a dark room bumping into things because there was no lamp to light the way? It's near impossible to navigate in the dark.

Just like the daylight brings the birth of a fresh new day, so the Light of Jesus brings a newness to the heart and mind. Light, both natural and spiritual, is a vital necessity of life. Nothing — natural or spiritual—can grow or thrive without it. We blindly walk darkened paths when we are without the light. We walk aimlessly with no sense of direction or purpose.

Jesus is the only One who can provide spiritual light. The Word says, "The Lord turns my darkness into light" (Psalm 18:28). If we want to find purpose and steer clear of the things that so easily entangle, we must embrace the spiritual light. Apart from the Light we can only grope around and hope we find what we're looking for.

JUNE 9

"My eyes stay open through the watches of the night, that I might meditate on your promises"
(Psalm 119:148).

We all have nights when our eyes suddenly fly wide open, and we think it's morning only to look at the clock and see that it's still the middle of the night. Falling back asleep always proves challenging. We toss and turn and wrestle with our pillows trying to ease back into dreamland. But nothing seems to work, and we lie there tired and frustrated.

Have you ever considered that maybe God might be purposely waking you up so He can spend some time with you? It's hard during the day sometimes for Him to get our attention. We're usually so busy we have no time to spare not even for a quick check in with the Lord. So, knowing He can only get our full and undivided attention in the wee hours of the morning, He touches us with a little insomnia. We can now use this time to talk to Him, pray, and reflect on His goodness. We can even use this time to glorify Him as we sing praises quietly in our heads.

We don't have to rely on counting sheep to get back to sleep. We don't need the TV, our tablets, or our phones. We just need to focus on the Shepherd, and He will give us perfect restful sleep.

JUNE 10

"You will keep in perfect peace him whose mind is steadfast because he trusts in you" (Isaiah 26:3).

Some people base peace on their current circumstances. If things are going well, all is right in their world. But throw a little monkey wrench in the mix, and suddenly that peace evaporates like rain on a hot sidewalk.

Peace is not the absence of chaos in your life. It's that feeling of knowing that you belong to Jesus and that He is in control of your life. The Word says, "Do not be anxious about anything" (Philippians 4:6). We are simply told to bring every concern, every problem, and every challenge to Him and He will give us the peace we are so desperate for. Talking out tough situations with a friend or family member won't provide the peace only God can give us. It may make us feel better temporarily, but ultimately God's peace will still elude us until we turn to Him.

When we feel anxious, the problem is not with the circumstances. The problem is that we insist on ruling over the circumstances. We want to be in control. We want to be able to fix it ourselves. We don't want to have to rely on anyone else. God's Word tells us that peace is only attainable if we give our concerns to Christ and trust in Him. There is no special formula or requirement to receive the gift of peace. Will you put your faith and trust in Him, so you can revel in His peace that truly surpasses all human understanding?

JUNE 11

"He performs wonders that cannot be fathomed, miracles that cannot be counted" (Job 9:10).

When people hear the word *miracle*, they tend to think of all the miracles Jesus performed during His time on earth. He made the lame walk, the tongue speak, and opened the eyes of the blind. The Apostles performed these same kinds of miracles after Jesus left them and ascended into heaven.

Who can watch a video of a tiny embryo from conception to a full-term baby and not think of the miraculous hand of God? Who can explain being the lone survivor of a plane crash where everyone else perished? Who heals someone with a terminal prognosis?

I have seen many miracles in my life. I call them miracles because I can't explain them scientifically or naturally. For instance, I survived a horrible diving accident as a teenager with nothing but a sore neck. Another time I was in a car accident where my head hit the windshield so hard I left half my hair implanted in it. I almost drowned as a child, *"But God"* ... nudged a lifeguard who spotted me at the bottom of the pool and pulled me out. These are all miracles that can happen only by God's grace and mercy.

I would definitely have to say that God is still in the miracle performing business. Don't ever think anything is too big or too hard for Him. The Word says that "All things are possible with God" (Mark 10:27). Our God is a God of miracles and a keeper of promises. Never doubt what He can do in your life!

JUNE 12

*"But those who suffer He delivers in their suffering;
He speaks to them in their affliction" (Job 36:15).*

Jacob's favorite son, Joseph, dealt with overwhelmingly difficult circumstances in his life. He was sold into slavery by his jealous brothers as a young boy. As a young man, he was falsely accused of adultery with the king's wife and imprisoned for thirteen years for a crime he didn't commit. Joseph suffered for years, alone and forgotten in the pit of a dungeon.

Through all this, Joseph never lost his faith and trusted that God had a plan and a purpose for his life. Fast forward to the end of the story, and we see that Joseph was ultimately appointed second-in-command to the King and placed in charge of all of Egypt. Because of Joseph's careful planning, he was able to provide food for the people during a severe famine in the land. He was restored to a place of great respect and honor after all that he suffered.

Joseph wasn't the only one who suffered in this story. His father mourned the loss of a son, and his brothers lived for years with horrible guilt. But they were also restored in the end when Joseph eventually revealed himself to them and said, "You intended to harm me, *"But God"* intended it for good to accomplish what is now being done, the saving of many lives" (Genesis 50:19).

Paul tells us to rejoice in our suffering because we know that God intends to use it for good one day. Like Joseph, God will use our pain for His honor and glory if we continue to persevere in our trials.

JUNE 13

"The Lord opened her heart to respond to Paul's message" (Acts 16:14).

The "her" in this Scripture verse was a Jewish woman named Lydia. She was a businesswoman who believed in God and followed the law. However, she was curious about this Apostle Paul, so she looked for him when he came to town to hear him preach. Because of Paul's message she was able to respond to the truth and accept Jesus as her Savior.

Why does it seem that God opens some ears to hear the gospel message and others remain closed? Why did He open Lydia's ears that day? I think the answer lies in the willingness of people to seek out the Truth. Lydia pursued Paul with the desire to really listen to what he had to say. She was actively engaged.

The New Living Translation of this verse says, "As she listened, the Lord opened her heart, and she accepted what Paul was saying." There seems to be a pre-requisite for the Lord to open our hearts: we have to make a conscious effort to expose ourselves to the Truth.

After Lydia's heart was opened, she was baptized, and she became "a worshiper of God." She then invited Paul to be a guest in her home. Lydia heard the Good News and responded. Have you had the opportunity to respond to God's Truth yet? If you haven't, don't sit idly by. Wise King Solomon said in Proverbs 8:17, "Those who seek me [God] find me." If you seek God, you will find Him.

JUNE 14

"In His hand is the life of every creature and the breath of all mankind" (Job 12:10).

Jesus' hands symbolize so much of His character. His hands serve as a powerful reminder that it took those humble hands being nailed to a cross for the forgiveness of our sins and life everlasting. Those scarred hands remind us that He is our Savior and salvation. He is our Redeemer and our Lord. Isaiah tells us that our names are engraved on the palms of Jesus' hands and that "By his wounds we are healed" (Isaiah 53:5).

Jesus' hands also represent love and healing. Gentle hands that cradle the faces of His children as He tells them how much He loves them. Strong hands that hold ours as He leads and guides us through the trenches of this life. Welcoming hands that are always outstretched to draw us near to Him. Soft hands that caress us and wipe away our tears. We are covered from our heads to our toes with God's beautiful handprints.

Psalm 31:15 says, "My times are in your hands." All the events and circumstances in our lives are in the faithful hands of God. Love, life, and eternity overflow from His hands into our hearts. We can reciprocate by offering God our own hands as we raise them high and give Him glory for all He has done for us.

JUNE 15

"I consider my life worth nothing to me if only I may finish the race and complete the task the Lord Jesus has given me—the task of testifying to the gospel of God's grace" (Acts 20:24).

God gives all of us important job to do while on this earth. It's really an easy job if you think about it. It simply involves opening our mouths and testifying to the gospel of God's grace. Another translation reads, "Telling others the Good News about God's wonderful kindness and hope."

To share the gospel of God's grace, we have to know what it is before we can talk about it. What exactly is the grace of God? The answer is found in Ephesians 2:8. It says, "For it is by grace you have been saved, through faith, and this not from yourselves, it is the gift of God—not by works so that no one can boast." Each one of us has been given this gift of grace from God, and all we have to do is untie it and share it with the world.

We are not testifying if we keep all the good things that God has done for us bottled up inside. We are called to talk about them to others with joy and boldness. This task is not optional. If we are Christians, we are responsible for sharing Christ with the world.

We have to strive to spend whatever time God has given us on this earth to fulfill His purpose. Let's cross that finish line in heaven knowing we did all we could to point others to Jesus and His saving grace.

JUNE 16

"The Lord's will be done" (Acts 21:14).

The Apostle Paul gives us a great example of this Scripture verse. Paul wanted to go to Jerusalem to preach, but the Apostles warned him that trouble awaited him there. They strongly urged him not to go. But Paul with his steady unshakeable faith and devotion responded, "I am ready not only to be bound but also to die in Jerusalem for the name of the Lord Jesus." Scripture says that the Apostles "gave up" and told him, "The Lord's will be done."

"But God" had another agenda for Paul and prompted him to go despite all the warnings. Sometimes we don't understand why God calls us to do something. The truth is that God doesn't need us to understand. He is only looking to see if we will be obedient to His call. His plan will be carried out regardless of our desires and opinions.

This passage in Acts should give us all great comfort. If we were in charge of our own lives, we would make a mess of it for sure. It's far better to leave things in God's hands and rest assured He will work things out for our good. I don't know what my future holds, but I know who holds my future. Praise be to God!

JUNE 17

"To the man who pleases Him, God gives wisdom, knowledge and happiness" (Ecclesiastes 2:26).

Someone once asked me if the Bible promised happiness. It was a great question, but I was not sure about the answer. Whenever that happens, and I don't know the answer, or I have questions, I go straight to God's Word. I see what the Bible has to say about the subject. When I did this, I discovered that God does indeed make that promise regarding happiness. But as I took a closer look at the verse, I noticed that there seemed to be a prerequisite for enjoying this divine happiness. King Solomon stated that it is only given, "To the man who pleases God."

So, what pleases God? How do we please God? We must understand the answers to these questions to truly understand the meaning of the verse. According to the Ten Commandments, the first requirement for pleasing God is to make Him the number one priority in our lives. We must seek Him first in all that we do and put nothing else before Him. We must be diligent about reading His Word and commit to having a personal relationship with Him.

The Bible is not full of great suggestions for happy living. We can't cherry-pick which commands we will adhere to and which we can let fall by the wayside. To please God, it's all or nothing. We can absolutely enjoy happiness as long as our lives include God. Where are you on the happiness scale?

JUNE 18

"I have chosen the way of truth. I have set my heart on your laws" (Psalm 119:30).

What is the way of truth? Maybe the real question should be: who is the way of truth? The answer is a person, and His name is Jesus. Scripture tells us that Jesus is "The Way, the Truth, and the Life" (John 14:6). Jesus is Truth, and no one gets to the Father—to heaven—except through Him. Jesus is our one-way ticket to heaven!

We have to make many choices throughout our lives. And we must live with the consequences of those choices. We can believe and trust that Jesus is the Truth, or we can continue to reject Him and face the dire consequences of that decision. There is only one choice when it comes to entrance into heaven, and it is via our Savior Jesus Christ.

Believers and unbelievers will have to stand in judgment one day. When believers stand before God, they will have Jesus standing beside them testifying to God on our behalf. Unbelievers will stand alone with no one to speak up for them. You never know what the future holds, so don't delay. Choose Jesus, and He will personally escort you through the pearly gates on that glorious day!

JUNE 19

"It was good for me to be afflicted so that I might learn your decrees" (Psalm 119:71).

Affliction is never pleasant. But sometimes God uses it to get our attention. He has to use something painful to get our focus back on Him. Scripture tells us that God is a jealous God. He will not compete with anyone or anything for our attention. We are on a slippery slope if we make anything in our lives more important than God.

We can also choose to see afflictions as God's mercies in disguise. Our biggest disappointments and heartaches serve as the best opportunities for God to do great things in our lives. There is a spiritual lesson in everything we go through. And most of the time, it is learning how to rely not on ourselves but on God.

Some of us have or will have a "come to Jesus moment" in our lives where we raise our hands in surrender and give our hearts over to Him. He wants us to run into His arms, and sometimes affliction is the best motivator. Will you keep your eyes on Jesus and rest knowing He loves you and only wants the best for you?

JUNE 20

"As for God His way is perfect; the Word of the Lord is flawless" (2 Samuel 22:31).

It took 1500 years and 40 different authors to write the Bible. It contains factual accounts of events, places, people, and dialogue. Historians and archaeologists have repeatedly confirmed its authenticity. There have been 300 prophecies about Jesus Christ that have already been fulfilled. To try to explain the Bible any other way than factual would be absurd. There are no odds high enough to dispute any of these facts and discoveries.

Christianity is the only religion that can prove itself. Thousands of people saw Jesus in person, witnessed His miracles, and watched as He ascended into heaven. People testified to His incredible healings and His mighty displays of power. There were family members, friends, religious leaders, and Roman soldiers who looked on as He was being tortured and hung on a cross to die. Hundreds saw Him and were with Him after He was resurrected from the dead.

What more proof can there be? The author Bill Bright sums it up perfectly. He writes, for those who do not believe the Bible, "This is not because they were unable to believe — they were simply unwilling to believe!"

It all comes back to choices again. What will you choose to believe? God invites all of us to investigate the Truth for ourselves. Keep an open mind as you do this. Be willing to have your beliefs challenged and your hearts transformed.

JUNE 21

"When times are good be happy; but when times are bad consider: God made the one as well as the other" (Ecclesiastes 7:14).

When God gave permission to Satan to attack Job, everything was taken away from him except a complaining wife and a few questionable friends. He was afflicted both physically and mentally. His pain was overwhelming, yet he never cursed or blamed God. His wife, being the encourager that she was, said to Job, "Are you still holding on to your integrity? Curse God and die!" Because of the strength of his faith and commitment to God, Job replied to his wife, "Shall we accept good from God and not trouble?" Job not only accepted his circumstances, but He continued to give thanks to God through them.

God doesn't allow us to suffer for no reason. The reason may be hidden in the mystery of His divine purpose and might never be revealed to us in this lifetime. However, we are called to trust Him regardless and believe that He is a God who only does what is in our best interests.

Things turned out pretty good for Job in the end. The Lord made him prosperous again and gave him twice as much as he had before. It says in Job 42:12, "The Lord blessed the latter part of Job's life more than the first." Job went on to live 140 years and was blessed with children to the fourth generation. We have to learn to accept the bad times as well as the good. Our circumstances should not determine our faith and commitment to Christ.

JUNE 22

"The mind controlled by the Spirit is life and peace"
(Romans 8:6).

Our minds control us; what we think, what we feel, what we do, our attitudes and behavior. They are all birthed in this incredible entity called the mind. It's a challenge to control our thinking sometimes. We tend to allow bad attitudes and ugliness to seep in. The famous author and speaker Joyce Meyer refers to the mind as a battlefield. She says there is a constant battle taking place in our heads. Satan wants to get in there and wreak all kinds of havoc to pull us away from Jesus. We can either banish these thoughts or entertain them. In other words, throw the bad ones out and only let the good ones in.

Controlling our minds to think the right way is an ongoing struggle. It takes time and practice to develop a Spirit-filled mind. The Bible says to "take every thought captive and make it obedient to Christ" (2 Corinthians 10:5). Cast aside anything that you know deep down is not pleasing to God. Tell Satan to "get behind thee" (Matthew 16:23). Nothing would give him greater pleasure than to put a wedge between Christ and us.

We can't develop a Spirit-filled mind on our own. Our minds are too easily influenced, and we need God's power and strength to keep them pure. Living the Christian life is all but impossible without the help of the Holy Spirit. The good news is that we have a loving God who is committed to seeing us win this battle and enable our minds to have the victory!

JUNE 23

"It is with your mouth that you confess and are saved" (Romans 10:10).

It's one thing to live with your faith and beliefs locked away somewhere safe in your heart, and quite another to confess those beliefs with your mouth. How does anyone know you are a follower of Jesus unless you tell them or show them? We talk about the weather and everything else under the sun, and yet, so few of us talk openly about our faith. It almost seems like a taboo subject in our culture.

Paul writes later in Romans 10:13, "Everyone who calls on the name of the Lord will be saved." The word *call* is a verb which requires some sort of action on our part. Salvation involves inward belief as well as outward confession. We must be bold and speak up for Jesus. We should be more concerned with speaking up for what and who we believe in than what others think of us or being accepted. Luke 9:26 says, "If anyone is ashamed of me and my words, the Son of Man will be ashamed of him."

God is so good and so faithful we should be shouting it from the rooftops. Our purpose here on earth is to give God glory. What better way than to speak up and tell others of all the wonderful things He has done for you!

JUNE 24

"We have different gifts according to the grace given us" (Romans 12:6).

God has given us each the ability to do certain things well. These abilities were given to us for one purpose: to meet the needs of others in our communities and in our churches. These gifts are to be used for His glory and not our own. We should never get caught up in our pride but acknowledge that we are only capable of achieving such things by the grace of God.

I was given the opportunity to lead a Bible Study that wasn't anywhere on my radar. It involved a lot of reading and preparation, and it would take up two mornings of my week. I knew I had the gift of teaching, but I just wasn't sure I wanted to make such a big commitment. Finally, one day it hit me—I was making it all about me and totally disregarding God. It didn't matter whether I had the desire or the time. I knew if I stepped out in faith and said yes to this invitation, He would enable me to do it successfully.

We tend to focus on ourselves without being aware of it sometimes. We make excuses; I'm too busy, I'm not very good at it, or surely someone else would be much more suited to it than me. We must put all that aside and lose our self-centeredness. God calls us to use our gifts by His grace and for His glory!

JUNE 25

"Love the Lord your God with all your heart and with all your soul and with all your mind and with all your strength" (Mark 12:30).

One of the Pharisees came to Jesus one day and asked Him, "Teacher, of all the commandments which is the most important?" Jesus answered, "Love the Lord your God with all your heart and with all your soul and with all your mind and with all your strength" (Mark 12:30). God's laws are not complicated. They can be reduced to two simple guiding principles: love God and love others. When you love God completely and care for others as you care for yourself, then you have fulfilled the very essence of the Commandments. Jesus said that these two commandments to love God and love your neighbor summarize all of God's laws.

People look at the word *love* and define it as a feeling or affection. It is neither. By God's definition, love is a choice. We can either choose to love Him and our fellow man, or we can choose not to. If we wait until those feelings of affection are stirred within us, we may never get around to showing love. Love involves action. We have to be intentional about loving God and others. Don't wait until you feel it. Demonstrate it, and the feelings will follow!

JUNE 26

"Run in such a way as to get the prize" (1 Corinthians 9:24).

What is the prize the Apostle Paul is referring to in this verse? It's not a medal or a ribbon that we would typically receive after finishing a race. The prize Paul is talking about is spending eternity with Jesus. The Apostle Peter calls it "a priceless inheritance for his children kept in heaven for us." 1 Peter 5:4 says, "And when the Chief Shepherd appears, you will receive the crown of glory that will never fade away."

Paul uses the analogy of a race to define our Christian walk. Our walk of faith is like a marathon. Just like the runner in the race, we have to keep a steady pace putting one foot in front of the other. We must persevere through the challenges and pain. There are no shortcuts, and like the runner, we can't veer from the course that's been mapped out. We have to keep our eyes on the finish line and stay focused.

The children's story about the tortoise and the hare gives us another great example. The hare believed he could win the race because he ran so much faster than the turtle. But the hare burned out halfway through, and the turtle slowly but surely kept going and won the prize.

We don't need to sprint towards the finish line. We just need to keep our eyes on the goal—the prize for which Christ has called us home!

JUNE 27

"Taste and see that the Lord is good" (Psalm 34:8).

Taste and see does not mean checking out God's credentials and see what you think. Instead, it is an invitation to experience God firsthand. When we take that first taste of God, we can't help but discover that He is a wonderful God. When we begin our Christian life, our knowledge of God is limited. But as we trust in Him, we experience His goodness, which whets our appetites to know Him better.

There used to be an old commercial for Life cereal that always stuck with me. Two brothers are sitting together at the kitchen table with bowls of Life cereal in front of them. The little one is reluctant to try this strange new cereal. His brother pleads with him to give it a try. Little brother is still aimlessly stirring the cereal around, head propped up with his hand and looking totally uninterested. Finally, the big brother pipes up one last time and begs, "C'mon, Mikey, try it. You'll like it!"

What a great analogy for this Scripture verse. You can't sit around trying to muster up the desire or the nerve to taste and see what God is all about. A great discovery is waiting for you if you just follow in Mikey's footsteps and pick up your spoon!

JUNE 28

"If anyone does not love the Lord—a curse be on him" (1 Corinthians 16:22).

The Apostle Paul sometimes preached some harsh but truthful messages. They were always right on the money. This verse, I imagine, was a tough one to preach as well as a tough one to hear. Paul was not one to tickle any ears. He was all about stating the facts and opening up people's eyes to the consequences of their choices.

This teaching was directed at unbelievers. He told the Corinthians that if they did not come to the Lord Jesus Christ that they would experience God's wrath. Of course, the same can be said for us today. Scripture confirms that if we reject Jesus, He will indeed reject us.

Loving God involves total involvement and commitment. It involves seeking Him, serving Him, and worshipping Him. Anything less than this is not authentic love for the Lord and carries with it the same warning we see in this verse. God sees right into our souls and knows our hearts better than we know ourselves. He can't be fooled. He knows the depth of our love and devotion to Him. What is He seeing in your heart today?

JUNE 29

"He died for all that those who live should no longer live for themselves but for Him who died for them and was raised again" (2 Corinthians 5:15).

Some people hold to the belief that Christ died for a chosen few. They think He selectively picked those who would get to be with Him in heaven. The Bible, however, doesn't say that Christ died for some. It says that "Christ died for all" (2 Corinthians 5:15). All of us who have accepted Christ's invitation of salvation will share eternity with God.

When we dedicate our lives to Christ, we give up living for ourselves. We need to sacrifice our wants and desires and live for His. How do we live for Christ? The answer can be summed up in one sentence: by making Him your number one priority in life, by living your life in such a way that everything you say and do is pleasing to God and brings Him glory.

Contrary to what our culture tells us, we were not created for our own happiness. News flash: life is not all about us! It never was, and it never will be. We were created to love and serve the One and Only True God. We were created to praise and worship Him for who He is and all that He has done for us. Because Christ died for us, we should no longer live to please ourselves. Will you give your life over to the One who gave you His?

JUNE 30

"In quietness and trust is your strength" (Isaiah 30:15).

God never designed us to live by our own strength. He created us to rely on Him for everything. Every need, every problem, every fear. Later in this chapter, it says, "For the Lord is a faithful God. Blessed are those who wait for Him to help them."

The Prophet Isaiah tells us that quietness and trust are key factors when it comes to strength. We have to be still—no worrying allowed—for trust to be effective. We need to trust at all times that God has everything under control. That alone should silence our minds and give us peace and comfort. Isaiah 40:29 says, "He gives strength to the weary and increases the power of the weak."

If we trust and believe in God's promises, we can be sure that our weaknesses will always be covered by God's strength. Scripture tells us that He has the power to quiet storms and calm the seas. He has the power to raise people from the dead. He has power that we can't fathom. He can surely handle whatever comes our way. So, when you are tempted to press the worry button, remember: "In quietness and trust is your strength."

JULY 1

"The life I live in the body I live by faith in the Son of God" (Galatians 2:20).

What does it mean to live by faith? We can certainly choose to be in charge of our own lives. We can try to survive in our own strength. We can attempt independence and make our own decisions. All that focus on self, however, does not line up with God's Word. God tells us to live by faith and to trust Him for everything. We must allow God to be the one in the driver's seat, and we have to take a back seat. It's a much smoother ride when Jesus takes the wheel!

We were not created to be left on our own. Why would we need God if we could manage everything ourselves? How prideful of us to even think that we can be self-sufficient. How many times have you heard someone say, "I don't need any help; I can take care of things myself," only to watch them crumble when life throws them a curveball? Who do those people turn to for support and comfort? Family and friends will always fall short of meeting our needs and expectations. *"But God"* never will. He is there for us in the good times and in the bad.

Living by faith is difficult sometimes. It's not easy to trust someone you can't see or might not know all that well. However, God's Word tells us to live by faith and not by sight. Faith must have an object, and the only object must be God. We need to live our lives by trusting in the Son of God who first loved us and gave Himself for us. God's sacrifice for us must elicit a response. And the only proper response should be to live our lives for Him, by faith, trusting in Him for everything.

JULY 2

"Live a life of love just as Christ loved us" (Ephesians 5:2).

If we think of all the ways that Christ loves us, and then we look at how that lines up with how we love others, I'm sure we would all fall short. Christ's love for us is unconditional. He loves us no matter what! Victories or failures matter not to Him. His love is constant and steady. He forgives the unforgivable and loves the unlovable. We can't earn His love by being good or doing good things. And we can't lose it when we mess up or disappoint Him. God can never love us any more or any less than He does right now!

If we are to be imitators of Christ, we have to ask ourselves some questions: Do I love my family and friends unconditionally or do I predicate it on their behavior? Do I love them when they hurt me or disappoint me? Do I love them when they are acting selfishly? Jesus even loved His enemies. As He hung dying on the cross, He asked His Father in heaven to forgive those who tortured Him and put Him to death.

Just as children imitate their parents, we should follow the example of our Father in heaven. Our love for others should be sacrificial. It should be the kind of love that goes beyond affection. It's easy to love those who love us. When you see a homeless person or encounter a cranky sales clerk, remember that God loves them just as much as He loves you. That is the quality of love that Christ has called us to and expects from us.

JULY 3

"For it has been granted to you on behalf of Christ not only to believe on Him, but also to suffer for Him" (Philippians 1:29).

The New Living Translation version of this verse says it is a privilege to suffer for Christ. Paul and the Apostles rejoiced that they were counted worthy to suffer for Him. Christian suffering should be considered a blessing according to God's Word. We are given the gift of faith as well as the gift of suffering. They will always co-exist with one another.

When Paul was in prison in Philippi, he wrote many of his letters which became books in the New Testament. As he sat chained up in cold, wet, dirty dungeons, he told his fellow inmates that what he was suffering was good because it was serving a wonderful purpose. It was serving to advance the gospel and bring people to Christ all throughout the country. His testimony encouraged the brothers, and they became more courageous and fearless in sharing God's Word.

Isn't that the purpose of all suffering? To be able to testify to God's goodness regardless of our circumstances? Every hardship we go through is a platform for our faith. It wasn't Paul's chains that brought God honor but the way he responded to them. He didn't get angry at God and complain but maintained a loving and positive attitude. Attitude is everything, especially when it comes to suffering.

JULY 4

"Remember O Lord how I have walked before you faithfully and with wholehearted devotion and have done what is good in your eyes" (Isaiah 38:3).

This verse was a prayer written by King Hezekiah when he thought he was dying and the end of his life was at hand. Like David, Hezekiah was a good king. He was faithful and wholly devoted to the Lord. Had God not saved His life, this prayer would have made a wonderful eulogy for the king.

Our culture today devotes itself to many worthless distractions. We dedicate ourselves to causes and pursuits that have no lasting value or significance. We tend to put wealth and success before faith and godliness. We idolize people or things that have no importance in the Kingdom of God.

God wants us to be wholeheartedly devoted to one person and one person only. Jesus preached a sermon on treasures in heaven that addressed this very issue. He said, "No one can serve two masters. Either he will hate the one and love the other, or he will be devoted to the one and despise the other." There can only be one person who is the object of our devotion and loyalty. Like King Hezekiah, we have to walk out our faith wholeheartedly for the sole purpose of honoring God.

JULY 5

"Now go; I will help you speak and will teach you what to say" (Exodus 4:12).

Moses is a wonderful example of how God uses ordinary people to do extraordinary things. When God gave Moses the mission to go to Egypt and ask Pharaoh to let His people go, he immediately started giving God excuses as to why he wasn't the right guy for the job. He told God that he was not a good speaker and couldn't possibly do what God was asking of him. *"But God"* ... told him that He would teach him to speak and tell him what to say. Moses was completely out of excuses at this point and surrendered to God's will.

Once, I was given less than eight hours of notice to speak to a ladies group at my church. I had nothing—not an inkling of an idea what to talk about. But this Scripture verse immediately came to mind, and it gave me total peace about the situation. It said, "Do not worry about what to say or how to say it. At that time, you will be given what to say, for it will not be you speaking but the Spirit of your Father speaking through you" (Matthew 10:19).

I wrote this verse down, put it in my pocket, and headed off to church with not a note in hand. When I got up to speak, I opened my mouth and out poured a twenty-minute message. *"But God."* Our God is so faithful and good! Trust in His promises, and He will never let you down.

JULY 6

"And the peace of God which transcends all understanding will guard your hearts and your minds in Christ Jesus" (Philippians 4:7).

God's peace is far more wonderful than the human mind can comprehend. His peace is different from the world's peace. God's peace is not found in self-help books or positive thinking. It is not the absence of conflict or suffering. It comes from believing that God is in control and that we can trust Him for everything. True peace is that inner tranquility that comes from giving all our cares over to God. He is far more capable of solving our problems and meeting our needs than we are.

Peace is a priceless treasure. Scripture calls it a gift of the Holy Spirit. We can't pursue it for ourselves. The only way to receive this gift is to receive the only One who can give it. Just like salvation, Jesus is the only path to peace.

The peace of God is pure satisfaction dwelling in our hearts. It overwhelms us with a grateful heart and a joyful attitude. If we want to experience this kind of peace, we must align our lives with Jesus. We must know Him, love Him, and be committed to Him. Only then can we expect the blessing of this unfathomable gift.

JULY 7

"Speak Lord, for your servant is listening" (1 Samuel 3:9).

At around the age of twelve, the prophet Samuel was helping a priest named Eli to serve in the Tabernacle. One night as they were both sleeping, God called to Samuel. Samuel, however, thought it was Eli calling to him. Three times the Lord called Samuel, and three times Samuel thought it was Eli. When Samuel finally went to Eli and asked him what he wanted, Eli told him it was not he who had called *"But God."* He told Samuel the next time he heard someone call to him answer and say, "Speak, Lord, for your servant is listening."

When you hear the voice of God speaking to you in your inner spirit do you answer like Samuel and answer, "Yes, Lord, I am listening"? Or do you pretend you didn't hear and ignore God's voice? Or maybe you chose not to hear because you might not have liked what God had to say or what He may be asking you to do? Do you use the filter test before you decide whether you will listen to His voice?

My mother used to tell me I had selective hearing growing up. I only heard what I wanted to hear. She frequently reminded me how badly I suffered from this affliction. Even now, sometimes I wonder if I am purposely hard of hearing when it comes to God's voice. Do I always listen when He speaks? Do I acknowledge Him right away? The God of the universe speaks to us personally, and yet we ignore Him. Our prayer and our response should always be like Samuel's, "Speak, Lord, for your servant is listening."

JULY 8

"And without faith, it is impossible to please God, because anyone who comes to Him must believe that He exists and that He rewards those who earnestly seek Him" (Hebrews 11:6).

Sometimes we get caught up in thinking that it's what we do for God that pleases Him instead of who we are. We think we must serve in countless ministries at church or chalk up the volunteer hours at the local soup kitchen for God to take notice of us. But He is not interested in our works. They do not buy us any favor with God. We can't earn any more love than God already has for us.

Scripture is very clear that even though acts of service should be the result of living out our faith, these aren't the things that truly please God. What pleases God is our godly character. He looks to see if we are kind and loving to others and if we are putting Him first in our lives. He looks for displays of patience and goodness. He also tests us to see if we will remain faithful and trust in Him. Who we are matters more to God than what we do.

God's love is always unconditional. It is given freely and abundantly. It can't be earned by acts of service or by trying to be a good person. If we truly want to please God, we must seek Him with all our hearts and truly believe He exists to love us. 1 Thessalonians 2:4 says, "We are not trying to please men but God." Our goal in life should be pleasing God and not people. He should always be our first priority.

JULY 9

"Before I was born the Lord called me; from my birth He has made mention of my name" (Isaiah 49:1).

How incredible is it to think that the God of the universe—the Creator and Sustainer of life—called us before we were even born? He knew what our names would be, whom our parents would be, what we would look like. He knew exactly how many days we would spend on this earth. He knew everything there was to know about us before we even took our first breath. The Savior of the world had His hand on us from the beginning of time. He had a plan and a purpose all prepared in advance for us.

If you really want to make Scripture personal, insert your name in the verse above when you read it. You can do this with any verse in the Bible to really make it come alive. It will seem like God is talking directly to you (which He is) and giving you better insight. Go ahead; put your name where the 'me' is in this verse. Doesn't it make a huge difference?

Some people don't care for their names, but maybe if they realized that it was given to them not by their parents but by the Almighty before they were born, it would make a difference. I used to tell people that my earthly father picked out my name, but I've learned through Scripture that it was my heavenly father who truly named me. Now I embrace my name, which I never did before, and praise God for it!

JULY 10

"Be joyful always; pray continually; give thanks in all circumstances, for this is God's will for you in Christ Jesus" (1 Thessalonians 5:16).

There is so much wisdom packed into this one little verse. Actually, one might describe this teaching by Paul as bedrock faith. Paul tells us that these three things are vital to a successful walk with Christ.

Being joyful really means to rejoice. Rejoice in the Lord always, at all times. Even when we don't feel like it, or we're having a bad day. There will be times when we don't feel like singing along in worship. *Sing anyway.* There will be times we don't want to have our quiet time and read our Bibles. *Do it anyway.* God will reward our dedication and perseverance with unspeakable joy.

Praying continually means just what it says—pray continually. Prayer was never intended to be formal, performed at a certain place or a precise time. Simply talking to God is praying and we can do it whenever and wherever. Think of it as an ongoing conversation with God that never ends.

The rest of this verse is a tough concept for some people. Does God really mean *all* circumstances? How can we possibly be thankful when we are hurting? Believe it or not, we can always find something small to be thankful for in any painful circumstance if we look hard enough. I was in the ER one time in excruciating pain. I found that I could at least be thankful that I wasn't blessing everyone with my lunch!

The minute we give thanks in a tough situation is when our hearts find peace, and we can trust God whatever the outcome.

JULY 11

"For we brought nothing into the world and we can take nothing out of it" (1 Timothy 6:17).

Death is an inescapable destination for every single one of us. We may question many things in life but dying is not one of them. We will all have to face it someday.

If we can take nothing away from our life here on earth, why do people focus on amassing great fortunes and working to have expensive things? Jesus tells us in Matthew chapter 6 that our treasures will be worthless in heaven. What good is building a financial dynasty if it will serve no purpose for eternity? Do we care that much about looking affluent and successful? At what point do we say that we are content with what we have? When does enough become enough? The Apostle Paul would answer it like this, "If we have enough food and clothing let us be content." Paul had absolutely nothing but the clothes on his back, yet he lived a totally satisfied life and was a successful teacher and missionary.

Jesus gives us His commands concerning wealth in His teaching, Treasure in Heaven. "Do not store up for yourselves treasures on earth. But store up for yourselves treasures in heaven. For where your treasure is there your heart will be also" (Matthew 6:19). Jesus is asking, "What do you hold most dear in your life?" If we value anything more than God, our treasures are in the wrong place. The only thing He will care about when we get to heaven is what we did with what He gave us and how we used it for His glory. Did we store up treasures in heaven by using what God entrusted to us, putting them to use to help others? Or did we squander His resources on ourselves? We leave this earth just like we came into it. By the grace of God and empty-handed.

JULY 12

"For God did not give us a spirit of timidity but a spirit of power, of love, and of self-discipline" (2 Timothy 1:7).

It is hard to fathom sometimes that the same Spirit that raised Christ from the dead also lives in us. That is amazing when you think about it. God, in His goodness, gave us a way to access His great power through His Holy Spirit. He knew we would need help to live godly lives.

A hairdryer lying on a counter is just an inanimate object. It performs no function. It doesn't become useful until it's plugged into a power source. We are just like that. We are unusable until we get plugged into Jesus. God is the electrical outlet, and we are the prongs.

How can we best plug ourselves into God? Two ways: prayer and His Word. Both will keep us charged up and ready to go to work for His Kingdom. His love will become our love. His strength will become our strength. His power will become our power. All we have to do is just plug into God!

JULY 13

"I have raised you up for this very purpose, that I might show you my power and that my name will be proclaimed in all the earth" (Exodus 9:16).

The Israelites were slaves in Egypt for 400 years. They were worked to the bone and horribly mistreated. When God went to work on freeing them from Pharaoh's grip, it was a long and laborious task. Pharaoh was as stubborn as they came, and he was not about to give up and let the people go. God sent devastating plagues, and Scripture says that after each plague, "The Lord hardened Pharaoh's heart, and he would not let the Israelites go out of his country" (Exodus 11:10).

I've always wondered why God kept hardening Pharaoh's heart so that he refused to cooperate. Could all that death and destruction have been avoided if only God hadn't hardened his heart? One day, the answer to the question hit me, and there was the *"But God"* staring me right in the face. It happened this way so that God's purpose and power would be evident. God would get the credit for the Israelites gaining their freedom, not Pharaoh.

We, too, can be like Pharaoh. We ignore the signs that God sends us because we want our own way, or we don't want to relinquish control. Pharaoh and his hard heart eventually ended up at the bottom of the Red Sea.

If you struggle with a hard heart, pray, and ask God to soften it. Your new life built on faith and trust in God awaits you on the other side of that parted sea.

JULY 14

"For prophecy never had its origin in the will of man, but men spoke from God as they were carried along by the Holy Spirit" (2 Peter 1:21).

Remember stenographers? They were the people who sat in front of the bosses' desk with pen poised over a steno pad ready to write down what he dictated. They usually used what was called shorthand, a method of rapid handwriting using simple strokes. Stenographers are a thing of the past now as technology rules our world.

This serves as a great analogy for how the Bible was written. Forty different writers composed the Bible, but they didn't author it. The words were dictated to them by the boss (God), and they simply recorded everything He said. In essence, they were the conduits God used to put His words on paper.

Back to the stenographer. After the boss dictated his letter and it was typed up, he would sign it, and off it went in the good old-fashioned snail mail. The recipient of the letter would never think to question its authenticity. He trusted that the signature was genuine. What reason would he ever have to doubt it?

The Bible, however, is treated very differently. Some don't trust the signature of the author. *"But God"* says His Word is Truth and Life and the only way we can gain access to our Father in heaven. The author of the greatest book ever written offers all people the hope of salvation and eternal life. Why not open your Bible today and grab a steno pad?

JULY 15

"We have different gifts according to the grace given us" (Romans 12:6).

God has given each of us the ability to do certain things well. These abilities are called gifts of the Holy Spirit and are unique to each individual. They have been given to us for ministering to the needs of others and ultimately for bringing glory to God.

How do we know what our gifts are? A combination of the answers to these three questions will usually point us in the right direction: What am I good at? What comes naturally to me? What am I passionate about? The responses melded together should be able to uncover our natural gifting.

Sometimes our goals in life may not necessarily line up with our gifts. What we have in mind may not be what God has in mind for us at all. We must be careful to make sure we are operating in the gifts God gave us versus the ones we desire. As a mental health advocate, I wanted to be a speaker, travel around the country, and talk about the sad state of mental health in our country and what we could do about it. *"But God"* obviously had other plans for me!

The Apostle Peter writes in 1 Peter 4:10, "Each one should use whatever gift he has received to serve others, faithfully administering God's grace in its various forms." We must be faithful with the gifts God has given us. Just as we should not squander our time, we should not squander our gifts and talents. If you still question what gifts you've been given, ask God and also ask other God-fearing people to answer those questions about you. Sometimes our greatest insights can come from others.

JULY 16

"Be active in sharing your faith so that you will have a full understanding of every good thing we have in Christ" (Philemon 1:6).

Giving your personal testimony is a great way to share your faith. No one can refute your own experiences with God. They can't negate your feelings or choices. They can't challenge the hope that lives in your heart. Testimonies are not debatable. They are what they are, and people should accept and respect them. To doubt someone's word is the same as accusing them of lying.

Share with others all the wonderful things God has done in your life. Talk about what a great and awesome God you serve. Proclaim His goodness and faithfulness in your life. Be ready for the questions people may want to ask. Practice your responses if you need to. 1 Peter 3:15 says, "Always be prepared to give an answer to everyone who asks you to give the reason for the hope that you have."

Is your faith on display or hidden in the depths of your heart? Are you willing to step up your boldness a notch and speak out even if you may face rejection or ridicule? Jesus faced these things every day, and yet He never wavered from the mission His Father gave Him. He preached the Good News no matter what! Are you sincerely committed to carrying out this same mission in your life?

JULY 17

"Are not all angels ministering spirits sent to serve those who will inherit salvation?" (Hebrews 1:14).

Angels often masquerade as people. Very rarely will an angel appear to someone in flowing white robes and wings like the kind we see portrayed in books or on TV. They most likely look just like you and me. It's that person who pulls over to help you change a flat tire in the pouring rain. It's that person who is the first one at the scene of an accident and pulls you out of the car. It's that person who anonymously pays for your lunch when you're short on cash.

Angels are defined as ministering spirits. Helpers. Providers. Other translations call them *servants*. We can all be servants of our fellow man and in doing so be an angel to them. We can look for opportunities to bless others and be that ministering spirit to them. We all have the potential to become angels.

My son had a life-threatening fall as a teenager. He fell a distance that statistics say should have killed him. *"But God"* he survived! In the hospital the next day, we noticed he had black and blue marks under his arms. We thought it strange and unexplainable. A few days later while I was reading Psalm 91, I found the answer to those mysterious black and blue marks. Verse 11 says, "For He will command His angels concerning you to guard you in all your ways; they will lift you up in their hands so that you will not strike your foot against a stone." We all believed from then on that an angel sent by God caught my son under his arms and saved our son's life.

Look for ways to be an angel to someone. Offer assistance when you see someone struggling. There are needs all around us if we just open our eyes!

JULY 18

"He is not here. He has risen!" (Luke 24:6).

These three words were spoken to Mary Magdalene by an angel sitting outside Jesus' tomb. The angel said to Mary, "Why do you look for the living among the dead? He has risen!" The angel then reminded her of Jesus' words before He died: "The Son of man must be delivered into the hands of sinful men, be crucified and on the third day be raised again."

It's interesting to note that of all the people Jesus could have chosen to appear to first, He chose Mary Magdalene. Not the Apostle John, "the one that Jesus loved." Not His mother or brothers. He chose a woman who had quite an unsavory reputation. We see throughout Scripture how Jesus seemed to regularly practice choosing unlikely candidates for important tasks.

God doesn't always use the most qualified person to carry out His plans. He uses simple ordinary people like you and me. Mary Magdalene didn't have any special qualifications, and yet she was able to play a vital role in the greatest event in all of history.

All of us are qualified to serve in the Kingdom of God. We have different assignments, but one is no more important than the other. We are all children of God and are considered equal in the eyes of the Lord!

JULY 19

"Acknowledge your guilt—you have rebelled against the Lord your God" (Jeremiah 3:13).

The prophet Jeremiah was appointed by God to bring judgment against the Israelites for their continued sin and idol worship. This mission of judgment was hard for Jeremiah to carry out because, despite their sins, he still loved the people. Before God leveled the blow, Jeremiah did point out to them that sincere repentance would stave off the impending wrath of God. However, they opted to continue in their sin to the point of sacrificing their children to foreign gods.

Of course, the story doesn't end here with the destruction of the Israelites. They eventually repented, and God forgave them and restored them as His chosen people. Only a merciful and forgiving God would do this after the people had so blatantly sinned against Him and rejected Him. There is only one word that can describe this restoration: grace!

Jeremiah tells us there is a prerequisite to receiving God's forgiveness and grace. We must first acknowledge our sin before Him and ask Him to forgive us. And then, just like the Israelites had to do, we must abandon our sin and change our ways. Penance without change is useless.

Don't be like the stiff-necked Israelites. Walk away from sin and let God cleanse you and make you whole again. Let Him restore you to oneness with Him just as He did the Israelites.

JULY 20

"Where you go, I will go, and where you stay, I will stay" (Ruth 1:16).

The story of Ruth and Naomi is such a beautiful example of love and devotion. Ruth was Naomi's daughter-in-law, and she was fiercely devoted to her. After Ruth and Naomi became widows, Naomi wanted to return to Israel to be near her people. Ruth could have returned to her homeland of Moab, but instead, she chose to follow Naomi. She said to her, "Don't ask me to leave you and turn back. I will go wherever you go and live wherever you live. Your people will be my people and your God will be my God. I will die where you die and will be buried there." What a picture of sacrifice and of the incredible bond they shared.

This story is also a great example of the importance of mentoring those younger than us. We should all be mentored and be mentoring someone else. This is what the book of Titus teaches us. The older women (and men) should be full of wisdom, strong in their faith, and lead godly lives. In turn, they should be an example to the younger ones. Role models are of huge importance as we seek to grow in our faith.

Do you have anyone in your life right now that is mentoring you? Likewise, have you offered to help someone else grow deeper in their faith? These kinds of relationships are vital to our spiritual development. You need to look no further than Jesus and His disciples to see how necessary the role of a mentor plays. The Father passed His wisdom down to His Son, who, in turn, passed it on to His disciples, who then poured it out into the world. Just like Naomi's faith trickled down into Ruth and encouraged her to dedicate herself to God, so we should follow in her wise footsteps.

JULY 21

"I will put my laws in their minds and write them on their hearts" (Hebrews 8:10).

Committing Scripture to memory can be challenging. God tells us to write His words on our hearts, but our minds may struggle to recall them. While out shopping one day, I came across a cute little blackboard that I thought would look perfect hanging on my kitchen wall. But what could I use it for? Grocery lists? Notes to the family? Suddenly, I heard God whisper an idea in my ear. Why not use it to write down Scripture verses? Great idea, Lord! That way I would have them right in front of me all day, so I could keep them fresh in my memory.

This simple little blackboard revolutionized my retention of Scripture. When the verses are right there in front of you, it's amazing how they just seem to tattoo themselves on your brain. Joshua 1:8 says, "Do not let this Book of the Law depart from your mouth; meditate on it day and night, so that you may be careful to do everything written in it."

I was able to share a Scripture verse recently with a friend that I had just written on my board. I was so excited that I remembered it so easily. She said it was just what she needed to hear that day and thanked me for the encouragement. That is why God commands us to learn Scripture and write it on our hearts. God knows what a blessing we can be to others who need to hear a special word from Him at just the right time.

JULY 22

"Let us consider how we may spur one another on toward love and good deeds" (Hebrews 10:24).

This verse reminds me of the concept of paying it forward. We do kind things for others, and they, in turn, pass that kindness onto someone else. Everyone gets the blessing all the way around. There is nothing like generosity to bring joy to the heart.

My husband and I were out for dinner one night, and we had an opportunity to pay it forward. We were able to anonymously bless a young couple sitting next to us who were celebrating their first anniversary. The waiter told us as we were leaving that they, in turn, bought a gift card on their way out to give to someone else. That's what Paul is talking about — "spurring one another on to good deeds." One kind act begets another kind act.

God expects us to share our blessings with others. He is generous with us and wants us to follow His example. Our good deeds don't have to be monetary. They can be as simple as holding the door for someone, letting someone go ahead of you in line, or taking a plate of brownies to the new family in the neighborhood. I love how the New Living Translation states it: "Think of ways to encourage one another to outbursts of love and good deeds."

We need to ask God to put divine opportunities in front of us to express these outbursts of love and good deeds. Pray for Him to bring someone to you so that you can pass a blessing along. You never know how many people down the road will be blessed because of your one act of simple kindness.

JULY 23

"For before he was taken he was commended as one who pleased God" (Hebrews 11:5).

This verse is referring to Enoch, the son of Cain and the father of Methuselah. The Bible really doesn't record much about Enoch except that he walked with God for 300 years, and when he died, "God took him away." We are told that he enjoyed a close relationship with God all his life. Enoch was known as "one who pleased God."

When it is my turn to be taken home, I want nothing more than to be celebrated for living a life pleasing to the Lord. I can think of no greater accolade. I want to hear, "Well done thy good and faithful servant" (Matthew 25:21). My accomplishments and my successes won't mean a thing.

This may be a good time to stop and take a spiritual inventory of your life. Is your heart in the right place? Are you focused on the right person? Will you hear the words "well done thy good and faithful servant" when you arrive at heaven's door? These are the questions in life that really matter.

JULY 24

"For when your faith is tested your endurance has a chance to grow" (James 1:2).

Everyone has their faith tested from time to time. No one is immune to trials and challenges. Some people think that when they become Christians, they will live problem-free lives. But God's Word says otherwise. Jesus said in John 16:33, "In this world, you will have trouble."

It's human nature to want to question God about why we have to suffer. We want to know why we have to go through such painful trials that rob us of our peace and joy. God's answer, according to Scripture, is that He wants to grow our faith, develop perseverance in us, and build up our character. While these things are all positive and good, sometimes they seem to fall short of supplying the hope that we need at the time. To conquer this frustration, we need to change our way of thinking and work alongside God and not against Him.

I have learned by walking through many fires that the question to ask God is not "why" but "what do you want me to learn from this experience? What lessons can I take away from this? What nugget of truth can I apply that will help me see things in a different light?"

God does not owe us any explanations. He is God, and we are not. He wants us to be overcomers. He wants us to put our faith and trust in Him and to rest in the fact that He has things under control. He wants us to learn to rely on Him and not on our own strength.

James tells us that trials will make us mature and complete in our faith so that we do not lack any good thing. Psalm 119:71 says, "It was good for me to be afflicted so that I might learn your decrees." Don't ask God "why" the next time you face trouble. Ask Him to help you understand what He is trying to teach you.

JULY 25

"If you really keep the royal law found in Scripture, '[Love your neighbor as yourself,' you are doing right" (James 2:8).

The royal law can be defined as the Law of Love. It's called royal because it is the supreme law that is the source of all other laws that govern relationships. It is a summation of all the laws. Jesus also called this law the Second Greatest Commandment, right after loving God with all your heart, mind, soul, and strength.

Loving your neighbor can be as easy as a smile, a wave, or a kind word at the mailbox. It's an offer to watch over their house and picking up their mail when they're out of town. It's an offer to come over for a cup of coffee or tea. It's just one person showing another person love.

I was recently watching a handful of men pouring concrete in my neighbor's driveway. They had been digging and shoveling dirt all week preparing the area. Every time I looked out my window, they were diligently working away. I sensed God was telling me to bake them some brownies and take them over. I was super busy, though, and really not in the mood for baking. He wouldn't let me alone, insisting I should turn the oven on and get busy. I finally gave in, knowing in my heart that it wasn't my agenda that mattered, but His.

When I delivered the brownies, the men couldn't have been more appreciative. They all gave me great big smiles and thanked me profusely. One said, "That was very kind of you, ma'am." The Royal Law is really very simple...a little love and kindness are all you need.

JULY 26

"Faith by itself, if it is not accompanied by action, is dead" (James 2:17).

James talks a lot about faith in action in this second chapter of his book. He talks about genuine faith and how it will naturally produce good deeds. Faith and action have to work together. Faith is not just the mere intellectual acceptance of certain truths. The word faith is a noun and also a verb, which implies action.

James says that faith without works is false faith. Faith and works cannot co-exist independently of each other. The Apostle John talks about love and deeds in the same way. 1 John 3:18 says, "Let us not love with words or tongue but with actions and in truth." Action follows true authentic faith.

We cannot earn our salvation by doing good deeds. No action of ours can save us. The Apostle Paul explains salvation as a gift as opposed to salvation that we try to earn. He tells us in Ephesians 2:8, "For it is by grace you have been saved —through faith—and this not from yourselves, it is a gift of God." We can't earn our way into heaven. Some people think that leading a good life is enough. But what is the definition of good, and how much good is enough?

You will find that if you have truly committed your life to Christ, you will naturally want to put feet to your faith. You will yearn to serve God and your fellow man. Action follows true faith. It's proof that Jesus is indeed the Lord of your life and that you have chosen to serve Him because of His gift of salvation to you.

JULY 27

"Out of the same mouth come praise and cursing. My brothers, this should not be!" (James 3:10).

In his writings, James was also passionate about the godly use of our tongues. He dedicated an entire chapter to the subject. He called the tongue a fire that corrupts the whole person. He said no man can tame it, and that it holds the power of life and death. We can either speak love, affirmation, and kindness into someone, or we can speak death by murdering them with our hurtful words.

Words can sting, betray, disappoint, and cause great pain. They can kill someone's self-esteem and mangle their confidence. We truly must be careful about every word that comes out of our mouths. We must make it a point to focus on the positive and building people up. It feels good to be able to speak life into someone. Affirmation goes a long way toward lifting someone's spirits.

I like to pray this prayer before opening my mouth: "Lord, please keep watch over the door of my lips" (Psalm 141:3). I ask Him to guard my words so that I can speak only what is helpful for others and what is pleasing to Him. I ask Him to help me to exercise grace when I am the target of a cursing tongue. Wise King Solomon gave great advice on this subject. "A gentle answer turns away wrath" (Proverbs 15:1). Let your tongue bring life and blessing to others as you seek to honor God with your every word.

JULY 28

"The prayer of a righteous man is powerful and effective" (James 5:16).

The Christian's most powerful resource is prayer. Some people use it as a last resort when all else fails. But it should be our first plan of action. God's power is greater than ours, so it only stands to reason that we should rely on Him in our time of need.

Prayer is often replaced these days with self-help books. Or the Internet. Or advice from a well-meaning friend or family member. Prayer should never be replaced by any of these things and should always be our first line of defense. Our automatic go-to.

There was a major event in our family years ago that led to an entire city praying for us. Our 16-year-old son was missing for three days. Our church held a prayer vigil and friends and neighbors came together to pray. A whole community was on their knees crying out to God in unison for our son.

God in His infinite mercy answered our prayers and our son was found. The prayers of the righteous are indeed powerful and effective! Our pain and suffering ultimately brought God to the forefront, and we were able to give Him all the praise and glory in the end.

When God answers a prayer for you, make sure He gets all the credit. This is the reason behind every trial and difficult circumstance we encounter. God wants to be brought into the light so His power and strength will be revealed.

JULY 29

"By His wounds, you have been healed" (1 Peter 2:24).

Brutal can only begin to describe the suffering and torture Jesus went through during the crucifixion. His body was battered, bloodied, and crumbling under the weight of the 300-pound cross He was forced to carry. The nails in His hands and feet were pounded through bone and muscle. The spear in His side was not a glancing blow but struck through to His internal organs. The only way any of these wounds could ever have been healed was supernaturally. And God did indeed heal every one of them.

We too have deep wounds that can only be healed supernaturally. Some of them are hidden within us, growing and festering as we try to ignore them. When Jesus rose from the dead, His wounds were healed. He still had the scars though. He showed them to the doubting Apostle Thomas as proof of His resurrection.

Jesus' scars are a promise to us that we also can be healed of our wounds and suffering. God can heal us in every aspect of our lives—physically, emotionally, and spiritually—if we simply ask Him. Scars are a great reminder of God's healing power. We should not try to cover them up but wear them proudly as they tell the story of God's mighty work in our lives. Just as Jesus' scars brought His Father glory, ours can do the very same thing.

JULY 30

"But the day of the Lord will come like a thief. The heavens will disappear with a roar, the elements will be destroyed by fire, and the earth and everything in it will be laid bare" (2 Peter 3:10).

Scripture always mentions fire when it talks about Jesus coming back. God destroyed the world once with water, but after that, He promised never to use water again to wipe out the earth. He placed the rainbow in the sky as a reminder to us of His promise.

The Bible refers to fire as a refining agent. This means burning all the impurities away just like silver and gold are refined. After this process, what is left behind is pure. Jesus is going to bring fire down from heaven to refine us as well. All the impurities of sin and evil will be burned away, and a perfect world will be left behind.

Scripture gives us another insight into fire in the story of three faithful men thrown into a blazing hot furnace by King Nebuchadnezzar. These men survived for two reasons: they were righteous in God's sight, and they refused to bow down to any other god except the One True God. Their faith literally saved them from turning to ash.

Paul says in 2 Thessalonians 1:7, "Jesus will be revealed from heaven in blazing fire with his powerful angels." Don't wait for the refining process. Choose to live for God now and avoid the heat.

JULY 31

"This is the confidence we have in approaching God: that if we ask anything according to His will, He hears us" (1 John 5:14).

I was scheduled to go on a vacation that I had been looking forward to for months. When I developed a serious back problem a few weeks before the trip, I started to wonder if I should still go. I was somewhat incapacitated, and my activity level was way down. But my friend had purchased the tickets, and I felt like I couldn't disappoint her. So, I began to pray that something beyond my control would happen to prevent me from going. I guess what I really was asking God was to give me a gracious excuse to keep me home.

Then one morning in my quiet time, the Lord showed me this verse and suggested that perhaps I should pray for His will to be done instead of mine. Truly, I was afraid of praying this way because of the possibility of not getting my way. Time was running out, however, so I changed my prayer to "Thy will be done."

It became obvious all too soon that God's plan was for me to go. Blessing always follows obedience, and this time was no different. I wasn't there long before God confirmed I was to be there by leading me to this Scripture verse: "Come with me by yourself to a quiet place and get some rest" (Mark 6:31). I ended up having one of the most relaxing vacations I've ever had as well as some amazing one-on-one time with God. He poured into me every day even when I was out walking, albeit at a snail's pace.

I had to relearn a valuable lesson through this experience. If we pray for God's will to be done and not ours, it is always what is best for us. I thought what was best for me was staying home. But in the end, I saw that God's plan was way better than mine. I do think our prayer requests must entertain God sometimes as we think we know what we need instead of Him.

AUGUST 1

"Look at the birds of the air; they do not sow or reap or store away in barns, and yet your heavenly Father feeds them. Are you not much more valuable than they?" (Matthew 6:26).

Every spring, there is a bird that flies into my backyard and makes a nest on a speaker in the upper corner of my patio. I don't know if it's the same mama bird that comes every year, as I know nothing about the memories or nesting habits of birds. All I know is that she spends weeks flying back and forth building her little abode and preparing for her young ones.

As I often do with nature, I try to relate the natural to the spiritual side of God's beautiful creation. From a changing leaf in the fall to sitting beside a quiet stream, there are analogies all around us. I think the comparison here is how the mama bird takes care of her little ones just like God takes care of us.

The baby birds have to rely on their mama for everything, just as we have to rely on our Heavenly Father for all of our needs. The mama loves her young and is fiercely protective of them. In the same way, God is passionate about His children and keeps them safe under His wings.

Mama bird knows exactly when it's time to take her little ones and leave the nest. She takes flight and expects they will trust her enough to take that leap of faith and follow her. God expects us to take those leaps of faith as well. We have to trust our Father enough to follow where He leads!

AUGUST 2

"No one knows about that day or hour not even the angels in heaven nor the Son but only the Father" (Mark 13:32).

It seems there is always someone predicting the end of the world. They seem to base their predictions on current events and wars and even astrology. The truth is that no one can predict any of this either by Scripture or science or the state of the world.

The Bible does talk about the end times and Jesus' return all the way from the Old Testament through to the book of Revelation. Scripture says that Jesus' return "will come like a thief in the night" (1 Thessalonians 5:2). Jesus' return is God's secret that no man can know or predict.

Preparation, not prediction, is what we should focus on when we talk about end times. Jesus told His Apostles in Luke 12:40, "You also must be ready because the Son of Man will come at an hour when you do not expect Him." Jesus is saying that being ready is the only thing that matters. Don't worry about the time or the details.

How can we prepare ourselves and others as we wait for this glorious day? If you want to be serious about preparing, pray and ask God to put people in your path with whom you can share your faith. It's hard to step out of our comfort zone, but think about that one life you could impact. One life at a time is all it takes to bring more residents into the Kingdom of God!

AUGUST 3

"The Lord lives! Praise be to my Rock! Exalted be God, the Rock, My Savior!" (2 Samuel 22:47).

This verse is part of what's called, "David's Song of Praise." He sang it after the Lord had rescued him from his enemies and from King Saul. The whole prayer is beautifully written and reveals David's passionate heart. He loved to sing and dance and praise the Lord. The Bible refers to him as a man after God's own heart.

David understood and trusted God's faithfulness. He tried to find safety in other people and places while he was on the run from Saul, but deep down, he knew that true security was found only in God. David wrote in verse 31, "He is a shield for all who take refuge in Him."

How do you worship the Lord and sing His praises? Do your passion and devotion shine through like David's? Would God refer to you in the same way He described this man who so openly and fervently loved Him?

David understood and appreciated God's goodness and character. He knew Him intimately because of the close relationship they shared. The more intimate we become with God, the more we will want to sing His praises like David. The desire of his heart to know God should be the desire of ours as well.

AUGUST 4

"Enable your servants to speak your Word with great boldness" (Acts 4:29).

Peter and John had just been released from a Roman prison. The first thing they did when they gained their freedom was to pray and thank God publicly and then ask Him to give them the strength to keep preaching the Word. They continued spreading the gospel despite the warnings of the Sanhedrin, Israel's highest court. They were on a mission from God, and nothing was going to stand in their way.

It takes courage to be bold. It takes bravery to maintain convictions. Boldness is not reckless or impulsive as Peter sometimes demonstrated. It is the ability to press on through our fears and do what we know is right. Courage didn't come naturally to the Apostles, just like it doesn't come naturally to us. They had to pray and ask the Holy Spirit to empower them. This serves as the perfect example for us.

Look for opportunities in your family and neighborhood to talk about Christ. You don't have to preach in a forum like the Apostles. If by chance you are faced with rejection, take comfort in Jesus' words in Matthew 5:11: "Blessed are you when people insult you, persecute you and falsely say all kinds of evil against you because of me. Rejoice and be glad because great is your reward in heaven." We can have the same boldness as Peter and John. All we have to do is ask the Holy Spirit, and He will provide it.

AUGUST 5

"Praise and exalt and glorify the King of Heaven because everything He does is right, and all His ways are just" (Daniel 4:37).

King Nebuchadnezzar enjoyed great success during his reign, but God had to humble him once for being prideful. His royal authority was stripped away, and he was sent out to live with the wild animals for seven years. Nebuchadnezzar was not angry or bitter. *"But God"* he praised and glorified the Almighty. He said, "Everything He does is right, and all His ways are just." The king was restored to the throne years later.

Some people don't exactly share the good King's attitude towards suffering. They question God's fairness and justice. They wonder about all the evils and atrocities in the world. Why all the pain and suffering? They struggle to align these things with a good and fair God.

It says in Deuteronomy 29:4, "But to this day the Lord has not given you a mind that understands or eyes that see or ears that hear." There are mysteries about God that we will never be able to understand or explain. But what we do know for sure is that God's promises are trustworthy. He is a good and faithful God, and He will never leave us nor forsake us.

We will never understand all of God's plans and purposes. We are only called to have faith and trust Him. Deuteronomy 29:29 says, "There are secret things that belong to the Lord our God." Although God does not tell us all we want to know, He has told us everything we need to know.

AUGUST 6

"Walk in His ways and keep His decrees and commands, his laws and requirements as written in the Law of Moses, so that you may prosper in all you do and wherever you go" (1 Kings 2:3).

These words were spoken by King David as his death approached. He was giving instructions to his son Solomon for what was to take place after he died. David stressed to his son the need to make God and His laws the center of his life to preserve the Kingdom. He admonished him to walk faithfully with all his heart and soul.

It's a challenge to walk in all God's ways. The world wants to corrupt us and lure us away from our faith at every turn. Society tells us we can have it all if only we indulge ourselves in the temptations of the world. We are also being deceived by the evil one who feeds us nothing but lies. He would like nothing more than to keep us away from God and destroy our faith.

Jesus said to His disciples, "What good will it be for a man if he gains the whole world yet forfeits his soul?" (Mark 8:36). Jesus is saying we can't have it both ways. We can't live by the world's standards and live for Jesus too. Living for earthly pleasures provides nothing in the end but an eternity alone. Living for Jesus and walking in His ways ensures us of the most beautiful highway to heaven and an eternity spent in the presence of the Almighty God.

AUGUST 7

"He must become greater, I must become less" (John 3:30).

John the Baptist was being questioned in this passage as he baptized new believers. The people wanted to know why some were going over to Jesus to be baptized. John replied, "I am here to prepare the way for Him. I am filled with joy at His success. He must become greater and greater, and I must become less and less. He has come from above and is greater than anyone else."

God must become greater than the importance that we place on ourselves. Many things can prevent us from putting Him first. Selfishness, pride, and vain ambition will definitely land Jesus in second or third place. Focusing on things that have no eternal value will always keep Jesus out of contention for your affections.

It's not about the *what* in life; it's about the *who*. Who am I going to devote myself to? Who am I going to follow? Matthew 16:24 says, "If any of you wants to be my follower, you must put aside your selfish ambition, shoulder your cross, and follow me." Following Jesus requires something of us. Shouldering a cross is hard work. Are you willing to grab hold of that heavy chunk of wood and sacrifice to pursue Jesus? Are you willing to become less so that He may become greater?

AUGUST 8

"The Lord will fight for you; you need only to be still" (Exodus 14:14).

We all know the story of God parting the Red Sea as Moses led the Israelites out of Egypt. They were hotly pursued by Pharaoh and his army when they came to a dead end, where they thought all was lost. Moses had been encouraging them to have faith and stand strong, but now it seemed they did, in fact, have something to fear as they faced this impasse. *"But God"*...

Moses reassured the Israelites by commanding them to "Stand firm, and you will see the deliverance the Lord will bring you today" (Exodus 14:13). They needn't worry about solving the problem because God had everything under control. They just had to stand still and believe that He would make a way for them.

Our battles are not ours to fight. God goes before us into every single one and protects us from our enemies. However, the victory can be ours only if we look ahead to Him and stay close behind. Our job is to be patient, trust in God's timing, and have faith that He is able to do all of our fighting for us.

Instead of giving in to despair when you come to a roadblock or hit a wall, remember to enlist the aid of the One who can part the sea and stand you on dry ground. He is waiting and willing to fight for you. He longs to give you the victory!

AUGUST 9

"For I seek not to please myself but Him who sent me" (John 5:30).

Everything Jesus did on earth was to please His Father in heaven. He did nothing of His own accord but only what God instructed Him to do. Jesus depended on the Father and did the work the Father sent Him to do. That was His sole focus and mission.

Some days I feel like I am all about pleasing myself. I wake up and think, "What do I want to do today?" Rarely do my feet hit the floor without plans for the day rolling around in my head. But what if the first question I was to ask myself was, "Lord, what do you want me to do today? How can I use my time wisely and for your glory?" I suspect my days would go in completely different directions.

Jesus was totally selfless. He didn't think about His needs or desires. He invested Himself in people. His Father was the example that Jesus followed. He treated others as His Father treated Him.

Who are you seeking to please today? What kind of example are you setting with how you spend your time? Are you focused on yourself or are you focused on Christ? Jesus is our perfect role model for whom we should be focused on. Colossians 1:10 says, "Live a life worthy of the Lord; please Him in every way." Our goal in life shouldn't be our own pleasure but living our lives to please God. Who are you living for today?

AUGUST 10

"Enter His gates with thanksgiving and His courts with praise; give thanks to Him and praise His name" (Psalm 100).

This psalm is subtitled, "A Psalm for giving thanks." If ever you want to thank God for His goodness, this is a great Psalm to reference. Read the words aloud and let them sink into your soul. There is a sense of gratitude that seems to permeate every line. Making such a declaration of thanksgiving will fill you with unspeakable joy and peace.

God's faithfulness is evident in every area of my life. I never doubt that He always has my best interests at heart and that His goodness will prevail. I know this because I know God intimately, and I have a solid history with Him that I can look back on and be reassured He has everything under control.

The Bible repeatedly proclaims that God is good, and He has shown me that goodness many times. I have no reason to ever doubt that God is everything He says He is and does everything He promises to do.

Not only is God good, but His creation is good. After He spoke the entire universe into being, He ended each day's work with the words, "It is good." Then after all was complete, He said in Genesis 1:31, "God saw all that He had made, and it was very good." Only a good God can create goodness. He created it, and it is part of His being. So, enter His gates with thanksgiving and tell Him what a good God He is.

AUGUST 11

"It is more blessed to give than receive" (Acts 20:35).

I love to give. Resources, time, attention...it doesn't matter. I just love to give to people. It makes me feel good inside. In fact, nothing brings me greater joy than blessing others. There are so many needs out there and so many ways in which we can help.

I haven't always felt this way, to be honest. I was very self-indulgent for many years. Shopping was my favorite past-time—buying shoes and clothes I didn't need. All that changed one afternoon when, out of the blue, I felt God ask me two questions: what are you doing with the resources I have given you and what are you doing with the time I have allotted you on earth? He was calling me out on how I was spending my time and my money. God was holding me accountable for the gifts He had given me.

I made some big changes in my life after that day. I don't frequent the mall much anymore. I use my resources for ministries I've gotten involved in. I have learned how not to squander my time. It is so easy to waste time in today's world with all the social media. You could spend hours on your phone or computer and have accomplished nothing. I think it really breaks God's heart to see how people misuse His precious gift of time.

Maybe you're feeling convicted right about now. What a perfect opportunity to make some changes and experience what a blessing it is to put your resources and your energy into the right places. You will soon discover that giving brings greater satisfaction than Facebook ever could.

AUGUST 12

"But you will receive power when the Holy Spirit comes on you" (Acts 1:8).

Underestimating the power of the Holy Spirit is easy. We tend to make it complicated, when really, it is as easy as breathing. The power of the Holy Spirit enables us to do something far greater than we can do with our natural ability. When you feel incapable of doing something, it opens the door for the Holy Spirit to come in and be that strength you need. His power is so strong that in the Greek the word *power* actually means dynamite! [3]

All believers have the Holy Spirit living in them, which means we always have access to this explosive power. Think about it. The same power that raised Christ from the dead lives in us as well! When we yield ourselves to the Holy Spirit, amazing things happen. Struggles are overcome. Battles are won. Prayers are answered more than we ever dared dream or imagine.

When you feel powerless in a situation or weak in your convictions, call upon your power source. The Holy Spirit will remove all doubt and fear and replace it with peace and strength. Jesus calls the Holy Spirit "the gift my Father promised" (Acts 1:4). Don't let this gift stay in the box; open it and use it as God intended.

---

3   The Greek word *dunamis*, meaning "power," is the root of the English word "dynamite."

AUGUST 13

"What is faith? It is the confident assurance that what we hope for is going to happen" (Hebrews 11:1).

I doubt that you have ever heard the statement *I wish I didn't have faith.* I've never heard anyone say that they regretted their faith. I often wonder how people get through the storms in their lives without faith. What is the alternative? Hand-wringing, heart-wrenching worry and anguish that keeps us up at night and robs us of all peace. Faith is the only thing we have to hold onto in the darkness.

Without faith, we have no hope. We can live without many things in life, but hope is not one of them. Faith is the seed that gives birth to hope. Faith enables us to accept God's plan for us no matter what it is.

Faith should never be swayed by disappointments. We can have confidence in a positive outcome, but it may not work out the way we expect it. God's plan will always take precedence over ours. If we feel certain that God is going to do a miracle, but the miracle doesn't come, it should not affect our faith. We can't think of God as a genie in a bottle nor should our faith be used as an instrument to manipulate Him. God's ways are not our ways, and His answers may look entirely different from what we expect.

I prayed for my back to be healed for months. I felt complete assurance that it would happen. However, the Lord revealed to me that healing can be a process. It doesn't always happen at once. Who am I to question God's timing, methods, or motives? Part of faith is to calmly accept delays.

AUGUST 14

"For the Son of Man came to seek and save the lost"
(Luke 19:10).

The story of Zacchaeus in the book of Luke is a great example of Jesus' mission while here on earth. He came to save the lost, and Zacchaeus fit that bill perfectly. He was a crooked tax collector who was among the most unpopular people in Israel. He was a Jew by birth but chose to work for the government of Rome. He was actually considered a traitor by his own people. They couldn't understand why Jesus would want to have anything to do with him.

Jesus loved Zacchaeus as He loved all people. He wasn't put off by his occupation or his reputation for gouging fellow Jews. Jesus asked Zacchaeus if He could come to his house for dinner. This invitation was all it took for Zacchaeus to give his life over to Jesus. Never had there been anyone who showed him such unconditional love and mercy.

Jesus came to save all of the lost, no matter what their background or previous way of life. Through faith, the lost can be forgiven and made new. However, it is only through Jesus that we can be rescued from our sinful life and be restored to Him. There is no other way. There is no other god, no other philosophy, no other cultural movement or belief that will reunite us with God in heaven. The Bible says Jesus is "the Only Way."

Jesus told Zacchaeus that day, "Today salvation has come to you" (Luke 19:9). It wasn't some complicated process. All Zacchaeus had to do was welcome Jesus into his home and into his heart. He once was lost but then was found. All he had to do was respond, "Yes Lord, I will follow you." Salvation is as easy as those six words. Yes, Lord, I will follow you.

AUGUST 15

"But this happened that the work of God might be displayed in his life" (John 9:3).

God never meant for us to understand everything in this life. God is Sovereign, and His goodness is unfathomable. For example, Job suffered injustice after injustice, and yet he said in Job 11:7, "Can you fathom the mysteries of God? Can you probe the limits of the Almighty?"

Why does God allow such pain and suffering in the world and in our own lives? We can use the story of Lazarus to help us gain some insight. Word was sent to Jesus that His dear friend was dying. However, Jesus delayed going to see him for two days. In the meantime, Lazarus died and was placed in the grave. *"But God"* ... Jesus finally arrived and called His friend to come out of the grave, and Lazarus walked out alive and well.

Why did Jesus wait so long to go to His friend? Jesus always has a reason for everything He does. In this instance, He wanted to perform this miracle so He could display His power and authority, so that others may see and believe.

Thinking about Lazarus may help us see that God works for good even in our darkest times. He sometimes does His greatest miracles through our hardest suffering. We can be certain that God is working even when we don't see anything happening. There is no downtime with Jesus. He is always busy working out His will in our lives.

AUGUST 16

"But I have had God's help to this very day, and so I stand here and testify to small and great alike" *(Acts 26:22).*

This verse was written by Paul as he was defending his faith to King Agrippa. Paul was constantly defending his faith both to the Romans and the Jews. The Jews plotted to kill Paul for preaching the gospel, just like they wanted to kill Jesus. Paul begins his defense with this statement: "And now it is because of my hope in what God has promised our fathers that I am on trial today" (Acts 26:6).

I can relate to Paul because I also feel I have had God's help to this very day. As I look back on my life, I can see God's hand of protection and mercy everywhere. His handprints are evident in every aspect of my life. Even when I wasn't walking with Him, He loved and cared for me. He never gave up on me even when I gave up on Him.

I wouldn't be where I am today without God's help. He has seen me through every valley and every storm. When I was lost, he came looking for me. When I was on the wrong path, He redirected my steps. He has heard my every prayer and seen my every tear. He has been with me every single minute of every single day. I have been the recipient of God's great love and mercy from the minute I took my first breath.

Psalm 46:1 says, "God is our refuge and strength, an ever-present help in trouble." We needn't worry that God will neglect His promises to us. He is with us in good times and in bad. He is the only hope we have to cling to. Don't look to others for help. Look to the Only One who can meet all of your needs all the time.

AUGUST 17

"For man's anger does not bring about the righteous life that God desires" (James 1:20).

People are so easily angered these days. Whether it's sitting in traffic or waiting too long in the grocery line, this emotion seems to erupt with very little prodding. Why does everyone seem so angry?

One of the reasons could be because we have evolved into such a 'me' centered society. We think it's all about us. Only our time, our opinions, our ideas are important. We have very little regard for anyone else's feelings. When someone happens to disagree with us, we take it as a personal affront. Disagreements then metastasize into character assassinations. It's a downward spiral where no one wins and somebody, if not everybody, walks away upset.

God doesn't say that we should never be angry. Jesus was beyond angry at the Jewish leaders frequently for their heretical living. We have a right to be angry at the injustices in the world. Horrible things happen every day to people; that should cause us to be filled with anger. But this is not the anger that James is talking about here. The anger that James is referring to is dysfunctional. It is specifically aimed at hurting or demeaning.

The Bible tells us, "Be quick to listen, slow to speak and slow to become angry" (James 1:19). Ask God to release you from any bondage of anger that lingers in your heart. Unresolved anger leads to bitterness, and bitterness is like a cancer that spreads through the whole body. Don't let that happen to you. Choose to let go of any unresolved anger today.

AUGUST 18

"When Moses' hands grew tired, they took a stone and put it under him, and he sat on it. Aaron and Hur held his hands up—one on one side, one on the other—so that his hands remained steady till sunset" (Exodus 17:12).

The Amalekites declared war on the Israelites as Moses was leading them through the desert to the Promised Land. During the battle, Moses noticed something very odd. When he raised his arms in the air, the Israelites were winning, and when his arms got tired and fell down, they went into losing mode. Moses knew they needed this victory for his nation, but he couldn't do it alone. His arms were like Jello, and he couldn't lift them up anymore. Luckily, he had his two friends, Aaron and Hur, sitting on the sidelines ready to step in and help him with the problem.

We all need friends like Aaron and Hur; friends who will stand beside us and hold us up when we start to fall; friends who will interrupt their day and step in at a moment's notice; friends who will come to the rescue when the phone rings in the middle of the night.

There is an old adage we've all heard: To have a friend you must be a friend. We must be willing to put ourselves out there even when it feels awkward or uncomfortable. It can be challenging to make friends, especially if you're an introvert or new to an area. We have to remember that God created us to be relational.

I had a friend who was new to the church and wanted to get to know people. So, every Sunday after service, she would go up to random women and ask them over for a cup of coffee during the week. Some took her up on her offer, and it wasn't long before new friendships were forged. One invitation was all it took to make a new friend. Don't be an island. Why not invite someone over for coffee this week?

AUGUST 19

"Your Word is truth" (John 17:17).

It's a real challenge for some people to accept God's Word as truth. I personally have never faced that obstacle. I feel like I was born with faith. It always seemed easy for me to believe the Bible. I never questioned whether the people were real, the events actually happened, or the places existed. Scripture says that faith is a gift of which I was a recipient at a very young age.

Faith is birthed in the heart and the mind. If these are closed off to God, then, of course, nothing will seem factual or relevant. The mind dictates what a person will choose to believe or not to believe. The truth is only apparent when we are open to receive it.

John 1:1 says, "In the beginning was the Word, and the Word was with God, and the Word was God." The Word not only refers to God's divine writing but to His son Jesus. He then states in 1:14, "The Word became flesh and made His dwelling among us." The Word was a man who came to earth to deliver us from sin and give us eternal life. This man Jesus walked, talked, and ate with thousands. This man is not a story of fiction but fact. Eyewitness accounts can't be disregarded in the court of law or when it comes to Scripture.

If you reject the Bible and its truths you are rejecting Jesus as well. God's Word is accurate and can be trusted. It just requires an open mind to receive it and believe it.

AUGUST 20

"For nothing is impossible with God" (Luke 1:37).

We have all had situations or circumstances where we think that something we really want to happen is just not going to happen. Even though we pray and ask God for a miracle, we still have this tiny doubt in the back of our minds that the answer will never come to pass. We want so much to trust and not doubt, but somehow, we let that sly devil creep into our minds and discourage us from truly believing.

God is in command of the whole universe. He has authority over everything. If our God can command all of nature, perform miracles, and raise people from the dead, why do we doubt He can perform these in our lives? Why do we hesitate to trust Him completely?

Genesis 18:14 says, "Is anything too hard for the Lord?" God spoke these words to Abraham and Sarah after she laughed upon hearing God's prophecy that she would have a baby. Sarah was decades past child-bearing years when God told the aging couple she would get pregnant and have a son. *"But God"* ...

Both the New and the Old Testaments are replete with accounts of God doing impossible things in impossible situations. The miracles of the Bible can be our miracles too. Ask God to increase your faith to believe in His mighty power and strength.

AUGUST 21

"If anyone considers himself religious and yet does not keep a tight rein on his tongue, he deceives himself and his religion is worthless" (James 1:26).

The tongue can be like a poisonous snake ready to strike at anyone at any time. Like the snake, the tongue is capable of attacking and killing in mere seconds. Things like slander, gossip, and insults can devastate a person with one blow. The Apostle James said, "Surely my brothers and sisters, this is not right. This should not be! Can both praise and cursing come out the same mouth?" (James 3:10).

The taming of the tongue is an impossible feat if left up to us. But when we involve God in the process, it is not such a daunting task. We are helpless to accomplish anything on our own. We need God's strength and power to help us address sinful behavior and overcome our weaknesses.

If you are facing a difficult conversation with someone, the first thing you need to do is pray. Pray that your words be spoken with love and gentleness. Pray that what you have to share would fall upon a soft, receptive heart. Begin the conversation with an affirmation. It immediately diffuses any atmosphere of hostility or defensiveness. Then end with another affirmation that will bring the exchange to a close on a positive note.

Wise King Solomon had much to say about the tongue in his book of Proverbs. But the one verse that sums them up is found in 18:21: "The tongue has the power of life and death." This is how much significance he placed on the tongue. We can either choose to speak life into a person or kill them with unkind words. Let us not deceive ourselves into thinking that what we say doesn't matter.

AUGUST 22

"Nobody should seek his own good but the good of others" (1 Corinthians 10:24).

Life is all about choices. According to this verse, the choice we have to make is whether to live self-centered or other-centered lives. Scripture is clear that the second option is the right one. Philippians 2:4 says, "Each of you should look not only to your own interests, but also the interests of others." This tells us that we need to put the needs of others before our own.

Our sinful human nature wants what we want when we want it. We tend to indulge ourselves and satisfy our own needs before we think of anyone else's. It takes deliberate focus and willingness to put others first.

One way you can accomplish this is to decide in advance how you are going to live your life. Jesus is our perfect example of selflessness. There is no place in Scripture where our Lord put His own needs or wants first. Other people always came first. No matter how tired or worn out He was, He always made the time to love, heal and encourage.

Ephesians 5:1 says, "Follow God's example in everything you do because you are His dear children. Live a life filled with love for others." Are you living a life that is focused on other's needs? Or are you more fixated on your own wants and desires? Life is indeed all about choices. Following Jesus' example will always help us make the right ones.

AUGUST 23

"It is God who arms me with strength and makes my way perfect" (Psalm 18:32).

The definition of *strength* is "powerful, firm, durable, and tough." It is also defined as the ability to resist attack. Satan is always on the attack. He is the father of lies, and he will do anything and everything he can to pull us away from Jesus. The place where he begins his attack is always in our minds. Our minds control everything—our thoughts, feelings, and actions. Satan likes to plant all kinds of negativity in our thoughts. Doubt, fear, and a critical spirit are three of his favorite weapons. We must not let him get a foot in the door, or he will throw it wide open and go in for the kill.

Jesus never let Satan get a toe in the door. Even when he was starving after fasting for 40 days and nights in the desert, Jesus held strong. Satan came and tried to tempt Him with food and tested His authority, but Jesus refuted every lie by quoting Scripture. The devil finally gave up and departed from Him.

The devil can't stand up under the name of Jesus. If you feel under attack, you don't have to fight the battle alone. Engage the power and the strength you have in Jesus. Use His example and retaliate with Scripture. Jesus told Satan, "Get behind me, Satan." He told him, "You are a stumbling block to me" (Matthew 16:23). Arm yourself with Scripture and fight like Jesus!

AUGUST 24

"Just as the Son of Man did not come to be served but to serve and to give His life as a ransom for many" (Matthew 20:28).

Jesus' teaching while on earth was based upon this foundational truth. The Apostle Paul echoes it in Philippians 2:7, "He made Himself nothing, taking the very nature of a servant." Even though Jesus was born a King, He humbled Himself to become a servant. He was, in fact, the greatest servant who ever lived.

Jesus' greatest act of servitude came in the form of a ransom. A ransom is an exchange of one thing for another. Jesus is known as our ransom because He exchanged His life for ours. Jesus gave His life so we would be forgiven of our sins and live eternally with God in heaven. A price had to be paid for our entrance into the Kingdom, and Jesus stepped in and paid that price for us.

There is no measure of gratitude that we could express for what Jesus has done for us. However, one thing we can do in return is to live our lives devoted to Him. We can put Him first in our lives just as He put us first in His. We can exchange our old life and our old ways for a new life in Christ. This new life is what will bring Him the most honor and glory for His incredible sacrifice for us!

AUGUST 25

"Whatever you have learned or received or heard from me, or seen in me—put into practice" *(Philippians 4:9).*

Our lifestyles must reflect our beliefs, or our testimony is worthless. Reading and studying God's Word is useless unless we apply it to our daily living. We have to let God's Word reprogram our minds. Whatever occupies our thoughts will dictate our words and actions. We must learn to filter out the bad and replace it with good. Romans 12:1 says, "We will be transformed by the renewing of our minds."

Our minds are like computers. We plug the information into the computer, and it memorizes and stores it. Then when we need to refer back to it, we pull it back up. This is how we should look at reading Scripture. We first have to upload God's Word into our minds before we can access it. We can't utilize what isn't there.

Jesus said in Matthew 7:24, "Therefore everyone who hears these words of mine and puts them into practice is like a wise man who built his house on the rock." We will have a solid foundation that cannot be wiped away if we build our lives upon Jesus. Jesus said, "The winds blew and beat against the house; yet it did not fall."

Our minds can only respond to and act upon what we've put in it. Just like the computer, it can only recall what has been entered. Make sure you only upload godly thoughts and words to avoid potentially damaging viruses.

AUGUST 26

"...like an eagle that stirs up its nest and hovers over its young, that spreads its wings to catch them and carries them on its pinions" (Deuteronomy 32:11).

This is one of the many delightful word pictures that fill Scripture. In this passage, God is compared to an eagle for many reasons physically and spiritually. The eagle is a large, powerfully built bird known for its strength and stamina. It can carry the heaviest load ever recorded by any flying bird. Its wingspan is immense. These definitions also describe our God, who is also strong and powerful and the one who carries our heavy burdens.

The eagle is also known for the care of its young. Eagles hover over the nest watching their little ones just as God hovers over us protecting us and keeping us safe. The eagle never rests from her maternal duties just as God never rests from His. If one of the eaglets should fall from the nest, the mommy eagle swoops down and catches it on her broad wings. She restores her young one to the nest and continues her task of protection. God's treatment of us completely mirrors the majestic eagle.

The eaglet that falls from the nest is also a good analogy of how God takes care of us. Could it be that God may allow us to fall from our comfortable places to teach us reliance on Him? This could also provide the perfect opportunity for us to learn how to trust Him for all of our needs. Psalm 55: 22 says, "Cast your cares on the Lord, and He will sustain you; He will never let the righteous fall." No matter what we can always rely on the broad wings of God to catch us and return us to the nest safe and sound.

AUGUST 27

"For the Lord searches every heart and understands every motive behind the thoughts" (1 Chronicles 28:9).

It is impossible to fool God. Nothing can be hidden from Him. He sees and understands everything. He knows how and what we think and the motives behind them. It makes no sense to try to hide our thoughts or actions from an all-knowing God. However, we should be joyful because God knows even the worst about us and loves us anyway. His love for us is totally unconditional.

Proverbs 16:2 says, "All a man's ways seem innocent to him, but motives are weighed by the Lord." What would be considered a wrong or inappropriate motive? To answer this, we must ask ourselves these questions: Does this choice I'm about to make glorify me or glorify God? Is this decision going to make me look better or will God get the credit for it?

If you want to serve in your community because you feel obligated, then your motive is questionable. If you want to volunteer at church so the pastor will notice and be impressed with your dedication, that, too, would be a suspicious incentive. Our serving, like our giving, should be done in secret to avoid calling attention to ourselves. Always remember it's not about us. We live only to glorify God by all that we do.

AUGUST 28

"Commit your way to the Lord; trust in Him, and He will do this" (Psalm 37:5).

The words *commit* and *commitment* have lost their integrity in today's culture. People find it rather easy to commit to things but following through seems to be the problem. The divorce rate is a perfect example of our failure to keep commitments. At the first sign of trouble, we find it all too easy to throw in the towel. We wrongly assume that marriage promises happiness, so when we become unhappy, we think that gives us license to move on to greener pastures.

A commitment should be viewed as a binding contract. It is a promise or a pledge to stay the course, no matter what. No exceptions. No excuses. No reneging. We made a commitment, and it is our responsibility to keep that commitment.

Commitments involve a lot of work. Healthy relationships take time and effort. This pertains not just to marriage but to our relationship with Jesus as well. If we've said "I do" to Jesus, then we have made a binding contract with Him, and we need to live our lives accordingly.

If you are struggling with keeping a commitment, the first place you need to turn is to God. He is ready and willing to step in and walk you through whatever it is you need to do to honor that commitment. God is for us! He wants to see us succeed in all that we do. We can be victorious in our commitments even when the world tells us they really aren't all that important. Don't follow the morals of today's culture. Work and sacrifice to keep the promises you've made. God will reward your efforts and bless the commitments you are honoring.

AUGUST 29

"The Apostles said to the Lord, 'increase our faith!'"
(Luke 17:5).

Jesus is teaching His disciples about forgiveness in this passage. He tells them to forgive everyone "seven times seventy." In other words, it doesn't matter how many times a person asks for forgiveness, it should always be granted.

The Apostles felt inadequate of measuring up to the standards Jesus was setting before them. They knew they needed greater faith to be able to do what was being asked of them. They were fully aware that such obedience was beyond their capabilities. So, they asked Jesus to increase their faith and help them to do what they knew they couldn't.

What humbleness their request displayed. Anytime we admit we can't do something on our own we are exhibiting true humility. Jesus admires a humble heart and loves it when we ask Him for help. It demonstrates that we are relying on Him and not on ourselves.

When you feel you lack in faith, ask God to increase it. We can also try to cultivate it ourselves. Reading His Word, praying, Bible study classes, and fellowshipping with other Christians are great ways to help faith thrive. God wants us to have a passionate faith that includes nurturing it on our own. Are you fully committed to growing your faith?

AUGUST 30

"He is good. His love endures forever" (2 Chronicles 5:13).

Sometimes people call into question whether God is truly good. You need to look no further than 9/11 to make one wonder if God is as good as the Bible claims He is. How can a good God let this happen? How can a God who professes to love His people allow such loss and tragedy?

How do we make sense of a child losing his battle with cancer? Why does a young father who is fit and healthy keel over from a heart attack while running a marathon? Who can make sense out of terrorism? How does this all fit in with a good God?

Contrary to what some may believe God is not the one responsible for pain and suffering. Our human nature causes us to want to blame someone for the injustices of the world, so we accuse God. The truth is that when sin entered the world through Adam and Eve so did evil, disease, and death. We live in a broken world where there will always be suffering and misery. Using God as a scapegoat is neither biblical nor fair. If we truly believe Scripture, we must trust that God is good!

AUGUST 31

"For physical training is of some value, but godliness has value for all things holding promise for both the present life and the life to come" (1 Timothy 4:8).

I love to exercise. I love to walk either on my treadmill or out in God's glorious creation. I will generally spend an hour or more working out a few days a week.

One morning I was rushing through my quiet time with the Lord to get to my beloved treadmill. I guess the Lord wasn't very happy about that, so He pulled His two by four out and whopped me over the head with it. Sometimes God has to get rather aggressive when trying to get my attention. This was one of those times. He said, "Wait a minute here. Are you telling me that the hour you spend working out is more important than the time you spend with me? Shouldn't I at least get the same amount of time that you seem more than willing to spend on yourself?"

He caught me fair and square. How could I put anything before my time with God? It doesn't have to pertain just to exercise either. It could be anything that takes up too much of your time in place of God. If your focus is more on you than it is on God, there is something amiss in your priorities.

Spiritual exercise should always come first. It's good to be healthy physically, but a healthy, growing relationship with Christ is far more important. God should get top billing every day. If our schedules dictate anything else, we might want to reevaluate our calendars.

SEPTEMBER 1

"On reaching the place, He said to them, 'Pray that you will not fall into temptation'" (Luke 22:40).

Those who don't possess a strong commitment to Jesus can easily fall into temptation. Such was the case with the Apostle Judas. He was tempted with money by the Jewish council to betray Jesus which he gladly accepted. How could one of Jesus' Apostles fall into such a trap and become a traitor? The only logical answer is that he must not have truly loved Jesus in the first place and possessed no loyalty to Him. Anyone who is so easily swayed certainly doesn't have the firm foundation needed to stand strong in their faith.

Judas was an easy target for Satan because of his lukewarm faith. He acted fully devoted to Jesus on the outside, but inside, his heart was far from Him. This is an example of just how easy it is for Satan to get a hold of us. Scripture says he scours the earth looking for his next victim. He wants nothing more than to see us turn on Jesus.

Jesus asked His beloved disciples to pray for Him not to fall into temptation. He knew the agony of the crucifixion awaited Him. He prayed, "Father, if you are willing, please take this cup of suffering away from me" (Luke 22:41). He also told His Apostles to pray that temptation would not overpower them. He knew they would be tempted to deny their relationship with Him.

We must remain steadfast against temptation. Pray for extra strength when you feel you are being attacked. Satan knows where you're vulnerable and knows your Achilles heel (your weakness). When he starts his antics, speak up and tell him you are devoted to Jesus. How different Judas' life would have turned out if only he had made this claim!

SEPTEMBER 2

"...always learning but never able to acknowledge the truth" (2 Timothy 3:7).

Some people love being students. They have a deep appreciation for education and enjoy learning to its fullest. Some invest serious time and money accumulating degrees and certificates. These types of people are what's known as 'professional students.'

Unfortunately, churches have their fair share of professional students. These people attend church to gain spiritual knowledge, but it makes no practical difference in their lives. They listen and may even take notes, but they leave it all at the front door after the service.

These professional churchgoers are missing the link that is needed for life transformation to take place. They fail to connect their head knowledge to their heart. The head is soaking up the facts, but the heart remains aloof. These people are listening but not really hearing. Jesus said in Matthew 11:17, "He who has ears let him hear." In other words, only a person who is willing to hear the truth will grasp it.

Faith is not a matter of what you know. It is a matter of the heart. It is opening yourself and allowing Jesus into your life in a personal way. It is believing in God, not just with the mind but with your whole being.

Jesus is more than just someone we can view from an academic standpoint. He is a person who wants to come live in our hearts and give us new life. He wants us to become professional students of His Word so we can apply the wisdom and knowledge we find there to our lives. How are you doing at being a student of the Word?

SEPTEMBER 3

"These people honor me with their lips, but their hearts are far from me" (Mark 7:6).

Jesus called the religious leaders of His day hypocrites because they "replaced God's commands with their own man-made traditions" (Mark 7:7). Ironically, the Greek word for *hypocrite* is 'play-actor.' Hypocrisy is pretending to be something you are not. It is a false representation of your true self.

Jesus called the Pharisees hypocrites because they worshiped God for all the wrong reasons. Their worship was not motivated by love but by a desire to appear holy. They wanted others to take notice of them for their high positions and strict adherence to their laws.

When we worry more about our reputation than we do our character, we are hypocrites. When we follow certain religious practices while allowing our hearts to remain closed off from God, this is hypocritical behavior.

There are still religious leaders and sects today who add their own rules and rites to God's Word. This leads to great confusion and division among believers. Following Jesus is not about a set of rules we have to keep. It's not about religious practices or observances. It's about giving up all nuances of religion and investing ourselves in a relationship with our Heavenly Father.

Bill Hybels wrote a book many years ago called, "Character is Who You Are When No One is Looking." Are you the same person at home as you are at church? Do you treat people on the street like you do members of your family or congregation? Do not be like the Pharisees and simply talk up a good game. Be the person you claim to be. Honor God not only with your lips but with your life.

SEPTEMBER 4

"But after Uzziah became powerful, his pride led to his downfall. He was unfaithful to the Lord his God" (2 Chronicles 26:16).

The Old Testament is full of modern-day applications. King Uzziah is one of hundreds of examples that fall into this category. King Uzziah became king of Judah when he was only 16. He sought the Lord, and God gave him success. The king reigned for 52 years, and in that time, he became very powerful. He built towers and dug cisterns, and he took care of the land and the people. "His fame spread far and wide, for he was greatly helped until he became powerful" (26:15).

Unfortunately, after the king became powerful, pride stepped in. He became unfaithful to God, which led to his ultimate demise. The Lord punished the king for not honoring Him and gave him leprosy. The king had to live alone and excluded from the Temple because of this and suffered from the disease until the day he died.

Uzziah's pride got the best of him, and he ended up losing everything he held dear. He was ostracized not only by God but his entire family as well. The lure of power and success can ruin us if we're not careful. Make sure that the name of God dominates your vocabulary and not the word "I."

SEPTEMBER 5

"Come follow me, and I will make you fishers of men" (Matthew 4:19).

During Jesus' day, there were approximately 30 fishing towns that surrounded the Sea of Galilee. It was the main industry in these small towns and a very lucrative one. The first Apostles Jesus called into His ministry were four fishermen from one of these fishing towns. He called Peter first, then his brother Andrew. James and John followed them. These men were just ordinary people. They weren't particularly well known in the community nor did they possess any special appeal or qualifications. *"But God"*... saw their potential and willingness to take on a very important mission.

Jesus told these men to leave their fishing businesses and begin fishing 'for people.' Jesus was calling them away from their successful businesses and families to follow Him. They didn't give Jesus any excuses for not feeling up to the task or the timing being bad. They simply got up and left everything to follow Jesus.

This passage is a great example of how Jesus calls ordinary people to do extraordinary things. We don't have to have the perfect resume for Jesus to use us. We only have to be willing to get up and follow Him. He has a purpose for all of us, but we have to be willing to walk away from our old life and follow Him, just like those first Apostles.

SEPTEMBER 6

"Love your neighbor as yourself" (Mark 12:31).

Who doesn't know this Scripture verse by heart? It's probably one of the first verses of the Bible that kids learn in Sunday school—love others as you would love yourself. Easy words to recite, but some of the hardest to actually live out.

The Samaritans in Jesus' day were foreigners who were hated and ostracized by the Jews. The Jews viewed all Samaritans as half-breeds and practiced open hostility towards them. They went as far as to cross to the other side of the street when one was approaching.

We live among Samaritans today as well. For no reason, they are faced with rejection and persecution. Being loved by a neighbor would be the farthest thing they would ever expect. Yet Jesus tells us to embrace them and love them unconditionally.

When we drive past a street corner and see a homeless person, do we look away in disgust? Do we snub the person who shows up in church dressed shabbily and not smelling so sweet? Do we hug an unkind person with the same affection we hug our family and friends? Jesus embraced every kind of people; the sick, the lame, the demon-possessed and the beggars sitting outside the synagogue. It didn't matter. Jesus healed and loved them all.

We are called to do the same. We don't know everyone's story and background. We don't know what kind of pain they may have had to deal with in life. Paul says in Romans 14:10, "Why do you judge your brother? Why do you look down on your brother? For we will all stand before God's judgment seat." Let's not judge but love as Scripture commands us to do.

SEPTEMBER 7

"And who knows but that you have come to royal position for such a time as this" (Esther 4:14).

Esther had just been appointed Queen by King Xerxes. However, on the advice of her cousin Mordecai, she had not revealed to the king that she was a Jew. One of the king's officials hated the Jews and convinced the king that they all should be put to death across the land. The king ordered it done. Mordecai overheard this plan and told Queen Esther. He told her she must go to the king and ask him not to do this horrible thing. Mordecai gave Esther a boost of confidence by telling her that maybe she was born, "for such a time as this." The Jews were facing annihilation unless someone intervened.

"But God" used Esther as that someone. She convinced the king to repeal his edict, which spared the lives of the Jewish people. Esther was responsible for saving her people at this appointed time.

Maybe God has you where you are "for such a time as this." I was down and out for six months due to major surgery. But just like Esther, God had a plan for me. He encouraged me to use this period of rest to finish this book you are holding in your hands!

If you are in a difficult place like Esther be assured that God is doing or is going to do great things through your situation. Be assured that this designated time will not be wasted. God has a plan and a purpose for everything. Maybe you are where you are right now, "for such a time as this."

SEPTEMBER 8

"God blesses those who realize their need for Him" *(Matthew 5:3).*

It is a glorious day when we finally come to our senses and realize our need for a Savior! We think we have it all together, we are firing on all cylinders, and as a popular T-shirt tells us, "Life is good." But then one day a storm blows into our lives, and we suddenly realize that we can't handle it on our own. Some people call this "a come to Jesus moment." This moment is one of the biggest blessings we'll ever receive.

Eugene Peterson writes this great paraphrase of Matthew 5:3,4,8. He says, "You're blessed when you're at the end of your rope. With less of you, there is more of God. You're blessed when you get your inside world—your mind and heart—put right. Then you can see God in the outside world."[4]

It takes humility to come to this realization. Our pride has to be squelched so we can be honest with ourselves. Pride is the biggest obstacle to faith. We have to let our guard down and be able to tell it like it is. It's okay to admit we need help. There is no shame in weakness. Jesus embraces our weakness, for it gives Him the perfect opportunity to show His strength. We wouldn't hesitate to ask for help at work if we needed it or at home when we get overwhelmed. What keeps us from asking Jesus for His help?

Psalm 18:6 says, "In my distress, I called to the Lord; I cried to my God for help. My cry came before Him and into His ears." God hears us when we call to Him. Shedding your pride and realizing your need for God is the most honest moment you will ever have with yourself.

---

4   The Message (MSG)
Copyright © 1993, 1994, 1995, 1996, 2000, 2001, 2002 by Eugene H. Peterson

SEPTEMBER 9

"Whoever acknowledges me before men, I will acknowledge him before my Father in heaven" *(Matthew 10:32).*

Talking about our faith in a public forum can be a frightening experience. It takes courage to stand up for your beliefs, especially around unbelievers and skeptics. It can be intimidating having to defend your faith to others. Yet, this is exactly what Jesus calls us to do. He tells us to acknowledge Him, and He will acknowledge us. However, He also openly tells us in the next verse, "Whoever disowns me before men I will disown him before my Father in heaven." Jesus never sugar-coated the truth!

I don't think Jesus expects us to stand up on a soapbox in the park or on a street corner and preach the Good News. However, I do think that He expects us to talk to people He puts in our path. These are called divine appointments. They are God-given opportunities for us to talk about Him and hopefully plant a few seeds of faith that will one day take root and flourish.

A few paragraphs back in this same chapter of Matthew, as Jesus is preparing to send His Apostles out on their first mission trip, He tells them, "Do not worry about what to say or how to say it. At that time, you will be given what to say; for it will not be you speaking but the Spirit of your Father speaking through you" (10:19). He is telling them not to worry about how to approach the subject, for at that specific time, God will give them the right words to say. The same is true for us. If we take the first step in acknowledging Him to others, He will do the rest.

SEPTEMBER 10

"Did not He who made me in the womb make them? Did not the same one form us both within our mothers?" (Job 31:15).

This is such a fitting verse to apply to all the racial upheaval we face in our world today. The truth is that human equality is based on creation. God created each one of us in the exact same way! We are born equal with no race or color being superior to the other. No one is less valued than the other in God's world.

How did we slide so far away from this truth? When did we decide that some of us were better than others? When did we let all this inequality nonsense get so out of control? More importantly, what can we do as Christians to repair the damage and bring people together?

It's interesting how tragedies can blur the boundaries of racism. A catastrophe can pull people of every color together in a heartbeat. There is no difference in skin color or nationality when people are drowning or homes are being swept away. Everyone unites for the common good of their fellow man.

Unfortunately, when the crisis is over, everyone goes back to their biases. Oh, how this must break the heart of our God to see such hatred and division! He didn't create us to be this way. He made us all from the same dust of the earth.

We must strive to do away with our self-righteousness and start treating all men as equal. Look for ways to bless and affirm those who may be different than you. Make the extra effort to pay a kindness forward. One kind act begets another.

SEPTEMBER 11

"Let us hold firmly to the faith we profess" (Hebrews 4:14).

How easily something can slip out of our hands if we're not holding on tight. The same is true of our faith. If we're not careful, it can easily slip away. Sometimes, we don't even notice until a need arises, and we then realize we haven't paid much attention to God or our faith lately.

There usually are some prior indications. One is a lack of peace and joy. We may feel off or feel that all is not well with our souls. Another red flag is the emptiness we feel from neglecting God. One more indicator might be priorities that have gone astray. We get busy with life, and the first thing that seems to disappear from our agenda is God. We replace Him with less important tasks or events.

Spending time with God and in His Word are prerequisites for keeping our faith firm. The Apostle Paul knew how easily we could be pulled away from our faith, so he addressed this in many of his letters. Paul knew firsthand the danger of not remaining steadfast in his faith. He knew he couldn't have survived all of his trials and mishaps without the power of God. He knew he had to cling to God for his very survival.

How firm is your faith? Do you see any red flags indicating some backsliding? If so, make the decision now to restore your faith to its proper place. God should always be our highest priority.

SEPTEMBER 12

"As a mother comforts her child so will I comfort you" (Isaiah 66:13).

A while back, I was having a difficult time dealing with a chronic pain situation and really needed some encouragement from the Lord. When I opened my Bible that morning, I came across this verse, or should I say the Lord put it in front of me. He whispered to me to put my name at the end of the verse. I read it again with my name attached, and I began to cry. I was overwhelmed with God's faithfulness and attention to my every need.

He then gave me this vision of my precious granddaughter falling down and scraping her knee. I immediately thought of what I would do, and I pictured it just as it unfolded. I picked her up and tenderly held her. I soothed her with my voice and my hands. I kissed her knee and brushed her tears away, reassuring her that it was going to be okay. I pushed back the strands of hair from her face with gentle strokes and planted another kiss on her forehead. I hugged her tight before I let her go and told her how very much I loved her.

God impressed upon me that morning that this is exactly how He comforts us. The only difference is that His comfort exceeds that of even our own children. His love and compassion go deeper than a mother's for her child.

When I think about it, this depth of love is unfathomable to me. I wonder how I am so deserving of such love. I feel unworthy of God showering such affection upon me. Yet, what a perfect picture of God's grace. Always giving us what we don't deserve and blessing us unconditionally. No one in my life is more generous and giving than my Savior. He is, by far, the greatest comforter I've ever known.

SEPTEMBER 13

"Is the Lord's arm too short? You will now see whether or not what I say will come true for you" (Numbers 11:23).

Moses was at the end of his rope with the Israelites and their constant complaining. Their latest complaint had to do with food. They were tired of the manna and wanted some meat. Moses seriously doubted that meat would be added to the daily menu. These grumblers didn't deserve it! What Moses failed to remember from experience was that human impossibility was an open door for the Lord to come in and demonstrate His great power. Pretty soon, the camp was three-feet deep in quail.

I knew a couple whose marriage was in complete shambles. Infidelity had destroyed their relationship. The wife met with an attorney soon after the incident to seek a divorce. *"But God"* had another plan. He told her that she had made a commitment to her husband, and she had to stand by it. He told her that if she trusted Him, He would heal their broken marriage.

The wife stayed, and, with the remorseful husband, she joined a small group at church who surrounded them with support and encouragement. They began praying together at night and reading their Bibles together. They sought God for healing and remained steadfast in their attempts to work it out.

This couple has been married for six years now and has three beautiful kids. They are leaders in their church and share their testimony as a way to encourage others. God's arm is never too short. He is a God of the impossible for all who trust and believe.

SEPTEMBER 14

"If anyone will not receive you or listen to your words, shake the dust from your feet when you leave that house or town" (Matthew 10:14).

Shaking the dust off your feet had a symbolic meaning in Jesus' day. It was meant to show people that they were making a wrong choice. It was a solemn warning that they were rejecting Christ, and there may not be another opportunity for salvation.

I had an acquaintance who challenged me in every conversation we had about Jesus and my faith. Her beliefs were very different from mine and included such things as false gods, mediums, and different paths to heaven. This friend continually denied every truth I brought up. She continued to stand boldly on her false doctrines.

I felt like a failure in my inability to get through to this woman. *"But God"* spoke to me in my frustration and told me that it was not my job to change this person. It was His. I was doing all I could to share the Truth with her, but ultimately the Holy Spirit is the one who brings a person to Christ. Our job is to just plant the seeds and pray they take root.

When you feel you've done all you can to open the eyes of an unbeliever, and yet you are unsuccessful, it may be time to shake the dust off your feet and move on. You are not abandoning them but simply moving out of the way to make room for God to do His work. You may be surprised when you get to heaven and see all the people that are there because you took the time to plant some seeds. Don't be concerned about the outcome. Just keep on sowing.

SEPTEMBER 15

"For we must all appear before the judgment seat of Christ that each one may receive what is due him for the things done while in the body whether good or bad" (2 Corinthians 5:10).

I really don't like to think about being judged one day on how I lived my life. The thought of standing before the God of the Universe to give an account of my life is intimidating, to say the least. But it seems there is no getting around it, as the Bible is very clear that we will all one day have to answer a few questions at the pearly gates.

The conversation might go like this: "Well (insert name), what have you done with this precious time on earth I have given you? How did you faithfully serve me and further my Kingdom? Did you bring honor and glory to my name?" You can be sure you won't be asked about how successful you were or how much wealth you accumulated. Our power and position won't mean a thing when we get to heaven. God is not going to care about our golf handicaps or the fact that we won the tennis championship. His questions won't pertain to our accomplishments. God will be looking for the "who" we were not the "what" we did. How did we treat others? Did we demonstrate love and kindness to people? Did we make God our first priority?

However, as faithful followers of Christ, we shouldn't fear standing before the Lord. Paul tells us in Romans 8:1, "There is no condemnation for those who are in Christ Jesus." For those of us who abide in Christ, there will be no remorse or guilt at the time of judgment. There will be no punishment or consequences. Jesus already paid the price for all of our sins, so our list of transgressions has been wiped clean already.

We will enter the Kingdom of God rejoicing that our time has finally come to meet Jesus. Nothing else will matter. No past sin, mistake, or failure will be brought up. The light and love of Jesus will be so overwhelming that it will be the only thing we'll have to face!

SEPTEMBER 16

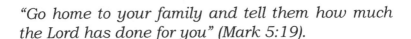

"Go home to your family and tell them how much the Lord has done for you" (Mark 5:19).

A man who was demon-possessed approached Jesus looking for help. Jesus took pity on him and commanded the evil spirit to come out of him. The evil spirit obeyed, and the man was set free. The man was so overjoyed and grateful to Jesus that he wanted to follow Him. But Jesus told him to go home and share the good news. Jesus wanted him to show everyone the miracle the Lord had done for him. Jesus told him to do this so that others may hear his story and believe in the One who healed him.

This example is for us today as well. When God blesses us with good things, He wants us to talk about them to others. Telling people about how Jesus has impacted our lives is one of the best ways to let our lights shine. God doesn't give us gifts so we can "hide them in a jar or under the bed" (Luke 8:16). He wants us to share them with the world so that He may be glorified.

Has God done a miracle in your life that you need to share? When opportunities present themselves, are you willing to speak up for Jesus? If we are open to these possibilities, we may be amazed at the people God will bring our way. Jesus said to, "Go and tell how much the Lord has done for you." Are you going to keep your Savior and your blessings bottled up or follow the same command that He gave to the healed man? Go and tell what the Lord has done for you!

SEPTEMBER 17

"He who has ears to hear, let him hear" (Luke 8:8).

Jesus made this statement often when He was preaching to the people on the hillsides or teaching in the Synagogue. He delivers it as a challenge—those who want to hear will open their hearts, and those who have closed hearts will turn a deaf ear. Hearing and listening are two very different things. We've all had the experience of tuning someone out when they're talking to us. We hear them speaking, but we really aren't listening to what they're saying. We can sit through a sermon in church on Sunday and come away with nothing because we were distracted or focused on other things. Even though we heard a voice speaking, we have no idea what was said. We were hearing but not listening.

Hearing is a sense. Listening is a choice. Jesus knew people would tune Him out, so He had to make it a point to challenge them to pay attention. It takes effort to truly be a listener of God's Word and not just a hearer. I keep a small notebook in my purse for taking notes during Sunday's sermons. It keeps me focused on the message instead of my to-do list or what's going on around me.

Thank goodness the Apostles and prophets just didn't hear God's voice but responded to it. The Bible would be non-existent if the writers' ears were not open to hearing God speaking to them. God wants us to be like them. He wants us to be ready and willing to listen as He teaches and instructs us. We can't tune out the teacher and recall the lesson. Open your ears and really listen for God speaking to you.

SEPTEMBER 18

"So because you are lukewarm—neither hot nor cold—I am about to spit you out of my mouth" (Revelation 3:16).

There are only two camps of people in the world: Jesus' and Satan's. You're either in one or the other. You can't have a foot in both although many try to. They proclaim to be Christians, yet they live their lives for themselves. Jesus calls these people lukewarm, and Scripture tells us that He has no use for them. Jesus said that He would spit these people out of His mouth. We are repeatedly told in His Word that if you aren't for God, you're against Him.

Our world today loves the gray area. Morals, ethics, values—all without borders or boundaries. Anything and everything goes as long as we're happy and it feels good. Jesus has no use for the people living in the gray area. You're either following Christ or following the world, which Satan rules. The lukewarm people may think they will see heaven one day, but Jesus tells them, "Then I will tell them plainly, 'I never knew you'" (Matthew 7:23).

The good news is that you get to exercise your free will and pick your camp. With which one are you going to put down your stakes and pitch your tent?

SEPTEMBER 19

"Salt is good. Have salt in yourselves and be at peace with each other" (Mark 9:50-51).

A preacher once used the analogy of bringing someone to Christ with the well-known adage, "You can lead a horse to water, but you can't make him drink." However, someone in the congregation had a different take on the old adage and called out, "Well preacher, that's not true. If you give him some salt, he'll be drinking in no time."

Just as salt is an essential ingredient for cooking and preserving, we can be salty Christians and help to make those around us thirsty for God. The Apostle Paul says in Colossians 4:6, "Let your conversation be always full of grace, seasoned with salt, so that you may know how to answer everyone." When we share with others about Christ, it is important to exercise grace in how we speak and what we say. We can lose our saltiness quickly if we are overbearing or disrespectful.

Salt is vital to one's bodily health just as it is essential for one's spiritual health. God tells us to keep a proper balance so we can live wholesome lives physically fit as well as spiritually fit for our work in the Kingdom. We should be sprinkling our salt wherever we go and flavoring it with the love of Jesus.

SEPTEMBER 20

"Whatever you do, do it all for the glory of God." (1 Corinthians 10:31)

We must be very careful not to glorify any people or things other than God. This is what God calls idol worship, and He says it is detestable to Him. God is the only one who is worthy of worship and honor. This is where the Israelites went wrong as they wandered through the desert for 40 years. They vacillated between worshipping God and worshipping idols. They created man-made objects to bow down to and turned their backs on the One True God.

This sin is so revolting to God that He made it the very first Commandment: "I am the Lord your God. You shall have no other gods before me" (Exodus 20). The Apostle Paul teaches us that we are supposed to do everything as an act of worship. In fact, our whole lives should be lived as one continual act of worship. Colossians 3:23 says, "Whatever you do, work at it with all your heart as working for the Lord and not men." This mindset will transform how you look at your job, your household chores, or any challenging task you face.

God takes great delight in us when He sees and hears us worshipping Him. 1 Thessalonians 5:16 sums it up this way: "Be joyful always, pray continually, give thanks in all circumstances for this is God's will for you in Christ Jesus." God's will is that we bring Him honor in all that we say and all that we do. How will you glorify God today?

SEPTEMBER 21

"I am the Lord who heals you" (Exodus 15:26).

Soon after Jesus entered the town of Bethsaida, a blind man was brought to Him by some townspeople. He took the blind man by the hand and led him outside the village. Jesus took His spit and rubbed it over the man's eyes. He asked the man, "Do you see anything?" The man's vision was still foggy as he reported seeing people who looked like tree trunks moving around. So, Jesus laid His hands on the man's eyes again, and the man quickly reported that he was seeing clearly.

It's interesting to note that the blind man wasn't healed completely when Jesus first put the spit on his eyes. It certainly wasn't because He couldn't do it the first time around. Even though the passage doesn't explain why God chose to heal the man in this fashion, we can be sure of one thing. Jesus always has a reason behind everything He does.

Jesus revealed to me through this story that healing doesn't always come all at once. Sometimes there are stages we have to go through. Sometimes it can be a long process. *"But God"* has His reasons for what we think is a prayer going unanswered. His timing is always part of a bigger plan He has for us.

Looking back, I believe that God delayed the healing of my body so I could finish this book. Otherwise, it might have taken me another 5 years to complete! I praised Him throughout my "light and momentary troubles" because I knew, in the end, He would be glorified. This is the ultimate goal of every trial we go through. To God be the Glory forever and ever, Amen!

SEPTEMBER 22

"Because you have turned away from the Lord, He will not be with you, and you will fall by the sword" (Numbers 14:43).

Our nation was founded on Christian values and principles. Our Pledge of Allegiance states we are "One Nation under God." "In God We Trust" is inscribed on our currency. Yet none of this seems to matter anymore. God is slowly and surely being removed from our country.

The Bible tells us that as wickedness escalates, the world we live in will become even more violent. It shouldn't be a surprise to us that God is not pleased with His creation. Why should He bless His people who have turned their backs on Him? There is nowhere in Scripture where you will find that God tolerates sin. In fact Proverbs 6:16 gives us a whole list of sins we are told that the Lord hates.

There is a life application we can take away from this unsettling verse, and it is this: we should not fear or be anxious about the enormity of evil. We should not nurture attitudes of defeat or apathy. Jesus tells us that we are overcomers and that is how we should live.

We may never be a Nation under One God again until Jesus comes back and rules the world, but it shouldn't deter us from the command He gave us in His Word to "Go out and make disciples of all nations" (Matthew 28:19). Our mission should not be affected by what is happening all around us. We can continue to make a difference for His Kingdom by turning people back to God and His rightful place of honor.

SEPTEMBER 23

"Blessed is the man who trusts in the Lord, whose confidence is in Him" (Jeremiah 17:7).

Humans have a natural tendency to worry. We think if we worry, we're in control because we're doing something. Worry is like a rocking chair...it goes back and forth yet never goes anywhere. Jesus wants to take our worry from us. 1 Peter 5:7 says, "Cast all of your anxiety on Him because He cares for you." He is able and willing to take our burdens and carry them. He wants us to let go and let Him take over.

Sometimes it can become an endless cycle of casting our cares on Him and then turning around a few days later and taking them back. This happens because we stop trusting God and feel the need to be in control again. God blesses our honesty when we tell Him that we need Him. When we take our problem to Him right away, He will help us get through it. He will provide what we need to persevere.

"Blessed is the man who trusts in the Lord." The word *trust* in Hebrew means confidence. Where do you place your confidence when the road gets rocky? In man or in the only One who can sustain you and see you through victoriously? David sums it up beautifully in Psalm 62:5: "Find rest, O my soul, in God alone; my hope comes from Him!"

SEPTEMBER 24

"The Son is the radiance of God's glory and the exact representation of His being sustaining all things by His powerful Word" (Hebrews 1:3).

I've always wondered why God gave Ezekiel such precise instructions on how to build His Temple. As I read through pages and pages of numbers, diameters, and widths, I couldn't help but wonder what the purpose was for all of these exact measurements. Why was it so important that it all be recorded in Scripture? I know the Word of God is as applicable now as it was then but how did this fit in with that truth?

Then I had an epiphany. I thought about how God's character reflects precision. He is a God of exactness. Everything He does and has done is exactly how it is supposed to be. He is always accurate and always definite in all that He says and does. His promises can be trusted exactly as they are written. He never wavers about any of His choices or decisions.

How do I incorporate this revelation into my understanding of God? Well, the most obvious answer is that if God is a God of minute details, then He cares about every little detail of our lives as well. Things we might think are trivial or insignificant He cares about! This tells us that being a God of exactness, He answers our prayers exactly the way they should be. God always knows the perfect solution.

SEPTEMBER 25

"Yet you heard my cry for mercy when I called to you for help" (Psalm 31:22).

One morning as Jesus was teaching in the Temple, He saw a woman bent over so far that all she could see was the floor. She had been crippled for 18 miserable years. She had no idea that Jesus was approaching her in the crowd because her only view was of her feet. Jesus took pity on her immediately, reached out and healed her. She stood up straight as a stick, and her gaze fell immediately on Jesus' face. Think about that for a second. Jesus' face was the first thing she saw in 18 years! I imagine she must have been overwhelmed with the sight before her eyes.

Jesus knows our needs even before we do. He sees and knows everything about us. Our needs may escape the notice of others but never Jesus. He wants us to rely on Him for our every need, so He purposely puts us in situations where we can do just that. He loves it when we look to Him and lean on Him for support.

It's a humbling experience to ask God for help when we've depended only on ourselves our entire lives. Proverbs 15:33 says, "With humility comes honor." God will indeed honor us when we honor Him by asking for help.

God rewards those who put away their pride and call upon Him. He is waiting for that call and ready to bless us with exactly what we need.

SEPTEMBER 26

"The Lord will guide you always; He will satisfy your needs in a sun-scorched land" (Isaiah 59:11).

I was heading home from Bible study one morning, and in my haste, I found myself going in the wrong direction. I was distracted by an errand I had to run, and I was already running late. When I realized I was headed the wrong way, I made a U-turn and began the drive across town to pick up the lunch I had promised my grandkids. I was frazzled, to say the least.

"But God" ... I hadn't driven very far when ... I couldn't believe my eyes. The restaurant I was heading for was right smack in front of me. I had no idea there was one so close. As I thanked God for this small miracle in my day, I was reminded again of the unending goodness of our God!

Looking back on this incident, I was able to see some spiritual analogies. I have learned through my many years of walking with the Lord that He is always in teaching mode. I discovered He often likes to use the small ordinary events in our day to impart these valuable lessons.

The insight I was given was about how easy it is for us to become distracted, not only when we're driving, but in our faith as well. We get caught up in life and veer off course. We think we're cruising along just fine when, in reality, we're heading in the wrong direction. A U-turn may be necessary to get back on track. God put a huge blessing in front of me when I turned my car around. He will do the same for you when you start heading in the right direction.

SEPTEMBER 27

"In the beginning, God created the heavens and the earth" (Genesis 1:1).

These first few sentences in the Bible tell us many things about God. He is revealed as being infinite—always existing—and He is referred to as the Creator. Isaiah 44:24 says, "I am the Lord, who has made all things, who alone stretched out the heavens, who spread out the earth by myself."

Scripture teaches us that before there was anything at all, there was God. He always was and always will be. We are told that God is Sovereign and is in control of the whole universe, past, present, and future. And He will continue to be in charge until the last page of history is written, and Jesus returns to abolish all evil and reign over the earth.

As believers, we can look forward with great anticipation to Jesus' return! The earth will be no more, but we will live eternally with God in heaven. Our rooms have been reserved, and the welcome mat has been laid out for us with our names written on it. Jesus declares in the last chapter of Revelations, "Behold, I am coming soon!" Amen, Come Lord Jesus, come!

SEPTEMBER 28

"I am the voice of one calling in the desert. Make straight the way for the Lord" (John 1:23).

Jesus said that no other man in the Bible fulfilled His purpose more effectively than John the Baptist. He stated in Matthew 11:11, "Among those born of women there has not risen anyone greater than John the Baptist."

John was the epitome of humbleness. He preached to the multitudes about the Messiah who was to come. Mark 1:7 says, "After me will come one more powerful than I, the thongs of whose sandals I am not worthy to stoop down and untie." In Jesus' day untying sandals was a service provided only by the lowliest of slaves when a person entered a home. John was proclaiming his unworthiness when he used this analogy so he could pay honor to the One who was to follow Him.

John the Baptist could have approached his mission much differently if he had so chosen. He could have appeared on the scene all puffed up and proud of himself for being the one picked to prepare the way for Jesus and having the privilege of baptizing Him. He could have easily called attention to himself and his ministry versus keeping the focus entirely on Jesus. However, John knew his purpose from a young age, and he always believed that Jesus was the Messiah.

The Word says that "John decreased that the Lord might increase." John took a back seat and forwarded all the attention to Jesus. Can you relate to John? Do you step back and allow others to have the spotlight, or do you tend to seek the limelight for yourself? We can learn a valuable lesson from John. Humility is what makes a person great. Why not untie some sandals today and experience the beauty of true humility?

SEPTEMBER 29

"Blessed are they whose transgressions are forgiven, whose sins are covered. Blessed is the man whose sin the Lord will never count against him" (Romans 4:7).

God is a God of forgiveness. There is no sin or failure that we can bring before Him that He will not forgive. He graciously wipes our slate clean and remembers our transgressions no more. If only we were this forgiving of ourselves and others!

Sometimes we tend to rehash old hurts from the past which makes forgiveness more unattainable. We tend to not only keep our baggage with us but keep it packed as well. We get comfortable lugging that heavy thing around and may not even realize how hard it is to carry because we've become so used to it. We may even feel more self-righteous as we rehearse all the injustices we have stored in that bag. We've carried that baggage around for so long it seems like it is a part of us!

God calls us to hand over that suitcase to Him and to forgive others as He has forgiven us. This command also includes those who haven't asked for forgiveness. The soldiers who crucified Jesus never asked Him to forgive them and yet before He breathed His last He had forgiven all of them.

Unforgiveness robs us of any chance for peace and joy in our lives. The good news is we can find healing and freedom in the arms of Jesus. Ask Him to help you have a forgiving heart. God wants nothing more than for you to walk without that suitcase in total freedom.

SEPTEMBER 30

"He thus revealed His glory and His disciples put their faith in Him" (John 2:11).

Jesus and His mother, along with the disciples, were at a wedding feast in Cana in Galilee. Weddings in Jesus' day were week-long festivals. Banquets would be prepared, and the week would be spent celebrating the new life of the married couple.

A problem arose towards the end of this particular feast. The wine had run dry. To run out of wine in those days was more than embarrassing. It actually broke the laws of hospitality. Mary went to Jesus and asked Him to fix the problem. He responded by telling the servants to fill six jars with water and then turned them into the finest of wines. The master of the banquet marveled at the choice wine served at the end of the feast because it was always the least expensive wines that were saved until last.

This first miracle is a wonderful example of Jesus' kindness and compassion. After Mary's request, Jesus at first replied, "My time has not yet come" (John 2:4). But out of obedience and respect for His mother and the willingness to provide for the needs of the people, He chose to carry out her wishes.

Are you being called to help someone in need right now? It doesn't have to be something as big as providing for a wedding feast. Small acts of love and kindness speak volumes. If Mary hadn't taken that step of faith and asked Jesus for help, there would have been hundreds of very disappointed wedding guests. Where or with whom do you need to take a step of faith today?

OCTOBER 1

"For I seek not to please myself but Him who sent me" (John 5:30).

It's good to evaluate our walk with the Lord periodically. It's important to be sure we are truly living for God and not living for ourselves and our own selfish desires. Living a God-pleasing life doesn't just automatically happen when we begin our walk of faith. It takes effort to have a healthy relationship with God and to stay on track.

We only get one shot at this life. There are no do-overs or mulligans. It is for this reason that we must be diligent about the condition of our spiritual lives. It is the most important part of our total being. Remember, whatever we let fill our minds will control our lives. Do we think about the things of God more than we do about ourselves and our own desires? Whatever occupies our minds and rules in our hearts will either mold us into godly people or self-focused and selfish ones.

The best way to maintain a healthy spiritual life is by spending time with God and reading His Word. Getting in a quiet place free from the chaos of life is crucial for maintaining a thriving relationship with Him. Study scripture, imprint it on your heart, and apply it to your life. This daily discipline will keep you centered and keep your mind focused on what's really important.

Be careful to guard your hearts and your minds. Protect them from the temptations and the lies the world wants you to believe. Do not seek to please yourself. Jesus sought only to please His Father, which is the standard we should follow as well.

OCTOBER 2

"If any one of you is without sin, let him be the first to throw a stone at her" (John 8:7).

The Pharisees in Jesus' day loved to judge others and pretend they were without sin. One day they brought a woman to Jesus who was caught in adultery and told Him that the law commanded such a woman be stoned to death. Jesus's response was perfect. He simply told the religious leaders to go ahead and stone her. But He told them to stop and think first and let those who have never sinned throw the first stone! When the accusers heard this, they slipped away one by one leaving the woman behind.

It is so easy to find fault in others. We can clearly see the sin in someone else's life, but we are blind to our own. We pray and ask God to fix them when, in reality, we are really the ones who need the fixing. Jesus teaches us about this kind of judgment in Matthew 7:3: "Why do you look at the speck of sawdust in your brother's eye and pay no attention to the plank in your own eye?" Jesus calls this type of judgment hypocritical, and we should have no part in it.

Our focus should always be on how we are living our own lives and not on how others are living theirs. Scrutiny has no place in a believer's life. The only judgment we need to be concerned about is our own when we stand before God in heaven and give an account of our lives. Will you be guilty of throwing any stones? Consider the Pharisees before you decide to pick up one and take aim.

OCTOBER 3

"If you hold to my teaching, you are really my disciples" (John 8:31).

Most Bibles today have the words Jesus spoke printed in red. What is the significance or symbolism behind this red lettering? The history behind it is interesting. Scholars in the late 1800s thought it appropriate that Jesus' spoken words be set apart from the rest of the text. They thought it would help separate Jesus' teachings from the surrounding writings. Also, they felt it was reverential in that the red would represent Christ's blood that was shed on the cross for us.

The red letters in our Bibles teach us everything we need to know about how to live the Christian life. They are full of wisdom and guidance. Jesus often taught with parables and word pictures, so people could better grasp the truth. He taught with infectious passion and grace and always in accord with His Father.

We are called to obey all of Jesus' teachings. We are told to "Fix these words of mine in your hearts and minds" (Deut. 11:18). Jesus also calls us to take His teachings and proclaim them to the world. Imagine if the Apostles kept everything Jesus taught them to themselves. The Christian faith would be non-existent today! It is up to us to have teachable spirits like the disciples so that we can go out and do the work God has given each one of us to do.

OCTOBER 4

"But this happened so that the work of God might be displayed in his life" (John 9:3).

Just like the Apostle Paul, God gave me a thorn in my flesh thirty years ago. And just like Paul, I prayed for God to remove it. *"But God"* kept referring me back to 2 Corinthians 12:9 which says, "My grace is sufficient for you; for my power is made perfect in weakness." Like Paul, my thorn remained, but I have learned through the years that His grace has indeed been sufficient in my suffering.

My thorn has been a lifelong battle with depression. I have struggled with it most of my life. I'm not afraid to talk about mental illness publicly. It is a disease that needs to be brought out into the open to remove the stigma that still surrounds it to this day. In many cases talking about it helps to relieve the undeserved shame and guilt that is associated with mental illness.

I have spent many days "in the pit," as David called his depression. My thorn encompassed a darkness that I never could have imagined. There were countless times I questioned Romans 8:28, which says, "And we know that in all things God works for the good of those who love him." "Where was the good?" I kept asking God. I couldn't understand how any of this emotional pain could work for the good.

"But God" revealed to me that my thorn could be used for His glory. He began to show me that I could use my affliction to help others simply be talking about it openly. I began to use my depression as a platform to help and encourage others with mental illness. I talk a lot about my faith and how Jesus plays a significant role in living successfully with the disease. Without Jesus, I know I would still be in the pit! I have learned that mental illness is an uphill battle unless you put your hope and trust in Jesus!

OCTOBER 5

"I was blind, but now I see" (John 9:25).

Who can read this verse and not be reminded of the famous hymn, Amazing Grace? The lyrics are most likely imprinted on every believer's heart. "Amazing grace, how sweet the sound that saved a wretch like me. I once was lost but now am found. Was blind but now I see." What was the writer of this hymn blind to and what did he finally see?

This Scripture verse in John is not referring to physical blindness but a spiritual one. We all live in darkness until the day we choose to believe in Jesus. After we make that decision, the scales fall from our eyes, and we are able to see life as we've never seen it before. We are able to see the Truth for what it is.

When our eyes are opened, we see life completely different. The world takes on a whole new look, and our perspective on everything changes. We have a newfound peace and a joy that we never experienced when we lived in the dark. Our newfound sight seems to permeate every part of our being and every aspect of our lives.

Are you spiritually blind and need to have your eyes opened? God's Amazing Grace is there for the asking. His grace is unconditional and available to anyone who wants to have their blinders removed and see the world through the eyes of Jesus. I can attest—there is not a better view in sight!

OCTOBER 6

"And so after waiting patiently, Abraham received what was promised" (Hebrews 6:15).

Is there anything more challenging or frustrating than waiting on an answer from God? We act like children whining and complaining about His delay. We try to come up with our own list of possible reasons why God is taking His good old time. Sometimes we even get a little testy and tell Him to hurry it up! Patience does not come naturally for any of us. It is a gift to those who are truly trusting in the Lord.

Father Abraham was very familiar with waiting. He and his wife Sarah prayed to God for a child for twenty-five years. Joseph waited seventeen years in prison before he was set free to rule over all of Egypt. David was on the run from Saul for twenty years. The Israelites wandered through a hot desert for forty years. There are dozens of examples in Scripture of how God's timetable is different from ours. Yet with all these examples, we still question His Wisdom when He is silent.

God has a reason for everything He does. Our job is not to figure out what those reasons are but to trust Him completely for the outcome. God is such a good God that when He does answer our prayers, He does it to the fullest measure. Abraham, Joseph, and David would agree wholeheartedly. Don't let the wait get the best of you. Stay focused on God, and He will bring that answer one day at the perfect time. Be assured that God is never late!

OCTOBER 7

"As He approached Jerusalem and saw the city He wept over it" (Luke 19:41).

Jesus' triumphal entry into Jerusalem before His death should have been a happy time for Him. He was being honored as the crowd gathered around Him. They laid palm branches down in front of Him as He rode in on His donkey. There was singing and dancing as the people praised and worshipped Him. Jesus should have been enjoying this grand show of affection, but instead, Scripture tells us that "He wept."

When Jesus looked out over His beloved city and His beloved people, He felt the fresh sting of reality and rejection. His chosen people had refused to accept Him, and He was overcome with sadness. Isaiah predicted this would happen hundreds of years before it took place. He said, "He was despised and rejected by men, a man of sorrows and familiar with suffering" (Isaiah 53:3).

Jesus shows us in this passage that He was very much a man as well as God. We see that Jesus experienced the same feelings and emotions that we do. The scene before Him is so overwhelming that He breaks down and cries.

Jesus still weeps over us today. He weeps every time one of His beloved children turns his back on Him. He weeps over the injustices in the world. He weeps when His people are mistreated. He weeps every time we weep! He understands our every emotion and is quick to console us as only He can. When you need comfort, run into your Heavenly Father's waiting arms, and let Him love you. He is holding a Kleenex ready to wipe away every tear and kiss the cheeks they've fallen on. If you are hurting, turn to the ultimate Comforter. You will experience comfort like you've never known it before.

OCTOBER 8

"Now faith is being sure of what we hope for and certain of what we do not see. This is what the ancients were commended for" (Hebrew 11:1).

The eleventh chapter of Hebrews is known as the "faith chapter." It contains wonderful examples of a number of our heroes of the faith in the Old Testament. These men were all highly commended for their faith and trust in God. They were absolutely confident of everything God promised them.

Abel was commended for his righteous living. Enoch was known as "one who pleased God." Noah built an ark when the land had never seen a drop of rain. Abraham became a stranger in a foreign land when God commanded him to pack up and move somewhere else. Isaac, Jacob, and Moses were all commended for their faith and obedience. God offered no explanations to these men before He called them into service. He simply said go and do, and they went and did. Even when it didn't make sense or involved suffering, the faith of all these men remained strong.

Will others remember you as a person of faith when your life comes to a close? Will you be thought of as a person who trusted God in every circumstance of your life? Your faith chapter will be written one day. The good news is that you can help write it by how you live your life!

OCTOBER 9

"In his pride, the wicked does not seek Him; in all his thoughts there is no room for God" (Psalm 10:4).

The very first commandment tells us that our God is a jealous God. He wants our full attention and doesn't like it when someone or something else becomes more important than Him. A jealous God demands exclusive devotion. He will not tolerate anything less. A jealous God will not put up with being in second place in your life. He wants all or nothing. In His mind, you are either all in, or you're not in at all.

What consumes your thoughts most of the time? Is it you and your agenda or is it God and His plan for the day? If there is no room in your thoughts for God, then pride is standing in your way. You have made yourself the number one priority in your life. Wise King Solomon had many things to say about pride. One is captured in Proverbs 11:2. He said, "When pride comes then comes disgrace, but with humility comes wisdom." If you can relate to this, it might be time for a little humbling and reassessment of your calendar. When we make it a point to put Christ first in our lives, He will always respond with blessings. A good thing to remember is TGIF—Today God Is First!

OCTOBER 10

"Yet I am not alone for my Father is with me" (John 16:32).

Jesus gave His disciples last-minute instructions right before His arrest and crucifixion. He told them that they would weep and mourn while the world rejoiced. But then He told them their grief would soon turn to joy. He used the analogy of a woman giving birth. He said after her baby is born she quickly forgets the pain and anguish of the delivery because of the joy of the new life she has just brought forth.

Jesus also told them that after His arrest, they would all scatter each to his own home and leave Him all alone at the crucifixion (except for John). He knew the disciples had faith but not enough to stand firm in the face of the impending events. Jesus knew they would fail Him, yet He wanted to reassure them that He would always be with them no matter what.

We are never alone. He is always with us 24/7. We may not feel His presence, but His Word promises us that He is right there beside us. Deuteronomy 31:6 says, "He will never leave you nor forsake you." God will never abandon us. If God seems far away, it isn't because He moved. We are the ones responsible for the gap between us. If you are sensing a void between you and God at the moment, now might be a good time to fill it back up. He hasn't moved one bit.

OCTOBER 11

"Again, Peter denied it, and at that moment a rooster began to crow" (John 18:27).

Can you picture Peter's face when he heard that rooster crow for the third time? It all came to pass just as Jesus predicted. The rooster confirmed what Peter was trying so hard to ignore. He had denied knowing his Master three times. Imagine his pain and devastation especially after he told Jesus in Matthew 26:35, "Even if I have to die with you, I will never disown you."

How did bold, outspoken Peter go from making such a powerful statement, vowing his very life to Jesus, to "I never knew Him"? How could Peter possibly have done such a thing? He was one of Jesus' closest confidantes. Peter, James, and John were known as the "inner three" among the disciples. They were Jesus' go-to guys.

While we might be inclined to be disappointed with Peter, we have to remember one very important thing. Peter was human just like the rest of us. Fear may get in the way of faith sometimes. This story is really not about courage in the face of danger. It's about forgiveness and second chances. Jesus appeared to His disciples after His Resurrection, and He had nothing but love for Peter. Despite Peter's actions, Jesus still loved and accepted him. He still had great plans for him.

God's love for us is unconditional. If you think Jesus could never forgive you for a particular sin, you couldn't be more wrong. It says in Jeremiah 31:34, "For I will forgive their wickedness and I will remember their sins no more." A clean slate is always available when we go to God and ask for His forgiveness. Don't let any crowing roosters stop you from getting that fresh start you've been yearning for.

OCTOBER 12

"You believe that there is one God. Good! Even the demons believe that and shudder. Faith by itself, if it is not accompanied by actions, is dead" (James 2:17-19).

There is such a thing as false faith. Just believing in God is not enough. James tells us that even the devil acknowledges that God is real. Genuine faith must include outward evidence. It has to involve an oral proclamation of our faith and trust in Jesus as well.

Some people mistakenly think that simply attending church is a good enough display of faith. Show up once a week and listen to a sermon and we're good to go. While church attendance is certainly an important part of our faith, it doesn't automatically mean we're Christians. What defines us as followers of Jesus is who we are the rest of the week. Do we live out our faith in our home and in our workplace? Are we known for our acts of kindness and the love we have for all people? Do we strive to accept and treat others in a godly manner?

Genuine faith must be evident for others to see. Our great Forefathers of the Bible were all called to put their faith into action. We are called to serve Him as well, not just to believe He exists. Don't just tell God you love Him—show Him!

OCTOBER 13

"Suddenly a sound like the blowing of a violent wind came from heaven and filled the whole house where they were sitting" (Acts 2:2).

It was the day of Pentecost, and all the Apostles were gathered together in one room. It was about seven weeks after Jesus' Resurrection and before His Ascension into heaven. It was in this room that the promised Holy Spirit would make His appearance and baptize them. *Breath* or *wind* is a symbol of the Holy Spirit, so when a great gust of wind swept through the room, it was a sign that He had indeed arrived. This was the fulfillment of Jesus' promise to send them a helper.

I had a spiritual encounter with the wind one day. I was sitting outside in my backyard distraught over the fact that my newest grandbaby was born with a life-threatening condition. I sat crying out to God with tears flowing and my heart aching. The wind was calm that day, but as I sat on that swing, a monstrous blast blew right over me. I knew right away that it was the Holy Spirit encouraging me to stay strong and trust God.

When I arrived at the hospital later that day, a nurse met me in the hallway and told me that the baby had made a sudden turnaround and was improving. From that day on, she just continued getting better, and today she is a normal healthy little girl.

It is easy to feel God's presence all around us as we relate to the physical world. Nature can speak to us and draw us closer to God. He is everywhere and in everything. What a comfort it is knowing He is always with us!

OCTOBER 14

"Wives, in the same way, be submissive to your husbands, so that if any of them do not believe the word, they may be won over without words by the behavior of their wives" (1 Peter 3:1-2).

Inferiority is never implied when we hear the word *submissive*. It is defined simply as respect and honor. We should treat all people in this manner. Peter is talking about using actions instead of words to win people over to Christ. We think we have to be theological experts to talk to others about Christ. This approach, however, can elicit strong differences of opinion and meaningless arguments.

Living our lives out loud for God is what makes an impact on people. Acts of random kindness and compassion are what people will notice. Taking an interest in those around you by encouraging and supporting them speaks volumes about you.

Jesus never pushed faith on anyone. He was always a gentleman. He didn't wave His scrolls around or put pressure on people. Jesus simply lived out His faith. His gentleness and loving spirit drew people to Him like a magnet. His deep compassion for others dominated His behavior.

Faith should live on the outside as well as the inside. A joyful expression will draw people to us as we smile brightly with the light of Jesus. Your countenance says everything about you. Are you wearing your faith for others to see?

OCTOBER 15

"We want you to know, O King that we will not serve your gods or worship the image of gold you have set up" (Daniel 3:18).

Everyone is familiar with the story of King Nebuchadnezzar throwing three men into the furnace for failing to worship him. These men were righteous and faithful to the One and only True God. This King was very successful, but he didn't believe in God. So, he commanded that a golden statue be erected for everyone to bow down to and worship. If anyone did not comply, they would be thrown into a furnace heated to maximum temperature.

The three men stood firm and would not conform to the king's edict. They told him, "If we are thrown into the blazing furnace the God we serve is able to save us from it" (Daniel 3:17). True to his word, the king had the men thrown into the fiery furnace. *"But God"* ... They walked out of that crematorium with nary a singed hair or hint of smoke.

We are faced with this same scenario in our world today. People are being forced to bow down and worship false gods and abandon their faith in the One True God. Christians around the globe are being tortured and executed for their beliefs.

Idols will continue to be thrown at us, but we as believers must remain steadfast in our faith. Jesus said in John 17:3, "Now this is eternal life: that they may know you, the only true God and Jesus Christ whom you have sent." We are to bow down and worship one God and one God only. To bow to anything else may bring a fiery consequence.

OCTOBER 16

"The wrath of God is being revealed from heaven against all the godlessness and wickedness and men who suppress the truth by their wickedness" *(Romans 1:18).*

Most people would prefer to view God as always gentle and loving. While He most certainly possesses these qualities, God is also a God of judgment. He will not tolerate sin and evil in His world forever. Scripture says His wrath will be poured out in the final days.

The prophet Hosea prophesied this would happen. He said, "There is no faithfulness, no love, no acknowledgment of God in the land" (Hosea 4:1). He couldn't have predicted the state of our world any better. When we began to remove God from our country, the downhill slide began. In verse 7 the prophet continues, "Because of this, the land mourns, and all who live in it waste away."

There are grave consequences for rejecting God. If we don't personally turn back to Him and the world refuses to embrace Him, the results, unfortunately, will not be pleasant. We don't want to think of God as angry or vengeful. But because He is who He is—the Author of Life and Creator of the Universe—He cannot and will not ever abide sin and evil. As God, He has every right to exercise His wrath.

The sobering truth is that we are all responsible for our actions and will be held accountable for them one day. Galatians 6:7 says, "Do not be deceived. God cannot be mocked." Don't ever think you can fool God. If He knows the number of hairs on your head, He certainly knows the condition of your heart.

OCTOBER 17

"If you seek Him, He will be found by you" (1 Chronicles 28:9).

A friend once told me that she thought I had a direct line to God because I shared personal things with her that God put on my heart. She said I must have a backdoor into the Throne Room. An "in" she called it with the Almighty.

Of course, this scenario is not possible. We are all on equal footing when it comes to prayer and accessing God. It is possible, however, that we may feel more out of touch with God because our existing relationship with Him is not strong. Are we in good standing with God? Do we pursue Him on a daily basis? These things may make a difference when it comes to hearing from God.

Recently, another friend and I had been praying together about something she needed direction for in her life. She was filled with great anticipation as we waited on God to answer her prayer. However, she became impatient, and one afternoon she called me and asked, "So, Cori, have you heard anything from God yet? Has He spoken anything to you about what I should do?" The words were no sooner out of her mouth when a Scripture verse flew in my head. It was the one above. "If you seek Him, He will be found by you."

I replied, "No, I haven't heard anything yet, but God did give me a Scripture verse for you." I shared it with her. I told her God wanted her to seek Him for herself. I explained that the best way to find God and to hear from Him was through His Word. The Bible holds the key to unlocking all the answers and direction we will ever need.

Are you actively seeking God or relying on others to spiritually feed you? Are you acting on the advice of others or listening to what God has to say? Why not pull out Life's user manual and let Him speak to you!

OCTOBER 18

"Let us come before Him with thanksgiving. The Lord is the great God, the great King above all gods" (Psalm 95:2).

How often do we set aside our laundry list of prayers and just thank God for who He is and not just for what He does for us? Do we ever spend our quiet time just praising and blessing Him?

One of the ways we can do this is to pray God's attributes back to Him. For example, we can start with: *God, thank you for being my Lord and Savior, my life-giver and sustainer, my Rock, my Foundation, my Hope, the Light of my life, my peace and joy.* You can continue with all the ways you may look at Him personally. *Our God is faithful, good, full of grace, forgiving, merciful, loving.* The depth of His character and how we can praise Him are infinite.

Worship God for who He is and what He means to you. When you thank Him, be specific. Thanking Him for everything is too vague. Just like God wants us to be detailed in our prayers, He wants us to be the same way in our thanksgiving. This method of prayer will revolutionize your relationship with the Lord. It takes the focus completely off of ourselves and puts it right where it belongs—on Our Great and Awesome God!

OCTOBER 19

"But you are a forgiving God, gracious and compassionate, slow to anger and abounding in love" (Nehemiah 9:17).

The ninth chapter of Nehemiah is a great summary of the Israelites trek through the desert. It is a powerful lesson on forgiveness and restoration. The Israelites repeatedly sinned by rejecting God throughout their forty-year exodus. When they realized their sin, they cried out to God to forgive them, promising to never abandon Him again. God, in His infinite grace, always forgave them, no matter how grievous the sin. However, their promises were short-lived, and it wasn't long before they were building idols again and casting God aside.

"But God" is always abounding in love and offers us unconditional mercy, compassion, and forgiveness. This is the very essence of who God is. He hasn't changed from the person He was in the Old Testament. God is the same God now as He was then!

Don't ever think you won't be forgiven for your sin and can't be restored back to God. We are never too far away that His love and forgiveness won't find us. We are never too lost that we can't be brought back into the fold. God always grants forgiveness when we come to Him with a repentant heart. His love is always unlimited and unconditional.

OCTOBER 20

"If anyone has material possessions and sees his brother in need but has no pity on him how can the love of God be in him?" (1 John 3:17).

Have you ever been to a homeless shelter? Have you ever gotten an up close and personal glimpse into how some destitute people really live? I never had these experiences until I visited a women's homeless shelter recently. It not only changed some misconceptions I had about the homeless, but it changed my perspective on many things in my personal life. My eyes were acutely opened when I walked in that room and saw all the cots lined up in rows with a few meager belongings scattered on top of each one. I saw children without coats and shoes. Threadbare blankets and broken toys were strewn about. What I encountered that day burned a permanent image in my memory.

I went home that day and felt sick when I looked in my closet. It felt wrong to have so much when there were people out there who literally had nothing. I cleaned out my closet with a vengeance that afternoon. Then I proceeded to tear apart every closet in the house and donated the items to a Mission in town. I once heard a pastor say that giving is only considered giving if it costs you something.

Jesus said in Matthew 25:40, "I tell you the truth; whatever you did for one of the least of these brothers of mine, you did for me." We glorify God every time we have a kind word or do a kind deed for someone else. When we love others God's love is returned to us sevenfold.

Is it time for a visit to a nearby homeless shelter to have your eyes opened like mine? Or maybe you feel led to reach out to someone in your neighborhood or place of employment. There are mission fields everywhere just waiting for us to get involved in. Nothing will bring more joy and peace into our lives than finding a cause or a person to invest our time and resources in. Making a difference in someone else's life is really making the most significant impact on yours.

OCTOBER 21

"...and being fully persuaded that God had power to do what he promised" (Romans 4:21).

God's character traits and promises are a common thread all throughout Scripture. Although I praise God for who He is and all that He has done for me, I don't acknowledge His promises as much as I should. I tend to take them for granted when, in reality, I should tell God how thankful I am for those promises every day.

I sat down recently and made a list of some of my favorite promises. These are the ones I tend to rely on the most on a daily basis:

- He will never leave me nor forsake me.
- He will fight my battles for me.
- He will bring good out of my trials and suffering.
- He will forgive me when I repent.
- He will be faithful even when I'm unfaithful.
- He will love me unconditionally no matter what.
- He will give me new mercies and grace every morning.
- He will enable the Holy Spirit to work within me.
- He will reward obedience and pour out blessings upon me.
- He will fill me with love, joy, peace, patience, kindness, goodness, gentleness, faithfulness, and self-control when I put Him first in my life.

Why not take a minute and jot down a few of your favorites to keep on hand when you need encouragement or need to share one with a friend? Over the years, I have shared these with many people who usually tell me it was just what they needed to hear at the time. God's promises are there to encourage us and to encourage one another.

If you need to rely on anything in this life, choose

to rely on God's promises. They will never fail you nor disappoint you. God means what He says and says what He means. That is the best promise of all!

OCTOBER 22

"Pride only breeds quarrels, but wisdom is found in those who take advice" (Proverbs 13:10).

Pride is the underlying cause of every quarrel. It feeds conflict, puts up walls, and drives distance between people. Our pride tells us we have to be right. Our pride insists that our opinions are the only ones that count. These attitudes are peace killers. The question we really should be asking ourselves in the heat of a battle is, "Do I want to be right or do I want to have peace?"

Humility is the opposite of pride and is essential for defusing an argument. Humility heals, where pride leaves behind wounds and scars. Remember, there is never a "but" after an apology. The "but" negates everything that was said before it. The proper response is "I'm sorry for..."; not "I'm sorry, *but...*" Choosing to love above all else is tough sometimes. But when hurts happen, reasons are not important. Weighing and balancing who was really at fault is pointless, non-productive, and prideful.

If you find yourself constantly arguing, examine your heart to see if there might be any element of pride lurking about. Its presence will affect every relationship you have. Stick to positive comments and be willing to admit your mistakes. Wise King Solomon said in Proverbs 12:15, 16, "A wise man listens to advice...but a prudent man overlooks an insult." It's a challenge, but it is possible to back away from a disagreement. Choose to be humble and happy versus prideful and perturbed!

OCTOBER 23

"You have made known to me the path of life; you will fill me with joy in your presence" (Psalm 16:11).

Joy is contagious. You can't help but feel happy around joyful people. You can spot them easily. They are usually the ones with a smile on their face and a spring in their step.

A friend's joy was the first thing that attracted me to Jesus. I was in a carpool with one such joyful woman. Every morning when she picked me up for work, she had the biggest smile on her face. No matter what was going on in her life, she exuded joy. I kept waiting for the day when she would show up in a rotten mood, but it never happened. Finally, I could no longer take not knowing the source of her joy, and I asked her why she always had so much joy. She didn't answer the why but instead gave me a name as the source of her resounding happiness. She introduced me to Jesus and said I could have that same joy if I gave my life to Him.

Because of this friend, I soon possessed the same joy by opening up my heart and asking Jesus to take up residence there. This Jesus who came to live in me brought enormous changes in my life. He gave me a peace and a hope that I had never experienced before. I thought I would never attain true fulfillment and contentment in my life. *"But God"*...

God put that friend in my life for a reason. I didn't even know her when I joined that carpool. *"But God"* knew her intimately, and He crossed our paths as part of His divine plan. People now tell me that I have that same contagious joy and they want to know how they can have it too. It's easy...just look to Jesus and welcome Him home!

OCTOBER 24

"If you confess with your mouth Jesus is Lord and believe in your heart that God raised Him from the dead you will be saved" (Romans 10:9).

Have you ever had someone ask you, "How do I become a Christian?" Paul explained it perfectly in this verse. He said salvation is as close as your own lips and heart. People think it is some complicated ritual, but it isn't. Scripture says if we believe in our heart that Jesus is Lord and confess with our mouth that we believe He died for us and rose again, we will be saved. It's as easy as that!

However, faith involves more than just Christian doctrine and knowledge. James spends the entire second chapter of his book dedicated to this very subject. A true commitment to Jesus professed inwardly will produce outward displays of love and gratitude. Faith is exhibited by how we live our lives and for whom we live them for.

Would someone looking at you and how you live your life be able to tell you're a Christian? Do your actions and words reflect what you say you believe? Do you talk about your faith to others? Is your appearance one of peace and joy?

We must take God's great message of salvation to others so that they can have a chance to respond to this Good News. How will your loved ones and neighbors hear it unless someone tells them? As Romans 10:15 says, "How beautiful are the feet of those who bring good news!" Think of one person who needs to hear this message and something you can do to help them along. People can hear the Good News through your actions. What are they going to hear as they watch you?

OCTOBER 25

"Everyone who drinks this water will be thirsty again but whoever drinks the water I give him will never thirst" (John 4:13).

There are two great nuggets of truth in this verse. The first is tucked behind the scene in a small town called Samaria. Jesus was on His way back to Galilee but decided to go through a region the Jews avoided because they wanted nothing to do with the Samaritans. They were considered half-breeds and extended open hostility towards them. However, this did not stop Jesus from passing through and stopping off at a well for a drink. He met a Samaritan woman there, and, after a series of exchanges between them, she came to recognize Him as the Christ. She was so excited, she went back to town and brought the people out to meet Him, and they too believed. Jesus' decision to go through dangerous territory brought many people to faith.

The second nugget of truth pertains to Jesus calling Himself the Living Water. He tells us if we drink of Him we will never be thirsty. All creation needs water to survive, or it will wither away and die. Jesus is saying that our faith is just like that. It is in constant need of nourishment, and if we don't provide it, it will dry up and be blown away by the wind.

Our spiritual bodies have to be fed just like our natural bodies. Growth can only take place when it receives the sustenance it requires. There are many ways to access the Living Water. Reading the Word of God is the best way to nourish ourselves. Open your Bible and let the Living Water pour His spirit into you. Drink deep every day and watch your faith grow and blossom.

OCTOBER 26

"I have trusted in the Lord without wavering" (Psalm 26:1).

The story of Abraham and Isaac is a powerful example of staying the course. Abraham always trusted in the Lord without wavering. One day, God told him to take his Son Isaac to the mountain and sacrifice him. Can you even imagine such a command from the Lord? But Abraham never hesitated. The very next morning, he saddled up his donkey with the necessities and left with his son to do what God had told him to do. Abraham never questioned God nor doubted that He had a purpose and a plan for this heart-breaking sacrifice.

Just as Abraham drew his knife back to slay his son on the altar, an angel called out to him, "Do not lay a hand on the boy. Now I know that you fear God because you have not withheld from me your son, your only son" (Genesis 22:12). Abraham chose obedience, and God rewarded him. It is a powerful illustration that faith doesn't argue or procrastinate but acts promptly.

How can we have faith like Abraham? Romans 10:17 says, "Faith comes from hearing the message, and the message is heard through the Word of Christ." Our faith can only increase when we are committed to reading God's Word and applying it to our lives. Abraham just didn't study the Scrolls; he lived them.

Passing God's tests is a huge faith builder. Abraham walked away with his son that day a much stronger man. Unwavering trust isn't built in the easy times; it's built on the battlefield of our lives. God spared Isaac from death to show His mighty power and to illustrate the blessings when we are truly faithful and trust in God's plan.

OCTOBER 27

"But they do not know the thoughts of the Lord; they do not understand His plan" (Micah 4:12).

We do not have the capacity to know the thoughts of God. He is Sovereign, and we are not. He has supreme power and authority over everything in the entire universe. How could our finite minds possibly think like His? The same applies to His plans for us. We may think we are in control of our destinies when in fact God ordains every step before it comes to pass.

God is in control of our lives from the moment of conception. He allowed our mothers to conceive and give birth to us. Even before we loved Him, He loved us and protected us. Even when we lived sinful lives, He never left our side. Even when we rejected Him and wanted nothing to do with Him, He still loved us.

We may not understand or accept God's plans for us, but we can be certain of one thing: His plan is much better than ours! God knows what's best for us better than we know ourselves. We have all said prayers that God didn't answer the way we wanted, but in retrospect, we saw that it was all for our good. His plans always trump ours!

When you don't understand what God is up to, be assured that He is in total control and you will reap the reward in the end. It's okay that God's ways are not our ways and His thoughts are not our thoughts. We can't be on equal footing with God nor should we expect to. God is God, and we are not. That should answer all of our why questions, past, present, and future.

OCTOBER 28

"But who are you O Man to talk back to God? Shall what is formed say to Him who formed it—why did you make me like this?" (Romans 9:20).

In this passage, the Apostle Paul is on his third missionary trip preaching to the Romans. He is irritated with them because they keep asking him non-pertinent questions. The Romans expected God to be accountable to them for His actions. They were full of pride and arrogance and thought they knew better than God. The fact is that God doesn't owe us anything, including explanations.

One of the things that people question God about is the way He made them. There might be things they don't like about themselves, so they ask God why He created them a certain way or gave them an affliction they're not happy about. Maybe they think they are not smart enough or pretty enough. They may even think, "God really messed up when He made me."

Complaining and comparing ourselves to others is, in essence, telling God that we aren't happy with His creation. The prophet Isaiah writes in 64:8, "We are the clay you are the potter; we are all the work of your hand." When a potter spins his wheel to form a pot, no two turn out the same. Each one is beautiful and unique. It is exactly the same when God puts us on His wheel.

Get rid of negative self-talk. Look in the mirror and tell yourself that you are God's masterpiece and that He treasures you. God doesn't make junk. 1 Timothy 4:4 says, "For everything God created is good." You have been beautifully and wonderfully made in God's eyes. Why not thank the Potter for the great job He did and enjoy being the person He made you to be?

OCTOBER 29

"Yet I will rejoice in the Lord. I will be joyful in God my Savior" (Habakkuk 3:18).

It's a challenge to be thankful and rejoice when you're immersed in disappointment. Sometimes it feels near impossible. In the back of our minds, we know that our faith isn't based on feelings or emotions, but it's hard to ignore those natural inclinations. Often, our perception tends to become our reality.

My husband needed to have a whopper of a kidney stone removed a few years back. The first operation was unsuccessful. A second one was scheduled which failed as well. When the third one was scheduled, I wasn't exactly rejoicing. *"But God,"* in His usual fashion, gave me the reminder I needed to hear the next morning during my quiet time. I ran across this Scripture verse in Habakkuk: "Yet I will rejoice in the Lord." Yet—no matter what or in spite of—I will choose to rejoice in the Lord. I went out to the kitchen and wrote the verse on my chalkboard, and every time I felt frustration creeping back in, I read that verse and thanked God for whatever came to mind. Gratitude will always relieve stress and bring peace.

A friend of mine takes this one step further. When she struggles with something, she writes an appropriate Scripture verse on a small piece of paper and puts it in the bottom of her shoe. She calls it standing on the Word of God. Isaiah writes in 7:9, "If you do not stand firm in your faith, you will not stand at all."

Stand firm and rejoice in the Lord for everything in your life. Joy is a choice we make. Choosing joy in the morning when you wake up is a great way to start the day. Say it to yourself as soon as you open your eyes. Today I will choose joy!

OCTOBER 30

"Because it is by faith you stand firm" (1 Corinthians 1:24).

We can feel empty in a number of ways. We can be drained physically, spent emotionally, or dying spiritually. We can even experience all three of these at the same time. They have a common thread, however, and it has to do with our relationship with Jesus. The further we are away from Him the more emptiness will fill our hearts. If we are off-kilter with the Lord, it will trickle down into every aspect of our lives.

Think about it like this. If something is amiss in your car's engine, it most likely will not run right. It will not function well until the problem is fixed. If a lamp loses electricity, it will not be able to give light like it's supposed to. Our spiritual lives work much the same way. If something is not working right in us, our whole physical and emotional being will be affected.

I have felt so empty at times I couldn't even pick up my Bible. I would even get mad at God for the pit of darkness I was in. My faith seemed anything but firm. *"But God."* I would cry out to Him, and He would whisper the following verse in my ear. It's found in 2 Corinthians 1:9, and it says, "This happened that we might not rely on ourselves but God!" He allows us to go through these times of emptiness to draw us closer to Him.

There is nothing more important than our spiritual lives. I repeat; there is nothing else in life that should take precedence over our faith. If this area of our lives isn't healthy, we will continue to struggle with emptiness and never be completely fulfilled. If you can identify with this, it might be God's way of drawing you back to Him. He will completely fill your soul when you turn to Him!

OCTOBER 31

"But each man has his own gift from God; one has this gift and another has that" (1 Corinthians 7:7).

I learned a very long time ago that the deepest satisfaction in life comes from serving God and others. When we make life about ourselves, we end up feeling empty, and everything feels meaningless. In the book of Ecclesiastes, King Solomon writes about the topic of meaningless things. In Chapter 2 he says, "Yet when I surveyed all that my hands had done and what I had toiled to achieve everything was meaningless, a chasing after the wind; nothing was gained under the sun."

We please God when we use the gifts and talents He has given us to serve Him. Some people struggle with knowing what their gift is and where to serve. I have found that it is usually a combination of passion and natural talent. Being passionate about a cause or a ministry is important for discerning where to serve God. I heard a pastor say that you know what your passion is by what moves your heart to tears.

My passion and strength is writing; therefore, I believe it is God's gift to me. This gift He has given me will serve Him by encouraging people to want to grow in their faith. I wrote this devotional with the sole purpose of bringing glory to God. That should be the intent of all of our gifts. They should ultimately be used to bring honor and glory to the King!

NOVEMBER 1

"You have heard that it was said, 'Love your neighbor and hate your enemy.' But I tell you: Love your enemies and pray for those who persecute you" (Matthew 5:43-44).

The teachers of the Law in Jesus' day had never heard teaching like this before. They were used to hearing sermons on Jewish laws, feasts, and rituals. This day, they heard something new. Jesus was preaching on how to live by faith in action. The crowd sat quietly, intrigued by His message.

Loving your enemies was not a topic frequently taught by the Scholars. The Jewish people lived in a culture much like we do today where certain ethnic groups were hated and ostracized. But Jesus spoke very clearly against such behavior. The heart of all of Jesus' teaching was love. Every one of us should receive the same consideration and kindness as the other. Scripture tells us repeatedly that all men are created equal and that He shows no favoritism.

One of the best ways we can love our enemies is to pray for them. It's amazing how prayer can transform our attitudes and opinions about people. It's hard to feel hostile towards someone you are praying for. Jesus knew there would always be evil and hatred in the world. He also knew His faithful followers were going to be persecuted for their faith. He specifically addressed this issue in Matthew 5:11 when He said, "Blessed are you when people insult you, persecute you, and falsely say all kinds of evil against you because of me."

When someone gives you a hard time about your faith, don't get into a debate with them. Just tell them you will pray that God will soften their hearts to the truth. It's actually a compliment when someone challenges your faith because it says that they have noticed something enticingly different about you. They were drawn to your Jesus light because you have something they don't. So, rejoice when you have to defend your faith. You are a light to the world!

NOVEMBER 2

"I wanted to see what was worthwhile for men to do under heaven during the few days of their lives" (Ecclesiastes 2:3).

Time is a precious commodity. We only get so much of it before it is taken away. Scripture says very simply in 1 Corinthians 7:29, "Time is short." Anyone who has children knows this quite well. Babies grow up so fast. It seems like in no time at all they are graduating from high school, and we find ourselves in a very quiet house.

We must always be aware of how we are using this precious gift of time. Are we wise about where we spend it and with whom we are spending it with? Every day that we open our eyes is a gift from God. It is another opportunity to make a difference in God's Kingdom. We don't know how many days God has pre-ordained for us. But whatever the number He expects us to use what He has given us wisely.

Procrastination is a ploy of Satan's preventing us from making good use of our time. We have great intentions to get involved and make a difference in the world, but we never get around to doing anything about it. We use the excuse that we'll do it tomorrow. But what if tomorrow never comes? What if we never get around to what's truly important in our lives? In hindsight, we never want to discover that we squandered the time God gave us on this earth.

NOVEMBER 3

"Unless the Lord builds the house, its builder's labor in vain" (Psalm 127:1).

Jesus is often referred to in Scripture as our firm Foundation. 1 Corinthians 3:11 says, "For no one can lay any foundation other than the one already laid which is Jesus Christ." If a house isn't built on solid ground, it stands a great chance of collapsing. The California coastline is a perfect example. Those homes were constructed on unstable ground, and many have slipped down into the ocean. There is only one foundation that is safe when building a home—one built on the solid ground of Jesus as the cornerstone.

The cornerstone is vital when constructing a building. The cornerstone is the starting point in the construction process and is often inscribed with a significant name or date. It is the first stone that is laid in place. Jesus is referred to as the Cornerstone in Scripture, because, just as buildings depend on their cornerstone to stand soundly, we need our spiritual Cornerstone to lay a solid foundation.

How do we build our homes—our lives—on Jesus? Paul writes in Ephesians 3:17, "And I pray that Christ will be more and more at home in your hearts as you trust in Him." Is Jesus at home in your heart? Have you invited Him to come in and live there? That is the starting point for building our lives on Christ our firm foundation. He will live in any heart that welcomes Him.

Leaving God out of your home and out of your life will weaken your family's spiritual foundation. In 1834, a pastor named Edward Mote wrote a Christian hymn containing these famous lyrics: "On Christ the Solid Rock I stand, all other ground is sinking sand."[5] Build your lives on Jesus, and you will always have a solid rock to stand on.

---

5   Edward Mote, *My Hope is Built on Nothing Less* (hymn, 1834), public domain

NOVEMBER 4

"Nevertheless, each one should retain the place in life that the Lord assigned to him and to which God has called him" (1 Corinthians 7:17).

As Christians, we are to live confidently for the Lord in whatever circumstance or station God has placed us. In other words, wherever we find ourselves right now is exactly where God wants us to be. This may not sound very encouraging for some who currently find themselves in a difficult or painful place. *"But God"* has put us where we are as part of His grand plan and purpose for us.

We don't always like the cards we've been dealt, but we can learn how to play them and win! Like a flower that grows through a crack in the concrete, sometimes we have to make the best of our situation and bloom where we've been planted. You may not realize it at the moment, but wherever God has you right now, you can be sure that vital life lessons are in process.

We always have choices in life. We can either choose to whine and complain about where God has us, or we can look at it as a teachable moment. We can ask God to show us more of what He wants us to learn exactly where we are. Also, we can focus on others, which will help get our minds off our own situation.

Learn to bloom wherever you are planted. You can't always change your circumstances, but you can always change your perspective. Look at all of life as a God-given opportunity to grow your faith and to positively influence others. Every obstacle opens the door to growing us closer to God and to practicing our gratitude skills. We can always find something we can thank Him for!

NOVEMBER 5

"For the Lord gives wisdom and from His mouth come knowledge and understanding" (Proverbs 2:6).

My friend was looking for a new job. She was changing career paths and, with no experience behind her, was having a difficult time breaking into the business world. Everyone offered their advice and opinions about what she should do and how she should do it. But this just caused her more stress and confusion.

Everyone meant well, but no one really knew what was best for this young woman and her future. *"But God"* always knows what's best for us. He knows our every desire and need. He is the only who can give us the right guidance and direction. He is the only one we should be listening to for advice.

The Bible says that wisdom is a gift and must be diligently sought after. We are told to simply ask God for this gift, listen to what He has to say and then act on it. No advice or direction is more valuable than God's. Don't turn to others when you have a big decision to make. People don't possess the knowledge that God does, and they can easily mislead you. The only one who really has your best interests at heart is God. Trust in Him for your future. He will lead the way if you ask Him.

NOVEMBER 6

"And a voice from heaven said, 'This is my Son whom I love; with Him, I am well pleased'" (Matthew 3:17).

Jesus needed affirmation just as we do. He was perfect, yet He was a man and had the same human needs that we have. He needed to be reassured from His Father that He was doing a good job and fulfilling the mission He was given.

The Father was well pleased with His Son because Jesus did exactly what the Father told Him to do. He was obedient in every way and looked only to glorify His Father in everything He did. The cross was the ultimate act of honoring Him. Jesus' death and resurrection fulfilled God's plan and purpose for His Son.

We all yearn to hear that God is well pleased with us. He most likely won't open up the sky and speak audibly to us as He did with Jesus. He speaks to us in more quiet ways through His Word. If someone comments that they don't hear from God, ask them if they read their Bible. It is the only book we can read where the author is right there with us.

The lesson we can take away from this is that obedience is what pleases God. It's easy to hang plaques on our walls with Scripture verses elaborately painted. But do we put them into practice? Do we follow God's instructions and commands? In the book of Exodus, we will find the Ten Commandments listed. These are not merely suggestions for how we are to live our lives. We are called by God to obey them. If we are truly committed in our faith and following His commands, we can rest in knowing that God is well pleased with us.

NOVEMBER 7

"There is but One God, the Father, from whom all things came and for whom we live" (1 Corinthians 8:6).

We live in a polytheistic world today. People acknowledge and worship many gods. Some don't even have names. They are just referred to as higher powers. Some are not people or powers at all, but things created by man that have been labeled as some sort of spiritual deity.

The Bible states that there is only One True God and He is the Creator of everything and everyone. This One True God not only created all of life, but He sustains and governs it as well. So why believe what the Bible says? Not only has it been proven historically, physically, and archaeologically, it makes one claim that no other religion can. The God of the Bible gave us His Son who died and rose to life again. No other god in history can make that claim.

There was a man named Jesus who walked the earth over two thousand years ago. He called Himself the Savior of the world—the Messiah—and the only path to eternal life. He not only preached this message, but He proved it by dying on a cross and then rising again three days later. There were hundreds of eyewitnesses. Many people touched Him, talked to Him, ate with Him, and walked with Him. These events were all well-documented and recorded in what is the greatest selling book of all time.

The Bible is not mere speculation. It contains facts that cannot be disputed, prophecies that cannot be denied, historical relics that have been documented and verified. What other religion—what other God—can make such claims? Jesus said in John 3:16, "Whoever believes in Him shall not perish but have eternal life." Open your heart to the One True God, and you will live eternally with Him in heaven!

NOVEMBER 8

"Many women were there watching from a distance. They had followed Jesus from Galilea to care for His needs" (Matthew 27:55).

Women were a very big part of Jesus' life and ministry. Many women followed Jesus during His time on earth. There were four women at His crucifixion. It was women who checked and attended to the tomb every day. It was on the third day after Jesus' death that a woman by the name of Mary Magdalene had the awesome privilege of seeing the Resurrected Jesus for the first time. Jesus didn't choose one of His beloved Apostles to appear to as soon as He rose, but a woman who simply loved Him with all her heart.

Each time Jesus chose a woman for a task or ministry, I believe He was sending a message. The culture back in Jesus' day was not very reverential towards women. They were considered inferior to men and not held in high regard. They were segregated from the men in the Temple and most other public events. They weren't permitted to be schooled, and they were not allowed to hold any office. Basically, women's roles revolved around domestic duties and raising children.

Jesus, however, respected and honored women as much as He did men. He played no favorites. He had no biases. God chose ordinary women to do His work just like He chose ordinary men. Jesus loves us all equally and unconditionally regardless of gender.

NOVEMBER 9

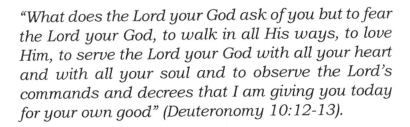

"What does the Lord your God ask of you but to fear the Lord your God, to walk in all His ways, to love Him, to serve the Lord your God with all your heart and with all your soul and to observe the Lord's commands and decrees that I am giving you today for your own good" (Deuteronomy 10:12-13).

Moses is giving instructions to the Israelites in this passage. He is telling the people what God expects from them. We can easily see that these commands would apply to us today as well. This is a great example of the beauty of Scripture. It is applicable regardless of the time it was written. God's Word is the same yesterday, today and forever. It is a solid truth that never varies or changes.

God expects believers to act according to what's written in His Word. He tells us that we must revere Him always, live by the standards He has set for us, love Him unconditionally as He loves us, serve Him wholeheartedly, and follow all His commands. Scripture tells us that if we claim that Jesus is our Lord and Savior, we must adhere to His expectations.

"But God." Thankfully we don't have to try to follow God's instructions all on our own. God gave us a helper—the Holy Spirit—to encourage us and keep us on the right path. God wants only good for us. He wants us to have lives full of love and joy and peace. We can have all these things if we walk faithfully and obediently to what He calls us to do.

NOVEMBER 10

"The Lord has sworn and will not change His mind"
(Hebrews 7:21).

Can prayer sway the mind of God? Should this be our motive when we pray? It sounds a bit manipulative, don't you think? The purpose of prayer is not to change God's mind but to lay our burdens at His feet and free ourselves from worry. Our prayers are meant to draw us closer to God, lean into Him, and trust in Him more completely.

Scripture tells us that God doesn't change His mind, but it does say that He relents at times. Psalm 106:44-45 says, "But He took note of their distress when He heard their cry; for their sake, He remembered His covenant, and out of His great love He relented." God relented from completely destroying the Israelites in the desert. He relented from destroying all of Sodom and Gomorrah and saved Lot and his family. God has the authority to pass judgment and relent according to His will. He is sovereign, and so are His responses to our prayers.

God's answers to our prayers will never come accompanied by detailed explanations. Who of us can fathom the mind of God? How do we know what is ultimately best for us? As Job wrestled with God over the devastating conditions of his life, his friend Zophar asked him, "Job, can you fathom the mysteries of God? Can you probe the limits of the Almighty?"

The mind of God is a mystery none of us will ever understand. But we can always rest in the fact that God's mind is always in tune with what is the absolute best for us. And that's all we really need to be concerned about.

NOVEMBER 11

"Impress these commands upon your children. Talk about them when you sit at home and when you walk along the road, when you lie down and when you get up" (Deuteronomy 6:7).

I was driving to the mall on a sweltering hot day with my five-year-old granddaughter in the back seat. As I entered the parking lot, I prayed out loud, "Oh Lord, wouldn't it be such a blessing if you could find us a nice shady spot to park in." No sooner had I finished my little prayer when I spotted a place right under a sprawling shade tree. I turned around to my precious girl in the back seat and said, "Look, sweetie, God found us the perfect spot." And then I added a big, "Thank you, Jesus!"

When we got out of the car, I continued sowing seeds of faith into her by making this incident an example of how much God loves us. I told her what a great God we have and how He takes such great care of us. I told her how He hears our every prayer—even the short ones that just pop up in our heads at the time.

Our little ones are sponges. They soak up everything we say and are watching everything we do. Look for ways to bring attention to God in front of your kids. Use examples from daily life to show off God's goodness. If you let your love for Jesus live out loud, it's highly probable your kids will too.

NOVEMBER 12

"We know that we are children of God and that the whole world is under the control of the evil one. We know also that the Son of God has come and has given us understanding so that we may know Him who is true" (1 John 5:19-20).

When atrocities are taking place around the world, it's easy to yearn for Jesus' return so He can put a stop to all the madness. It seems violence is escalating every day and we are helpless to do anything about it. To say we live in scary times is a huge understatement.

Some people wonder where God is in all this suffering. How can a good God allow such evil to go on? First, we must realize that God is not the source or the cause of all the horrible, wicked things that go on in our world. Scripture tells us that God is a good God and a good God couldn't possibly be responsible for inflicting such evil. Scripture also tells us that the world temporarily belongs to Satan and is subject to his power. Satan is the one we can blame for causing such mayhem.

"But God" ... will have the final victory when Jesus comes back to avenge all the wrongs and cast out all evil. Satan may be having a field day now, but his time is coming when he will be thrown into the lake of fire forever. And peace will finally rule and reign on the earth through all eternity. Alleluia!

NOVEMBER 13

"Then Nathanael declared, 'Rabbi, you are the Son of God; you are the King of Israel'" (John 1:49).

Nathanael was a skeptic—a tire kicker. This Apostle needed to test things out first before he made a commitment. He was the fifth Apostle Jesus called to follow Him. It was Philip who quickly ran to Nathanael and told him, "We have found the One Moses wrote about in the Law and about whom the prophets also wrote—Jesus of Nazareth, the son of Joseph" (John 1:45). Nathanael scoffed at Philip and replied, "Nothing good ever comes out of Nazareth." And then Philip did the best thing anyone can do with a tire kicker. He extended an invitation to come and meet Jesus.

Philip knew that if he could just expose his friend to Jesus that he would believe. And that is exactly what happened. He took Nathanael to meet Jesus, and the rest is history. Nathanael walked away from this encounter proclaiming that this Jesus was indeed the Messiah that was prophesied about by the Old Testament prophets.

This event highlights the importance of evangelism. Everyone knows an unbeliever who just doesn't buy into the whole Jesus thing. But have we personally taken the time to introduce them to Jesus? We could invite them over for coffee and share what God's done in our lives. We could invite them to church or maybe even a Bible study.

We can't make believers out of skeptics if we are not willing to invite them into our lives. Philip and Nathanael were friends first before Philip brought him to Jesus. Do you have any Nathanaels in your life that need to be introduced to the Messiah? We can all be like Philip if we truly care about others' salvation!

NOVEMBER 14

"He must become greater; I must become less" (John 3:30).

These words were spoken by John the Baptist as he was explaining to the people his subordinate position to Jesus. Some tried to put Jesus and John on equal ground, but John consistently proclaimed that Jesus was God's only Son and the only way to eternal life. He told the crowd that Jesus was far greater than he.

The life application from this verse can be summed up in four little words—it's not about me! Our selfish natures tend to make us lean in that direction. We want what we want when we want it. And make it quick while you're at it!

It takes a concerted effort to put others before ourselves. We all want to be happy, have good relationships, and make an impact on the world. But these goals can only be accomplished by applying the four little words mentioned above. We can't be number one and expect to live God-pleasing lives. Focusing our attention outward instead of within is key for Jesus to become greater in our lives while we become less.

John the Baptist knew his place. His job was to prepare the way for the man who was going to save the world. This was John's legacy. His focus was on Jesus and not himself. What will your legacy be? Those four little words will help you in creating yours.

NOVEMBER 15

"When a Samaritan woman came to draw water Jesus said to her, 'Will you give me a drink?' The Samaritan woman said to Him, 'You are a Jew and I am a Samaritan woman. How can you ask me for a drink?'" (John 4:7-9).

Jesus was a rebel. He stepped out of the boundaries of Jewish customs and laws so that He could help people. The story of the Samaritan woman is a great example of this. Jesus didn't care that Jews didn't associate with Samaritans. He wasn't concerned with edicts and regulations. People were always His main focus.

Jesus struck up a conversation with a Samaritan woman (talking with them was also not permitted in the Jewish culture) that in the end led her to believe that Jesus was the true Messiah. She was so excited that she ran back to town to tell everyone. John writes later in verse 49, "Many of the Samaritans from that town believed in Him because of the woman's testimony."

Because Jesus put more emphasis on relationships than He did laws, an entire town was saved. Jesus also performed miracles on the Sabbath, which was strictly forbidden. How many people would still have been blind or lame if Jesus' hadn't broken the rules? There are no boundaries where ministry is concerned.

There are lots of Samaritans in our world today. Do we steer clear of them or do we break down social boundaries and go after them? It takes great boldness and courage to be a renegade. Why not be a rebel like Jesus and go for it?

NOVEMBER 16

"If you hold to my teaching, you are really my disciples. Then you will know the truth and the truth will set you free" (John 8:31-32).

The Apostle John records more of Jesus' teachings than any of the other Gospel writers. John walked and talked with Jesus for three years and heard every sermon He ever preached. He told others who Jesus was, what He came to do, and why He came to do it.

In this passage, Jesus is teaching about freedom—the kind of freedom that comes from abandoning your old life of sin and accepting a new life rooted in Jesus. Second Corinthians 3:17 says, "Now the Lord is Spirit, and where the Spirit of the Lord is there is freedom."

Today people crave freedom from the burdens of this life, but they look in all the wrong places to get relief. They mistakenly think that other people can provide the things that only Jesus can. When we were created, we were made to walk in the freedom that Jesus came to give us. Only Jesus can help us abandon our lives as slaves and live our lives completely free.

Do you feel like you need to be set free from some unhealthy choices or hurtful people in your life? Or maybe thoughts that are chaining you to your past? Jesus doesn't want you to carry those burdens around anymore. He wants you to let go of the ties that bind you. You will never be bound again once Jesus sets you free. You will walk in total freedom for the rest of your life. Jesus said, "He whom the Son sets free is free indeed!" (John 8:36).

NOVEMBER 17

"Be careful not to do your acts of righteousness before men to be seen by them. If you do, you will have no reward from your Father in heaven" (Matthew 6:1).

I used to make and donate blankets to the Cancer Center of our local Children's Hospital. I would tie Scripture verses to every single one and pray for each child as I made them. God had clearly given me this ministry a few years ago, and I embraced it wholeheartedly. As time went by, however, I became discouraged. I realized that when I went to drop off the blankets, the nurses didn't even know my name. I simply handed them over, and they said thank you. I felt unappreciated, and I began to question my commitment.

So, I prayed and asked God to either encourage me or close the door on the ministry. *"But God."* The next time I took the blankets in, they asked me my name and my phone number. I left feeling a little more encouraged. Then two days later, I got a phone call from a public relations person who told me that a local news channel wanted to do a story on my blankets. They aired a segment once a week called "Angels in Our Midst," and they were interested in my story.

While I was excited that God had answered my prayer with such a wonderful affirmation, I knew what I had to do. The verse about letting your giving be done in secret was running through my head like a ticker tape. I politely declined the offer, explaining that the Bible tells us that our giving should be done anonymously. She understood, and that was the end of it.

I got more joy out of being obedient to God's Word than I ever would have sitting in front of a TV camera holding a blanket. God had taught me that even if no one else noticed my hard work, God did and that's all that counted. God let me see that I was making a difference for His Kingdom. Don't worry about your good deeds being acknowledged by others. God sees them, and that's all that matters.

NOVEMBER 18

"If any one of you is without sin, let him be the first to throw a stone at her" (John 8:7).

The Pharisees were always doing their best to trap Jesus by accusing Him of disregarding the Law. One day, the Jewish leaders brought a prostitute to Him and challenged Him to stone her to death in accordance with the Law. Jesus challenged them right back by saying, "All right, go ahead and stone her. But let those who have never sinned throw the first stone!"

We are so quick to point out the sins of others without ever looking in a mirror. Are any of us without sin? Then who are we to condemn others? Jesus didn't condone the woman's sin by saving her from death. He forgave her and told her to go and sin no more. We are always to love the sinner but hate the sin.

Just as Jesus challenged the Teachers of the Law, He challenges us. He also confronts us when we judge others instead of offering grace and forgiveness. He wanted the Pharisees to understand that love and forgiveness were more important than following the rules. Lives are what matters—not laws.

God never wastes a teachable moment. Those moments may not be pleasant, much like the prostitute's experience. In the end, however, she walked away with a clear understanding of grace and mercy and a clean slate. If you feel like pointing a finger at someone, just know that God may turn that finger right back around and shine the spotlight on you!

NOVEMBER 19

"Blessed are those who have learned to acclaim you, who walk in the light of your presence O Lord" (Psalm 89:15).

Happy are those who acknowledge God and walk in the Light of Jesus. This is where we find true meaning and happiness in life. We will never find contentment within ourselves. We must look outside of ourselves to feel fulfilled on the inside.

Jesus taught in Mark 8:36, "What good is it for a man to gain the whole world yet forfeit his soul?" What good does it do to acquire things and achieve success if we're not truly happy? We are gaining the world and losing our souls.

God has given us the freedom of choice. He allows us to pick and choose who or what we will follow and who or what we will devote our lives to. He lets us be the one in charge. Our choices are our own, not God's. We can't blame Him for the unhappy consequences that occur because of the poor decisions we made.

Life itself doesn't give us meaning and purpose. God is the only one who can do these things. The Bible teaches us very clearly how to give meaning to our lives. It tells us to let go of the world, grab hold of Jesus, and walk with Him hand in hand through life. Then, and only then, can we expect to experience real happiness and fulfillment in our lives.

NOVEMBER 20

"When Jesus saw her weeping and the Jews who had come along with her also weeping, He was deeply moved in spirit and troubled...Jesus wept" (John 11:33, 35).

Jesus' dear friend Lazarus had just died and had been in the tomb for three days. His sisters Mary and Martha were standing outside the tomb overcome with grief when Jesus walked up to them. He looked upon them with His loving eyes and tender heart, and He began to weep right along with them. Their pain and loss became His pain and loss. His love for His friend and compassion for the sisters was overwhelming, and he reacted as any person would.

Many look upon Jesus as an emotionless God. But they forget that Jesus was also a man and experienced everything from a human perspective. He knew pain like we know pain. He felt sorrow like we feel sorrow. He felt frustration and anger the same as we do. When we suffer, He suffers right along with us. He is in tune with our every emotion.

Because Christ lives in us, He feels what we feel and knows exactly what we need at any given time. He becomes our strength when we are weak and our hope when ours is slipping away. He gives faith to the faithless and comfort to the hurting heart. Christ will hold our tissues when the grief overcomes us, and He will rejoice with us as we celebrate our blessings. God is involved in every aspect of our lives. That is something for which we should all rejoice and be grateful!

NOVEMBER 21

"He came to Simon Peter, who said to Him, 'Lord, are you going to wash my feet?' Jesus replied, 'You do not realize now what I'm doing, but later on you will understand.' 'No,' said Peter, 'You shall never wash my feet.' Jesus answered, 'Unless I wash you, you have no part with me'" (John 13:6-8).

The Apostle Peter was one of the most outspoken of the disciples, which sometimes was unfortunate for him. At the Last Supper, he told Jesus that he would not allow Him to wash his feet. Can you even imagine the scene? Peter arguing with Jesus. I bet you could hear a pin drop in the room.

This conversation could be interpreted as Peter acting undeserving of such a humble act of service by his Master. But in keeping with his personality, he was most likely challenging Jesus. This was not Peter's first attempt at disputing Jesus' plans. When he was told about the impending crucifixion, Peter confronted Jesus and said, "Never Lord, this shall never happen to you!"

Peter's heart was always in the right place, but sometimes his tongue and his actions got in the way of his faith and convictions. How often do we act like Peter? We get caught up in our pride and think we know better than God and try to tell Him how things should be. We don't want to do it His way.

We all fall on our faces at times. *"But God."* He is always there to pick us back up and extend forgiveness. Peter's actions didn't interfere with God's plan for Him. In Matthew 16:18, Jesus says, "And I tell you that you are Peter and on this rock, I will build my church." We are all flawed, but God's purpose will always prevail, even when we try to tell Him our way just might be better.

NOVEMBER 22

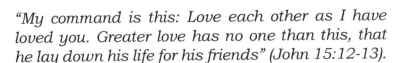

"My command is this: Love each other as I have loved you. Greater love has no one than this, that he lay down his life for his friends" (John 15:12-13).

We can't love others as God loves us without His help. His love is perfect, unconditional, and full of grace and mercy. God's love for us is so great that He willingly laid down His life for us so that we can spend eternity with Him. He was willing to die so we might live. What greater love could there ever be?

Could we put our lives on the line like that? Could we sacrifice our lives for anyone as Christ did? Could we submit to the same pain and suffering that He endured? That depth of love seems unfathomable, doesn't it? Yet, this is the kind of love that we are told to have for others.

We are incapable of this kind of love on our own. The only way we can love like Jesus is to pray and ask God to love others through us. We must ask the Holy Spirit to be the conduit that takes Jesus' love and channels it into others. Jesus loves us no matter what, and so we should extend that same grace to others. God's love is not predicated on performance. It is unconditional.

These three words, "no matter what," are crucial for loving others. We must love *no matter what*, forgive *no matter what*, and accept *no matter what*. There are no *ifs* or *whens* or *buts* in love. Our capacity to love others will always fall short. God's love is perfect and ready to be poured out on all of us. We were created to be vessels of love for the glory of God!

NOVEMBER 23

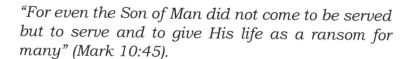

"For even the Son of Man did not come to be served but to serve and to give His life as a ransom for many" (Mark 10:45).

I was talking to a friend one day about serving and asked her if she was involved in any outreach or volunteer programs. I was excited to share with her how I was trying to put the gifts God gave me to good use to serve in His Kingdom. Her response not only surprised me, but it made me wonder if other people shared her same sentiments.

She told me that serving just wasn't her thing, and she had no time for it. I suggested ideas that could be a good fit for her. I said that often God uses our trials to open up doors to help others. I reminded her that she had gone through a significantly painful time in her life that she could definitely use to comfort and encourage others.

Still failing to convince her, I finally reverted to scripture (duh!) and told her that according to God's Word, serving was not optional. Jesus' whole ministry was based on serving. His sole purpose, while He walked the earth, was to serve others.

Maybe you can use a difficult time in your life to help others. God never wastes any of our experiences. He desires for us to find ways to serve Him and bring Him glory through them. Is serving the Lord a priority in your life or are you still waiting for that perfect opportunity to come along? This is not a time for waiting patiently but action!

NOVEMBER 24

"The angels came to present themselves before the Lord, and Satan also came with them" (Job 1:4).

When I first read this verse, a confusing thought came to my mind. Why are the angels announcing Satan's arrival? Why would God send His messengers to do such a thing?

I decided I needed to find the answer to my question. The first thing I did was pray and ask the Holy Spirit to give me clarity. Then I employed the tools I use for studying Scripture. I began by looking at the cross-references in the margins. Then I read the study notes at the bottom of the page (a good study Bible is essential for the serious student). From there I would look up the word *angel* in my concordance to see if any additional verses pertain to the subject.

By digging further into the passage, I answered my question as well as learned some other truths. I discovered in 2 Corinthians 11:14 that, "Satan himself masquerades as an angel of light." That made me think that if Satan could imitate angels, then he must have his own band of masquerading helpers.

God's angels couldn't have announced Satan's arrival because the verse didn't read they were angels "of the Lord" which is how they are usually referenced in Scripture. Also, how could holy beings ever be associated with Satan? Holiness cannot abide with evil.

The lesson to be learned here is not about angels. The lesson is for us not to gloss over something that doesn't make sense when you're reading God's Word. Pause and take the time to do the research and educate yourself. With the help of the Holy Spirit and a good study Bible such as the Life Application Study Bible or the New Living Translation, you will open up a whole new level of understanding of Scripture.

NOVEMBER 25

"But if we hope for what we do not yet have we wait for it patiently" (Romans 8:25).

God's timing is a mystery. Sometimes He may answer a prayer relatively quickly, and sometimes it may take months or even years. Regardless of how long it takes, Paul tells us we must wait patiently.

In Acts chapter 12, there are many examples of how God's timing is perfect. We find the Apostle Peter confined in a Roman prison hoping and praying for divine intervention. His fellow disciple James (John's brother) had just been killed by the sword, and so Peter knew he may be facing the same fate. His trial was coming up soon and time was running out.

"But God." The night before his trial God sent an angel to free him and take him out of the city. At the last minute, hours before his probable execution, God stepped in and rescued him. A last-minute answer to prayer, but an answer nonetheless! We will never understand God's timing, but He doesn't expect us to. He just wants to see if we will remain hopeful while waiting.

God always has a plan and a purpose for everything we go through. God may have wanted Peter in that prison to share the Good News with his fellow prisoners and guards. Who knows how many people may have been brought to faith in Christ because of God's delaying Peter's freedom.

NOVEMBER 26

"He is the Lord; let Him do what is good in His eyes"
(1 Samuel 3:18).

Eli was a judge and a high priest in Israel. He had two sons who were wicked and evil. They blasphemed God and cared nothing about the consequences of their sins. God called them contemptible, and He planned to put them both to death on the same day.

Upon hearing God's plan, Eli's response was much like Job's responding to all of his suffering by saying, "Shall we accept good from God and not trouble?" (Job 2:10). Eli said something very similar. He responded, "He is God; let Him do what is good in His eyes."

We must understand that there are consequences to our behavior. God will never let sin go unpunished. He tests our faith by how we respond to our trials. Will we have the mindset of Job and Eli? Will we maintain the attitude that God is good all the time and that everything He does is for a greater purpose? Our response to God's actions reveals what's in our hearts and minds.

How will you respond the next time you face a trial or difficult circumstance? Will you respond like Eli and Job? Remember, God is good all the time no matter what! You can count on it.

NOVEMBER 27

"However, each one of you also must love his wife as he loves himself and the wife must respect her husband" (Ephesians 5:33).

Many psychologists will tell you that respect is the number one need for men. Because of the way God wired them, they need to be held in high esteem and affirmed for who they are and all they do. Just like our relationship with our Heavenly Father, we want to honor our husbands for what they mean to us and not just for the things they give us. We should always affirm the person instead of the action.

Here is a skill I try to put into practice with my husband. It's called the 80/20 plan. In marriage, we tend to focus on the 20% that's wrong with our marriages instead of the 80% that's right. We tend to give more credence to the minority rather than the majority. Instead of finding things to be thankful for in our husbands, we are stuck in the 20% by finding fault and getting caught up in the small stuff.

Showing respect for our husbands is also exhibited by asking for their opinion. This makes them feel extremely valued and intelligent. They will see that we really do care about what they think and have to say.

When you find yourself caught up in a disagreement with your spouse, think 80/20. Look for the good and steer away from anything else. There is something good in every situation if we take a minute to look for it. Wives, make it a point every day to say something uplifting and respectful to your husband, and watch how doing something this small will transform your marriage.

NOVEMBER 28

"God is not a man that He should lie; nor a Son of Man that He should change His mind. Does He speak and then not act? Does He promise and not fulfill?" (Numbers 23:19).

God appointed Saul as the first King over Israel. Samuel anointed him as leader, and the Spirit of the Lord came upon him in power. However, Saul disobeyed God and soon found himself out of favor with Him. 1 Samuel 15:11 says, "I am grieved that I have made Saul king because he has turned away from me and has not carried out my instructions."

Did God make a mistake choosing Saul as king? Did He change His mind about His choice after Saul sinned and turned away from Him? Scripture tells us that God doesn't make mistakes or change His mind. Nothing man does or doesn't can thwart the divine plans of the Father.

God gave everyone free will. Adam and Eve exercised theirs in the Garden of Eden and ate from the forbidden tree. Moses demonstrated his when he murdered an Egyptian. David gave into his own will and committed adultery with Bathsheba. God gives us free rein to make our own choices, good or bad, and then face the consequences.

What God promises, He fulfills. What He has spoken in His word can be counted on and trusted in. God never changes, but He gives us that option if we choose it. We have the opportunity to change our lives for the better at any time. However, real change is only possible through Jesus.

Do you need to see a change in your life? All you have to do is call on Jesus, and you are well on your way!

NOVEMBER 29

"Whoever believes in the Son has eternal life but whoever rejects the Son will not see life for God's wrath remains on him" (John 3:36).

In this chapter of John, Jesus is talking to Nicodemus about the Son of God who was sent from heaven to save us and give us eternal life. John the Baptist also foretold that Jesus was the Son of God sent to give us eternal life.

Eternal life does not just refer to the future. It isn't just referring to the life we will have in heaven one day. John uses the word "has" in this verse, which indicates the present tense. He is saying that once we receive Jesus into our hearts, we will live experiencing eternal life with Him from that point on. We will be joined with Him as one, communicate with one another, and bask in the light of His presence. The joy we will experience with God in eternity we can also have here on earth with His Son. We can enjoy the same intimate relationship with Him now as when we arrive at our final home.

What great news! We don't have to wait to enjoy God's presence. His presence is here with us now. Eternal life began at the moment we said "I do" to Jesus. It's no wonder all the angels are constantly singing God's praises in heaven. They are celebrating eternity just like we should!

NOVEMBER 30

"So, David triumphed over the Philistine with a sling and a stone; without a sword in his hand he struck down the Philistine and killed him" (1 Samuel 17:50).

The Philistine in this passage is the giant Goliath who wanted a faceoff with David. Goliath stood over nine feet tall and was covered in full body armor when he went out to meet a lone, unclad David. Goliath also sent a shield bearer ahead of him just for safe keeping. Goliath couldn't have been more prepared or protected.

Then there was David, who was lacking in stature but certainly not in courage. David had faith in God that could move mountains. He felt confident that he could kill the giant with just his faith and a slingshot. David shouted to Goliath, "You come to me with sword, spear, and javelin, but I come to you in the name of the Lord Almighty—the God of the armies of Israel whom you have defied" (1 Samuel 17:45). David wanted to make the point that weapons don't bring victories—faith in God does!

"But God" went before David into the battle and enabled him to slay the giant with just one stone and one perfect shot from a small slingshot. David trusted God, even though everyone else didn't think He stood a chance against such a towering menace. David's actions constituted the meaning of the word faith as found in Hebrews 11:1: "Faith is being sure of what we hope for and certain of what we do not see."

Is there a giant you need to slay in your life? Have you asked God to go ahead of you into the battle? He wants you to enlist His help in the war. Victory will be yours if you trust Him for what you do not see and for what you are hoping for.

DECEMBER 1

"He who walks with the wise grows wise; but a companion of fools suffers harm" (Proverbs 13:20).

Paul writes in the book of Titus about the importance of training up those under us. He encourages us to guide those less mature in their faith and to teach them how to live confidently trusting in God. King Solomon echoes Paul in this Proverb about living among the wise.

A young college student in my Bible study class invited me to coffee one day. At first, I thought it strange that this young girl would want to spend time with a grandma! Then I remembered Paul's words about training up the young. So, I responded yes, and off we went.

As the conversation flowed during our time together, I realized that I was the one who was being ministered to. Her amazing testimony touched me to the core and opened my eyes to the wisdom someone so young could possess. I then realized that mentoring could go both ways. The young could absolutely give new insights and revelation to the mature.

When we choose to spend time with those who have the right focus and lead God-pleasing lives, we are following some wise advice. When we are the companion of fools, we will suffer harm. Pick your company wisely, as your character will reflect the character of your closest friends.

DECEMBER 2

"A cheerful heart is good medicine, but a crushed spirit dries up the bones" (Proverbs 17:22).

I have an uncle who was blessed with a naturally witty personality. He has a keen sense of humor and is usually great entertainment whenever he's around. He can always make me laugh with all of his jokes and stories.

When he became a widower, he struggled on his own. He was getting up in years and his two daughters worried about him, so they convinced him to move to an assisted living home. He wasn't very happy about it because he was of the opinion that retirement homes were only for old people. He had just turned 85!

When I visited him after he moved, I was so happy to see how well he was interacting with the other residents. His funny quips and infectious laugh drew people to him like a magnet. He made them laugh and they, in turn, brightened his day. The scene reminded me of the Scripture verse Proverbs 19, "A cheerful heart is good medicine."

It dawned on me later that God had a purpose for my uncle in that place. His fun personality was just the right pick-me-up his fellow geriatric friends needed. He brought great joy to all who came in contact with him. My comical uncle served as a wonderful example of two great spiritual truths: we can absolutely bloom where we are planted, and we are never too old to be used by God!

DECEMBER 3

"The wrath of God is being revealed from heaven against all the godlessness and wickedness of men who suppress the truth by their wickedness" (Romans 1:18).

God's wrath is not a popular subject. Maybe it's avoided because some people think that God is only sweetness and light and couldn't possibly judge or condemn anyone. Some may think of God's wrath as happening only at the end of time. While His judgment will take place one day in the future, Paul tells us in this verse that God's wrath also is taking place now. God has already poured out His wrath on those who have done evil and turned their backs on Him. A perfect God will never tolerate sin and wickedness now or ever.

The world's rejection of God today has brought His wrath upon the entire world. It is happening all around us as hatred and intolerance abound. God's children are killing each other and living life without any boundaries or morals. Unthinkable suffering is happening all around the globe.

God is allowing us to reap what we've sown. He is allowing us to experience the consequences of the evil we've exploited in our world. We have ignored Him and turned to false idols. We have totally ignored the First Commandment which tells us to worship the One and Only True God and put nothing or no one else before Him. His Word says He will tolerate nothing less.

God's wrath is real, and it's now. We may not be able to save the world from destroying itself, but we can make sure our lives are in proper alignment. And, as God's Word commands, we can pray without ceasing. We can pray for our country. We can pray for the whole world to repent and turn back to God. Jesus tells us in Matthew

10:32, "But whoever disowns me before men I will disown him before my Father in heaven." We must embrace Jesus now if we want to be acknowledged in the end by our Father in heaven.

DECEMBER 4

"Shall we accept good from God and not trouble?"
(Job 2:1).

Have you ever had a time in your life when you thought, "I hate my life?" Be honest. I have had several of those moments. What bothered me the most about them was that I felt as if I was insulting God just by having those thoughts. After all, He created me and gave me a wonderful life, and for me to say I hated it must bring Him great disappointment.

I had one of those episodes just recently. I was suffering from chronic pain and wasn't able to do much but lie around. All the things I loved to do I couldn't, and I was not a happy camper, to say the least. As I cried out to God one morning, this is what I heard Him whisper to me ever so gently: "Beloved, it's ok. I understand your frustration. Having these feelings doesn't hurt me because I know your heart, and I know you really don't mean it. In fact, I know that you love your life but just not where you are right now. I get it. I want you to think about my friend Job, and maybe it will encourage you. He persevered through horrible pain and loss because he loved and trusted me. You can choose to do the same. Always remember that nothing you say or do could ever make me walk away from you or love you any less!"

After a week of crying about my poor life a family member appeared and told me to get up and put my shoes on because we were going for a walk. Whoa, what? Didn't they know I was in horrible pain and couldn't possibly take a spin around the block?

"But God." As I started walking a strange thing started to happen. I began to feel better. So, every day from then on, I made it a point to get out for a walk. God knew exactly what I needed. Are you trusting God to take care

of your struggles and get you back on your feet? If you want to see improvement, you have to be willing to get up, put your shoes on and take that spin around the block!

DECEMBER 5

"We are therefore Christ's ambassadors as though God were making His appeal through us" (2 Corinthians 5:20).

God chose each one of us to be ambassadors for Christ while here on earth. An ambassador is a representative of something or someone. We are called to live our lives in such a way as to represent God and the gospel message. Political ambassadors represent their country and serve it with the utmost dedication. Christians are to act in that very same manner as they seek to serve God.

Never compare your serving with what others are doing. People mistakenly think that serving the Lord only counts when we get involved in a homeless ministry or become a missionary in some far-off country. But we are not all called to the same work. We can still be Jesus' ambassadors by working behind the scenes.

I heard a woman comment at church one day that she wanted to serve, but because of her physical limitations, the only thing she could do was make phone calls, and that didn't seem like very much. I reminded her that Scripture says God looks equally at all who are serving. Everything we do for God, no matter how small we think it is, brings Him great honor and glory. Always remember that we serve an audience of one. In our service to Him, God is the only one we need to be concerned about.

DECEMBER 6

"For we are God's masterpiece. He has created us anew in Christ Jesus so that we can do the good things He planned for us long ago" (Ephesians 2:10).

I had the chance to view many masterpieces when I was in Italy a few years ago. Museums were full of the works of famous artists such as Da Vinci and Michelangelo. Each painting was a rare treasure and extremely valuable. No two were alike in their beauty or in the story that they told. They were priceless pieces of perfect art. If something were to happen to them, they could never be replaced.

These artist's masterpieces serve as a great analogy of how God made us and what He thinks about us. Yet some people don't see the beauty that God created when they look in the mirror. They don't see their worth or the lovely image staring back at them. They are so distracted by their perceived faults that they can't see God's wonderful workmanship.

I know a young mom who instills powerful truths into her young children every night when she puts them to bed. After they pray, she holds them close and whispers to them, "You are beautiful. God adores you. He has a special plan for your life. You will do great things for Him one day. You will be a light to the world." She sows these values into them at a young age because she wants them to know early on that they truly are masterpieces created by God and He has a special purpose for them.

The next time you look in the mirror, tell yourself, "I am a child of God. I am dearly loved. I was created as a beautiful work of art. I am a rare treasure. I am valuable. There is no one else like me." These inspiring words will not only transform how you see yourself but how you view others as well. We are all God's masterpieces!

DECEMBER 7

"My times are in your hands" (Psalm 31:15).

Beautiful Queen Esther was given the task by God to save the Jews from annihilation during the reign of King Xerxes. It's interesting to read the story of how she went about this assignment. Instead of coming right out and asking the king to spare her people, she invited him and his evil official to a banquet. In fact, she held two banquets for them before she brought her request before the king. I wonder why God had her delay this request and go about it as she did.

This might suggest that God had some unfinished business to attend to before Esther made her move. One such order of business concerned Haman, the king's wicked official. He had to be brought down because he developed a huge problem with pride. The Word says that "Pride always goes before destruction" (Psalm 16:18), and that's exactly what happened to old Haman. He is a good example of what the sin of pride can do to your life.

The other issue that needed to be taken care of before Esther put her request in to the king had to do with her uncle. Mordecai revealed an evil plot to kill the king, so the king wanted to honor him for his loyalty to the throne. Mordecai ended up greatly rewarded for his faithful actions.

When the king finally heard Esther's request, he rescinded the order, and the Jewish people were spared. God gave Esther this moment in time to accomplish His will and to save His people. Like Esther, we should always be ready and willing to be used by God.

DECEMBER 8

"Whoever can be trusted with very little can also be trusted with much" (Luke 16:10).

Picture a little girl standing in a room clutching a small raggedy teddy bear to her chest. Jesus walks in with a big smile on His face holding something behind His back. It's a larger teddy bear adorned in a beautiful dress with lovely ribbons and bows. Jesus pulls the bear out and extends it towards the little girl, but she only shakes her head and hugs her little bear even tighter. Jesus wants her to give up her small tattered bear for the better one He has for her. She looks at Jesus with sad eyes and simply responds, "But I love this one."

Isn't that just like us? God asks us to give up something we love, but we are reluctant because we like what we have and are comfortable with it. We never stop to consider that He may have something bigger and better for us waiting in the wings. Scripture calls us to trust and obey without hesitation. Isn't that the very essence of faith?

When God asks you to give up something be assured that He always has something better in store. He closes the door to some things in our lives for our good but then opens another and blesses us more than we could ever imagine. Don't be afraid to give up your tattered bear— God has something much better in store if you just trust Him.

DECEMBER 9

"Is there anything too hard for the Lord?" (Genesis 18:14).

Our faith can easily be weakened by doubt and fear. The Apostle Thomas lacked the faith to believe that Jesus had risen from the dead until he saw the nail marks in His hands and the hole in His side. When he finally did, he said, "Lord, help my unbelief." Sarah struggled with the same problem after she overheard God tell her husband Abraham that she would yet have a son in her old age. She laughed out loud which prompted the Lord to respond, "Is anything too hard for the Lord?"

We all struggle with unbelief at times. A situation or circumstance may seem so impossible that we doubt God can even fix it. We may think that God is incapable of such a monumental task. *"But God."* There is absolutely nothing that is too hard for Him. If He can move mountains as Scripture tells us, He certainly can take care of our little foothills.

Sarah waited years to hold that baby boy in her arms. Even though God was true to His Word and did the impossible, He did it in His timing and in His way. Sarah's lifelong desire was fulfilled but certainly not when she expected it to be.

If you need a mountain moved, be patient. Trust that when God does start moving that hill, something glorious is about to take place. Never give up hope because there is nothing that is too hard for the Lord!

DECEMBER 10

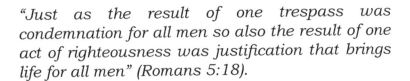

"Just as the result of one trespass was condemnation for all men so also the result of one act of righteousness was justification that brings life for all men" (Romans 5:18).

Adam and Eve's disobedience in the Garden of Eden brought condemnation on the world forever. God's plan for them was to live their lives carefree and happy in paradise with Him. Then, with one bite of forbidden fruit, everything changed. In that single moment, the garden was no longer perfect, and death and evil were introduced into the world. Their sin made an eternal life with God impossible.

"But God" thankfully had a plan. He sent His only Son Jesus to be the Savior of the world and set things right. When Jesus died on the cross, He took all of that sin, from Adam and Eve on, and crucified it with Him. This one sacrificial act restored eternal life to all believers. "Therefore, there is now no condemnation for those who are in Christ Jesus" (Romans 8:1). Believers can now look forward to a glorious future in heaven with God.

Jesus' death gave us life. It gave us a better life here on earth as well as life everlasting. We are righteous because of Jesus. We are justified because of Jesus. We can live in Him now and live with Him through all eternity. One selfless act of love reconciled a broken world back to the paradise that is waiting for us in heaven!

DECEMBER 11

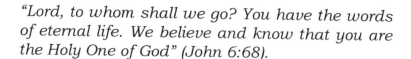

"Lord, to whom shall we go? You have the words of eternal life. We believe and know that you are the Holy One of God" (John 6:68).

Many abandoned Jesus because they did not agree with His teaching. They found it unfathomable and foreign to everything they believed in. Even some of His disciples professed it to be hard teaching. Many people found it was easier to walk away than to make an effort to understand it.

Jesus asked His disciples if they also wanted to leave Him. Peter spoke up and said they had nowhere else to go because they knew Jesus and believed in Him. The word *know* doesn't just mean they knew of Him; it meant that they had an intimate relationship with Him. They trusted that Jesus was whom He claimed to be. Their love and reverence for Him kept them by His side.

This Scripture passage also describes modern-day people. Some hear the gospel message, but because they don't take the time to fully comprehend it or find out who Jesus is, they walk away. Some have pre-conceived opinions and are not interested in backing up their false beliefs with the truth. They are content to live life in the here-and-now and with what they believe and not be too concerned about the real truth and their future.

Peter asked Jesus a pertinent question that applies to all of us today. Where shall we go when our lives are over if we don't know Jesus? How will we share in eternal life with God? The answer is found all throughout Scripture. If we truly believe that Jesus is the Son of God and died for our sins, we will experience the fulfillment of all of His promises!

DECEMBER 12

"And I will do whatever you ask in my name so that the Son may bring glory to the Father. You may ask me for anything in my name, and I will do it" (John 14:13).

When Jesus says we can ask for anything, we must remember that we have to ask according to God's character and His will. God will not grant anything that is contrary to His nature, His will, or His Word. We cannot use Him as a magic formula or a genie in a bottle to fulfill our wants and desires. If we are sincerely following God and our motives are pure, then our prayers will be heard and will be answered according to His plan.

If God seems to be delaying an answer to a prayer, you have to trust that He hasn't forgotten you. God doesn't waste time and always makes good use of our waiting periods. He is always in teaching mode and gives us bits of wisdom and truth in every situation we go through. He wants to see us grow into our full potential, so we can be who He created us to be.

When I'm waiting on God, I pray and ask Him to fill me with His peace. As long as I have His peace I can get through anything! I can rest and believe that God has everything under control. I can live worry free with my joy and hope intact. God is always in the process of refining our faith and increasing our ability to persevere. If you are struggling with something, tell Him and ask Him to fill you with His peace that passes understanding. That is one prayer He is more than happy to answer every sincere heart.

DECEMBER 13

"Love must be sincere. Hate what is evil, cling to what is good. Be devoted to one another in brotherly love. Honor one another above yourselves" (Romans 12:9-10).

Love isn't just a feeling or a word that connotes affection. It means so much more. It encompasses loyalty, commitment, compassion, dedication, selflessness, respect, and humility. It's a word that embodies everything that is good and right. Love in its very essence describes God and is God.

Many books have been written on the topic of near-death experiences. One such book told the story of a physician who was in a coma for five days, and in that time, he described being in heaven. There was the brilliant light and seeing loved ones, which other people have mentioned in similar experiences. But in this particular account, the word the man used the most to describe the overall feeling he had in heaven was love. He felt overwhelmed by love. He said he had never felt such an intense love in all of his life.

The book of 1st John talks all about God's love. God created us to love others just as He loves us. God's love always involves a choice and an action. Will you choose to show love or wait for the feelings to come before you express it? Don't confuse emotions with love. We can choose to love people no matter how we feel. We have access to the Holy Spirit who gives us the power to do what we can't do on our own. If you need a little help to love someone ask the Holy Spirit to empower you. One of my favorite Scripture verses is Philippians 4:13. It says, "I can do all things through Christ who gives me strength." We are capable of doing anything through Christ!

DECEMBER 14

"Each of us should look not only to your own interest but also to the interests of others" (Philippians 2:4).

I like to have an agenda every day. I can be flexible, but sometimes that flexibility lacks grace. I had one such day recently. I was in the middle of a project when my phone rang. A friend asked if I minded doing her a favor. My first thought was, "Oh no, there goes my day." I wanted to make up an excuse of why I couldn't help, but the Lord wasn't too happy about my selfish attitude and convicted me quickly. With my friend still on the phone, He whispered in my ear, "Life is all about relationships and putting others before yourself. Are you going to just read and write about it or live it?"

It's hard to put other's needs and desires before our own, just as it's hard to put God first sometimes. We want to get the to-do list out, and we get anxious if things aren't getting done timely. Meanwhile, our most important task, which is spending time with the Lord, gets postponed later and later until finally, He's at the bottom of the list.

There is a hierarchy in life when it comes to priorities. Picture a pyramid and at the top of the pyramid is God. Under Him comes your husband and then your family. Under them are the needs of others. We sit at the bottom of the pyramid as we are called to put all those above us first. The problem is that some people get the order confused and get the top and the bottom places reversed.

I can attest from experience that life runs a much smoother when we keep God at the top of that pyramid and put others before ourselves. Who is at the top of your pyramid? Do you need to change places with anyone?

DECEMBER 15

"Who is man that you are mindful of him?" (Psalm 8:4).

Have you ever asked yourself why the God of the Universe cares so deeply for His children? Have you ever wondered why God is so good to you and so faithful? We are so undeserving and yet He blesses us beyond measure. One day after feeling so overwhelmed by His goodness, I couldn't help but ask Him why He blessed me so abundantly. His response came quickly. He whispered, "Because, beloved, I love you."

As overwhelming as God's love is for us, we were not created simply for God to love us. In fact, it's completely the other way around. We were made to love Him, have a relationship with Him, and to glorify Him. This is why we were created and the reason for our existence. We are alive because of Him and for Him. As shocking as it may sound the world doesn't revolve around us! God is at His rightful place in the center of everything.

God is always attentive to us, but we are not always mindful of Him. Our minds may be occupied with hundreds of other things during the day besides God. Being mindful of Him takes effort and is something we must train ourselves to do. It should be basic training for every Christian.

DECEMBER 16

~~~~~~~~~~~~~~~~~~

"The Lord had opened a door for me, I still had no peace of mind" (2 Corinthians 2:13).

I always thought that when God opened a door that meant we were supposed to walk through it. I never really gave any consideration to the idea that maybe this was not always true. When I read this chapter in 2 Corinthians, Paul's words opened my eyes to some great insights concerning this subject.

Paul had many opportunities to preach, but he couldn't possibly accept them all. Even though the doors were opened to him, he had to use the wisdom and discernment God gave him to make his decisions about where to go. God's direction for us can never be assumed by a simple open invitation. We should always spend time in prayer before proceeding.

I once prayed that God would open the door for me to have a serious relationship with someone that I knew wasn't right for me. God allowed me to have my way, but as hard as I tried, I couldn't shake the doubt that had crept into my mind. My heart told me deep down that this relationship was not going to work out. However, despite this uneasiness, I moved forward and made a commitment. It ended up as you might expect when we choose to ignore our lack of peace after making a decision. Yes, God had left the door open for me, but I didn't use my spiritual barometers before walking through it.

God gave us the gift of discernment for a reason. When we choose to go our own way without consulting with God, we are trusting only in ourselves. We should never commit to something that doesn't feel right even if the door has been opened. If peace eludes us, there is a reason behind it. We would be wise to follow that inner voice rather than go ahead with something we might regret later.

DECEMBER 17

"I am the Good Shepherd. The Good Shepherd lays down His life for the sheep" (John 10:11).

When shepherds wanted to rest their sheep for the night, they would corral them in a circular pen made of tightly placed stones. Interestingly, there was no physical gate covering the opening to the pen. So, the shepherd would lie across the opening so he could protect his flock from dangerous animals and thieves. Lying there in the gap also prevented his precious flock from escaping. He guarded his sheep with his life.

Jesus is our Good Shepherd. He is also the gate by which we must pass through into the pen of salvation. Further along in this chapter, Jesus explains it very clearly: "I tell you the truth. I am the gate for the sheep. Whoever enters through me will be saved." Jesus is the only pathway into the pasture of God's Kingdom. If we want to enter, we must go through Him. There is no other way.

Our Good Shepherd laid down His life for us. He chose to die so that we could live. All those who have entered through the gate will live one day in the most beautiful green pasture we could ever imagine. Psalm 100:4 says, "Enter His gates with thanksgiving and His courts with praise." One day, we will dance and rejoice in beautiful green fields with our Savior! Alleluia!

DECEMBER 18

"I will give you every place you set your foot as I promised Moses" (Joshua 1:3).

The story behind this verse is remarkable. The Israelites have finally arrived at the precipice of the Promised Land. Moses has died, and his aide Joshua has been ordained by the Lord to lead the people. Even though God said He would give them every place they set their foot, He never mentioned anything about it being a walk in the park. He never told them that their final destination would be an easy acquisition or that it wouldn't involve battles and bloodshed.

"But God." He reassured them that He had everything under control and to be strong and courageous. He told them that He would go before them into the battle and they would have the victory. As encouraging as this must have been to the Israelites, they still would have had to exercise great faith and trust as they followed Joshua into the bloody battle to take over the land.

Do not lose sight of this application for us today. God always fulfills His promises, but we should be aware that it is not always going to be smooth sailing. God doesn't say anywhere in His Word that there wouldn't be any opposition or obstacles to overcome on our journey to heaven. Everything God told Joshua to do back then we must also do. We must be strong, courageous, and trust in Him as we go through life. If God planned it, He will make it happen. Keep your eyes on Him, and He will bring you into the new Promised Land in heaven.

DECEMBER 19

"At first the disciples did not understand all this. Only after Jesus was glorified did they realize that these things had been written about Him and that they had done these things to Him" (John 12:16).

This passage of Scripture concerns the events of Jesus' Triumphal entry into Jerusalem. Jesus was entering the city for the final time before His crucifixion. The people were throwing palm branches on the ground in front of Him as He went by, which was common in those days during celebrations and victories. The people were overjoyed, as they thought they were about to crown Jesus as their king. This day is often referred to in the Christian world as Palm Sunday. It marks the beginning of the week-long events that would lead up to Jesus' crucifixion and Resurrection.

The Apostles hadn't yet fully grasped all that was taking place at the time. It wouldn't come together for them until after Jesus rose from the dead. His words would then become crystal clear as they recalled Jesus' teachings.

Does our faith waver when we don't fully understand what Jesus is doing in our lives? Is our faith strong enough to withstand uncertainty when encountering challenges like the disciples were about to face? Their faith was born out of the intimate relationship they shared with Jesus. They had spent the past three years with Him, and their bond was strong.

That's what happens when we spend time with God. We get to know Him, and our bond becomes strong. We trust Him even when we don't understand everything that's happening. We may not see the big picture at the time, just as the disciples were blind until God's plan was fulfilled. We are not called to understand everything but just to have the faith to believe in the outcome.

DECEMBER 20

"And my God will meet all your needs according to His glorious riches in Christ Jesus" (Philippians 4:19).

There are hundreds of wonderful illustrations of this verse all throughout Scripture, but one recently caught my attention. It takes place in 1 Kings Chapter 17. It's the story of God sending Elijah to the widow to get food. He asked her for bread and water, but she said she had no bread, only a small amount of flour and oil. Elijah told her to go ahead and make the bread because the Lord was going to supply all the flour and oil she needed. Elijah and the widow were soon enjoying a feast.

God also allowed Elijah to heal the woman's son, who was sick and dying. Elijah prayed and asked the Lord to let life return to the boy. Soon he was up and sitting in his mother's lap. This widow had faith that God was working through Elijah to meet her needs and restore life back to her son. She trusted this holy man of God and extended the invitation for him to stay for as long as he wanted.

God can and will do what He says He will do in His Word. He promises to meet our needs and He will. We just have to be like the widow and have faith and trust that He will indeed provide for our every need.

DECEMBER 21

"Be joyful always, pray continually, give thanks in all circumstances for this is God's will for you in Christ Jesus" (1 Thessalonians 5:18).

I am a pet lover. I love my dogs and treat them like children. I'm sure many people can relate. Pets love us unconditionally. They always greet us with a toy in their mouths and a wagging tail. They bring great joy into the home. They can also bring unbelievable heartbreak, as I recently experienced.

I was home alone when our 14-year-old Viszla had a stroke. He was in pretty bad shape, and I didn't know what to do. My husband was out of town, so I called my son-in-law to come over. We agreed the end of his life was at hand, and we needed to make that awful decision. I asked my son-in-law to take him to be put down for me, as I was unable to go down that road.

As I was holding my sweet baby and saying goodbye, this Scripture verse in 1 Thessalonians came to mind. Lord, I thought, how can I possibly give thanks in this circumstance? My heart is breaking!

A few days later as I was rethinking this verse, a revelation came to me. One blessing I saw immediately was that my husband was not home at the time. He had a special bond with this dog, and I think God spared him the pain of having to put him to sleep. The second positive thing I saw was that I was able to have a great bonding experience with my son-in-law. He held me so tenderly while I cried and never faltered in what I asked him to do.

We can always find something to be thankful for even in heartbreaking situations. It can be the smallest thing, but that's okay. The important thing is that we are obedient to God's Word, and that's what counts.

Remembering to give thanks will make all the difference in the world as we seek to cope with the struggles in our lives.

DECEMBER 22

"...every creature of every kind will come to you to be kept alive" (Genesis 6:20).

When God told Noah to build the Ark, Noah never questioned the command. He simply listened to God's instructions and got started. He had faith that God would enable him to complete the task down to the very last detail.

As I contemplated this passage, I had to wonder if Noah ever stressed about this project and wondered how in the world he was supposed to capture two of every kind of creature to bring onto the boat. But just in the nick of time, Noah was blessed with a huge *"But God"* moment when God told him that the animals would come to the boat on their own! God met Noah's needs down to the very end of his assignment.

Noah had complete faith in God from the very beginning. He trusted that God would provide all he needed to get the job done. Looking back, we see that Noah was rewarded for his obedience and faith in God's Sovereignty as he and his family were the only ones that survived the flood.

The lesson we can glean from this is that we never have to worry about living life alone. God is able to provide exactly what we need when we need it. We don't have to worry about how things are going to work, but simply trust in God and His plan. He will always take care of us no matter what!

DECEMBER 23

"Blessed is she who has believed that what the Lord has said to her will be accomplished" (Luke 1:45).

After Mary was with child, she went to visit her cousin Elizabeth. Elizabeth was also expecting a child with her husband Zechariah, and this baby would someday play a huge part in Jesus' life. When Mary greeted Elizabeth, the baby leaped inside of her. Elizabeth was filled with the Holy Spirit and exclaimed to Mary, "Blessed is the child you will bear! Blessed is she who has believed that what the Lord has said to her will be accomplished."

John the Baptist was born to Elizabeth a few months before Jesus. But it's not often you hear John the Baptist mentioned in the nativity story. But it could actually be considered the prologue because of the timing and circumstances. Elizabeth was up in age and had been barren all of her life. "But God." She suddenly finds out that not only was she having a baby, but she was having the baby that the Old Testament prophesied about. Elizabeth's pregnancy preceded the greatest miracle in all of history.

God's plan for John the Baptist was "to prepare the way for Him" (Luke 1:76). John divinely knew what God had in store for him. He knew he was to preach a message of repentance as well as the salvation of God. He never lost his focus or the purpose of his mission.

Are we not all forerunners for Christ as John was? Do we not all share the same responsibility for preaching the good news as he did? How are we paving the way for others to find Jesus? John the Baptist embraced the plan God had for him. How are you embracing yours?

DECEMBER 24

"Glory to God in the highest and on earth peace to men on whom His favor rests" (Luke 2:14).

The shepherds are lying out in the fields guarding their sheep one quiet night when all of a sudden, an army of angels appear. There is glorious light radiating everywhere, and the angels are singing beautiful praises to God. They are on a mission to bring the good news about a Savior. They tell the star-struck shepherds that a Messiah is born that night in the town of Bethlehem. Wow! What a birth announcement!

The shepherds were afraid at first, but their fear soon turned to joy as the angels bid them come and see the baby for themselves. The shepherds would be the first ones to greet the Lamb of God who would one day take away the sins of the world. After seeing this baby Savior, the shepherds made haste to spread the great news of His magnificent birth.

Without this silent and holy night, our salvation and eternal life in heaven with God would have been impossible. This baby would someday change the world forever. He would soon become the greatest man who ever walked the earth. The most significant event in history had just taken place, and there was great rejoicing both in heaven and on earth.

How are you celebrating this joyous event? Have you thought about what kind of birthday gift you would like to bring to the party? Jesus really only wants one gift from each of us, and that is to commit our lives to this baby King. That would be the greatest gift anyone could ever give Him.

DECEMBER 25

"I bring you good news of great joy that will be for all the people. Today in the town of David a Savior has been born to you; He is Christ the Lord" (Luke 2:11).

The word *Savior* in Hebrew means "deliverer." The Jews in the Old Testament were waiting for the Messiah—the deliverer—who would rescue them from the tyranny of the Roman government. However, they were anticipating an earthly King, not a heavenly one. They weren't expecting an eternal, immortal, Sovereign King who was born to a young peasant girl and not in a house of royalty.

The prophet Isaiah predicted Jesus' birth 700 years before He actually arrived in a stable in an obscure little town called Bethlehem. There are hundreds of prophecies in the Old Testament that foretold Jesus' birth. And each one came to pass exactly the way it was prophesied. What a powerful testimony to the timing and accuracy of Scripture.

Jesus came that we may have new life—everlasting life. John 6:40 says, "For it is my Father's will that all who see His Son and believe in Him should have eternal life." Those who put their faith in Christ—in a baby born in a lowly manger—will be resurrected from physical death to eternal life with God. That is the reason we celebrate Christmas. It commemorates not only the birth of a King but our spiritual birth as well.

DECEMBER 26

"Do not judge or you too will be judged. For in the same way you judge others you will be judged and with the same measure you use it will be measured to you" (Matthew 7:1-2).

I had my first experience as a juror recently. I learned a lot about our judicial system as well as received a much-needed lesson on judgment. Sometimes as Christians, we mistakenly think we are less likely to sin, or we compare our sins to others to assess how we measure up. However, Scripture says that all sin is equal and we all fall short.

The defendant standing trial that day had what I perceived as a bad attitude. His body language was not one of humility or even interest. He seemed apathetic, and my mind immediately started forming all kinds of preconceived ideas. I seemed to fall very easily into the trap that Jesus had warned us about in this verse. I had judged this man solely on how he looked and how he presented himself. Thank God I was quickly convicted of my sin! After repenting, I looked over at the man again, and I saw someone completely different. I saw sadness and a softness that I hadn't seen before.

My fellow jurors and I all agreed the man was innocent of all charges. When the verdict was read to the courtroom, he looked over at us and mouthed the words *thank you*. It was odd, but a feeling of love for this stranger came over me as he exited the room. I wanted to run after him and wrap my arms around him and tell him how sorry I was that he had to go through this awful experience.

I thanked the Lord later for this teaching moment. I prayed and asked that He would give me eyes to see only the good in people. I asked Him to help me see others with acceptance and love. It's so easy to succumb to judgment. We need to see people as Jesus sees them—children of God and deserving of His love.

DECEMBER 27

"Go home to your family and tell them how much the Lord has done for you" (Mark 5:19).

Jesus spoke these words to a man who was demon-possessed one minute and talking normally the next. Jesus performed a miracle by commanding the evil spirits to come out of him. The evil spirits obeyed, and the man was set free. The man was so overjoyed and grateful to Jesus that he wanted to follow Him. But Jesus told him to go home and share the good news with his family. He wanted him to tell everyone what the Lord had done for him. Jesus told him to do this so that others may hear his story and believe in the One who had healed him.

This example is for us today as well. How will others come to faith if we don't open our mouths and talk about Him? Just as we would tell others about a doctor who has cured our physical ailments, we should talk about Christ and how He has healed our hearts and souls.

How often do you talk about your faith to others? Do you share the great and marvelous things God has done in your life? Do people even know you are a Christian?

God wants us to glorify Him by talking about His goodness and faithfulness. That is how we go about making disciples of all nations. We bring God great honor every time we speak about Him and testify about our faith.

DECEMBER 28

"Let your gentleness be evident to all. The Lord is near" (Philippians 4:5).

The Apostle Peter would never have been described as a gentle person. He had a hearty, robust personality and was naturally bold and outspoken. He was sometimes gruff and unfiltered, so Jesus had to rein him in at times when he crossed the line. Peter was the proverbial bull in a china shop.

What do we do if gentleness doesn't come naturally to us? How do we attain this fruit of the Spirit? The answer is found in the question. We can't attain anything on our own without the Holy Spirit working in us. Gentleness, like all the other fruits, is given to us as a gift when we live our lives by faith and obedience to the Word of God.

What if our every word and deed reflected the caring, compassionate character of Christ? What if we all spoke to each other as if we were speaking to Him? Oh, what a different world it would be!

If you lack gentleness pray and ask God to help you in this area. God loves an on-fire Christian, but we must be careful to channel all that energy and eagerness with a heart of humility and gentleness.

DECEMBER 29

"Let your conversation be always full of grace" (Colossians 4:6).

The Lord recently tested me on this Scripture verse. He opened up an opportunity for me to put grace into action. I was in a situation where I had to make the choice of reacting in anger or put this Scripture into action. This example may seem frivolous to some, but not for a woman; I can assure you of that.

My hair stylist appeared to be distracted at one of our monthly appointments. She inadvertently cut my hair way too short, and to make matters worse, she completely botched my bangs. I think I might have gasped when she finally spun me around in the chair and I looked in the mirror. One section of my bangs was completely missing! She apologized profusely, but I was not very happy, to say the least.

I had a choice to make at that point. I could stomp out of the salon with a promise to never return. Or I could have said something hurtful to make her feel even worse than she already did. But I got it right for once and chose grace and downplayed the whole incident. I told her not to worry about it because my hair grew fast and I could work with the bangs. I even made a quip about the money I was going to save because I wouldn't need a haircut for quite some time.

My husband took one look at me when I got home and told me I needed a new hairstylist. I told him that everyone has a bad hair day now and then. I reminded him that none of us is perfect, and we are all in desperate need of grace. Wouldn't we have wanted to be treated with the same mercy and understanding?

"But God." I arrived at church the next morning and found that people were actually complimenting my hair!

Isn't that just like the Lord? He takes a bad situation and turns it into a blessing. He took all my self-consciousness away and replaced it with peace and confidence. We always have a choice where grace is concerned. How will you extend it to someone who needs it today?

DECEMBER 30

"The Lord does not look at the things man looks at. Man looks at the outward appearance, but the Lord looks at the heart" (1 Samuel 16:7).

David's calling to be the King of Israel is quite remarkable. God instructed the prophet Samuel to go to Bethlehem to anoint the next King. He told him to go and find a man named Jesse and to choose a king from his seven sons. The Lord reminded Samuel to make sure he didn't look at their outward appearance but at their character.

After Samuel found Jesse and met all of his sons, God told Samuel to reject them all. So, Samuel asked Jesse, "Are these all the sons you have?" Jesse replied that there was still one more, but he was just a small shepherd boy out tending the sheep. Samuel told Jesse to send for him. As soon as Samuel saw him, God told him he was the one. He told him to rise up and anoint him as King.

Here was a 15-year-old shepherd boy that God had just chosen for His next King. God saw David's heart and knew He was the one. Jesse may have been perplexed by Samuel's choice, *"But God's"* plans defy understanding sometimes.

Have you been called out of your comfortable environment to do something for the Lord? It's easy to get stuck where we are and become complacent in our serving. Maybe now is the time to put down your shepherd's staff and follow where God is leading.

DECEMBER 31

"He who began a good work in you will carry it on to completion until the day of Christ Jesus" *(Philippians 1:6).*

David was thirty-years-old when He took the throne. He waited fifteen years for God's plan to come to fruition. Those fifteen long years were unfortunately wrought with great suffering. *"But God"* in His perfect timing eventually brought David to his rightful place.

David must have wondered why he had to go through all that waiting. He was anointed king one minute and then suffering through trials and pain the next. However, year after year, David persevered and never lost sight of His calling. David didn't know what the future held, but he knew who held the future.

Sometimes when God gives us a job to do, it takes time for it to all come together. We have no idea why it's taking so long to take shape, but it could be that God is testing us to see whether we'll hang in there and trust that He's got things under control. Like David, we have to be willing to follow blindly sometimes.

David was content in whatever circumstances God placed him. He didn't question Him or give up; he just kept trusting and moving forward. The truth is that God would never have given up on David and His plan for him just like he will never give up on us. God's plans can never be thwarted. If you think you're not up for the task, just remember David. That fifteen-year-old shepherd boy waited quite a while to become Israel's greatest King. He never lost sight of His destiny or His great desire to serve God!

Made in the USA
Coppell, TX
11 December 2020